P9-CLG-190

State Making in Asia

State Making in Asia examines state-making projects from a uniquely Asian perspective, highlighting the particular combination of institutions and ideologies embedded in Asian state making and demonstrating their distinctiveness from the Western experience. It underlines the variety and hybridism of Asian forms of the state and emphasizes the need to incorporate Asian patterns of historical change in our theorization about modern state making. Drawing on this alternative analytical framework, the book provides a comparison of Asian nations that accounts for their development in a non-Eurocentric perspective.

State Making in Asia offers new empirical and conceptual material based on original research within the field. Including contributions from leading authorities in state theory and Asian history, this book will be a valuable resource to scholars of Asian politics, history and international relations.

Richard Boyd is Reader in the Law and Society of Japan at Leiden University, the Netherlands.

Tak-Wing Ngo is Lecturer in Chinese Politics at Leiden University, the Netherlands.

Politics in Asia series
Formerly edited by Michael Leifer
London School of Economics

State Making in Asia

Edited by Richard Boyd and Tak-Wing Ngo

LONDON AND NEW YORK

First published 2006
by Routledge
2 Park Square, Milton Park, Abingdon, Oxon OX14 4RN

Simultaneously published in the USA and Canada
by Routledge
270 Madison Ave, New York, NY 10016

Routledge is an imprint of the Taylor & Francis Group, an informa business

© 2006 Richard Boyd and Tak-Wing Ngo for selection and editorial
matter; individual contributors, their contributions

Typeset in Times New Roman by
RefineCatch Ltd, Bungay, Suffolk
Printed and bound in Great Britain by
Biddles Ltd, King's Lynn

All rights reserved. No part of this book may be reprinted or
reproduced or utilised in any form or by any electronic,
mechanical, or other means, now known or hereafter
invented, including photocopying and recording, or in any
information storage or retrieval system, without permission in
writing from the publishers.

British Library Cataloguing in Publication Data
A catalogue record for this book is available from the British Library

Library of Congress Cataloging-in-Publication Data
State making in Asia/edited by Richard Boyd and Tak-Wing Ngo.
p. cm.—(Politics in Asia series)
Includes bibliographical references and index.
1. Asia—Politics and government. 2. State, The. I. Boyd, Richard.
II. Ngo, Tak-Wing, 1962–. III. Series.
JQ24.S73 2005
321'.0095—dc22
2005013350

ISBN10: 0–415–34611–8
ISBN13: 9–78–0–415–34611–5

Contents

Contributors

Richard Boyd is Reader in the Law and Society of Japan at the University of Leiden, the Netherlands.

Sity Daud is Lecturer at the Center for Historical, Political and Strategic Studies, National University of Malaysia, Malaysia.

Ann Frechette is Associate in Research, Fairbank Center for East Asian Research at Harvard University, United States.

Tak-Wing Ngo is Lecturer in Chinese Politics at the University of Leiden, the Netherlands.

Mark Ravina is Professor of Asian History at Emory University, United States.

Shamsul A. B. is Professor of Social Anthropology at the National University of Malaysia, Malaysia.

Jenn-hwan Wang is Professor of Sociology at the Sun Yat–Sen Graduate Institute of Social Sciences and Humanities, National Chengchi University, Taiwan.

Laurence Whitehead is Official Fellow of Nuffield College at the University of Oxford, United Kingdom.

R. Bin Wong is Director of the Asia Institute and Professor of History at the University of California in Los Angeles, United States.

Preface

This is the second volume in a series of publications that aims to return power and history to a central position in the study of Asian politics. The volume takes issue with the projection onto Asia of a simplified Weberian conception of the modern state. That conception owes much to an idealized understanding of the European state which is robustly indifferent to the particularity of states in Asia. Ironically, Weber himself warned against reading off the states of Asia from a Western text. He was sensitive to the difference of Asia and of the need to locate the state in its historical and cultural specificity – a need all the greater where the states in question have known their own autochthonous political development long before the colonial experience. The critical need is therefore to reconnect the state to the history of its own making as the indispensable means to reveal its contemporary form and meaning.

In this volume we greet with caution and circumspection the claim that states in contemporary Asia are very much the same as the modern state in Europe, and that accordingly concepts evolved in Europe are naturally applicable. We argue that if we draw back the curtains to reveal the actual trajectory of state making in specific Asian countries rather than to conceal this behind theories of radical imposition and so on, it will clarify the what, how, and the why of the modern state in contemporary Asia. Moreover, such an approach will also encourage us to view the state not as a fixed point outside of politics and time – the indicted reification effect of the state-as-independent variable approach – but as a process without end, as institutions and relationships embedded in other institutions and relationships, subject to internal dissension, competing pressures, and the gamut of centrifugal forces, and constantly in need of repair, renewal, and reinforcement.

Our motivation for this volume begins with a sense of dissatisfaction with the overwhelming preoccupation with economic growth and the associated state-as-independent-variable approach in the study of Asia. On the one hand, the growth paradigm has grabbed and held the political science of Asia by the throat for more than 25 years, leaving it little enough breath to do much more than say which nations have succeeded or which nations have failed to develop and what has been the 'contribution' of politics to these. Of course, the importance of growth and development is not to be denied. But there are problems and issues that are not reducible to economic success and failure. In particular, questions of the state, politics, and power cannot be captured in measures of efficiency and effectiveness. On the other hand, the state-as-independent-variable approach to the analysis of Asia has no past, no personality, and no politics. It is, to be blunt, ahistorical, antipolitical, overgeneralized, and reductionist. This is unacceptable even when it is not the state but the growth of the Asian economies that is the object of inquiry since the explanation in this second case returns precisely to the unspecified, untheorized, and little-understood 'state'.

Impatience with this state of affairs prompted us to engage in a long-term project on the political economy of Asia in comparative and historical perspective (PEACH). The hope is that the project will marry a rigorous social science approach to a concern with long-run history as well as language and culture. The aim is to produce a richer and reinvigorated study of Asia. The first concrete result of the PEACH initiative was a conference held in Leiden in June 2002 on the theme 'Revisiting the Asian State'. More than sixty scholars, among them anthropologists, historians, sociologists, political scientists, and political economists, gathered to debate a wide range of topics covering many of the countries of Asia. One of the most rewarding features of the event was the strong sense we gained that our reservations – about the narrowness of debates and the urgent need to broaden the research focus – were shared by colleagues working on the region. Shortly thereafter, for all the richness and variety of contributions, it became apparent that one of the key areas of concern is precisely the need to emancipate the study of Asian political economies from the growth paradigm. This has resulted in the publication of the first volume, *Asian States: Beyond the Developmental Perspective*, edited by Richard Boyd and Tak-Wing Ngo (London: RoutledgeCurzon, 2005).

The conference was followed up by a roundtable on 'Competing Perspectives on the State in Developing Countries', which took place in March 2004. The roundtable served to sharpen our awareness of the different approaches and paradigms deployed in the study of the state country by country. The contributions of participants at the roundtable, we gratefully note, have had a significant impact in shaping the themes of the two volumes. A further opportunity to pursue some of these ideas was made available by the Netherlands Institute of Advanced Studies (NIAS), which hosted a group of scholars working on East Asia and Latin America engaged in a country-to-country comparative study of power, conflict, and development. The collaboration was gratifyingly intensive. Of the observations that emerged critical was our sense that long-run processes of socioeconomic change generate prodigious problems of social conflict and social control. Governments assuming responsibility for the task of industrialization must manage (or fail to manage) the resultant conflict. Where power and authority have yet to be securely institutionalized, social conflict and social cleavages will be closely associated with bids for power and leadership. The particular modalities by virtue of which governments seek to manage this conflict, together with their consequences, are crucial determinants of development outcomes. The argument is articulated in the forthcoming volume *Political Conflict and Development in East Asia and Latin America*, edited by Richard Boyd, Benno Galjart, and Tak-Wing Ngo (London: Routledge, forthcoming 2006). The volume additionally questions the emphasis on the institutional and cultural bases (such as insulated technocracy, policy deliberation councils, pilot agencies, and policy instruments) for stable growth. It reminds us that the nature and potential of any instrumentality is refracted through political struggle.

We see these studies as a first contribution to the repoliticization of the comparative political economy of Asia which seeks moreover to ground the Asian political economies upon a basis that acknowledges their autochthonous politics and power relations, their unique histories, and the particularity of how these mesh and clash with Western political modernity. The payoff, as the research progresses and deepens, is a comparative exercise that will contribute to a theorization of the state and the politics of economic exchange (market) in Asia and feed back into theorizing about these in the West.

We understand that this kind of sustained endeavour demands tireless institutional and intellectual support. Fortunately, we have had both, as well as many reminders that good ideas are the product of many heads. In the process we have accumulated many debts to institutions and individuals who have extended their help in one way or another. Financial support has come from the International Institute for Asian Studies (IIAS), Royal Netherlands Academy (KNAW), Netherlands Organization for Scientific Research (NWO), Leiden University Fund (LUF), and the Research School of Asian, African and Amerindian Studies (CNWS) at Leiden University. We owe a special thanks to Wim Stokhof, Director of IIAS, for his unflagging support of the project and to colleagues of IIAS for their invaluable logistical help. We are grateful to numerous friends and colleagues for their insight, patience, questions, and criticism. They include most notably: Tony Allan, Chang Mau-kuei, Martin Doornbos, Maria Edin, Mustafa Erdogdu, Benno Galjart, Sheldon Garon, William Guéraiche, Stephan Haggard, John Haley, Kevin Hewison, Bob Jessop, Hagen Koo, Jan Newberry, Amit Prakash, Richard Robison, Garry Rodan, Alvin So, Olle Törnquist, Charles Tripp, Geoffrey Underhill, Bridget Welsh, Willem Wolters, Wu Yongping, and Zhang Xiaoke.

An earlier version of Chapter 2 has appeared in Mark Ravina, 'State-making in global context: Japan in a world of nation-state', in Joshua A. Fogel (ed.), *The Teleology of the Modern State: Japan and China* (University of Pennsylvania Press, 2004). We are grateful to the University of Pennsylvania Press for its permission to reprint the chapter here. We gratefully received the assistance of Gina Rozario and Tobias Keller in preparing the manuscript for publication.

Richard Boyd
Tak-Wing Ngo
Leiden, 2005

1 Reconnecting the state to the dynamics of its making

Richard Boyd and Tak-Wing Ngo

There is an increasingly widespread sense in the study of the states of Asia and other regions outside of Europe that the state cannot be assumed to conform precisely to a Western blueprint. The observation has both a normative and a descriptive aspect. With respect to the first, it is no longer accepted that the modern state, as configured and understood in the West, is the ultimate and final destination of modern political development; with respect to the second, it is equally doubted that a reading of the Western state can provide a proximate and adequate description of the states of the rest of the world. The observation is of great importance precisely because of the entrenched and pervasive nature of the views challenged; that is to say, there is a deeply rooted sense in social science that the modern state, which evolved in Europe, is the privileged form of political modernity and there is, no less, a tendency to view 'states elsewhere' as more or less close and adequate facsimiles of the Western state. These views have fashioned how the states of the world beyond Europe have been studied: their histories have been understood as obstacles to be overcome in a story of the coming-into-being of the modern state, while their contemporary form and meaning is treated as a variant upon the Western theme. We take issue with these views in the present volume: we side with those who argue that the states of Asia and elsewhere have to be understood in their particularity, and that, if we are to grasp this particularity, we must reconnect states to the history of their making. We must treat the state as the product of a history of state making. We conclude by noting that, while it is neither our intention to divide ontologically the world of politics into a Western and non-Western realm, nor to argue that there is a single and distinctive Asian state, it is our intention to recover the important particularity of states that has been obscured by the uncritical overgeneralization and projection of understandings captive to Western forms.

Why study state making?

The last ten years have witnessed a great renewal of interest in the study of state making worldwide. On the face of it, a concern with state making requires neither explanation nor justification: the state remains the dominant, if contested, political form in the modern world, and scholars, accordingly, are interested in the processes that have led to its emergence. However, whereas once interest in excavating the making of the modern state was confined primarily to Europe, latterly the exercise has been repeated in respect of South Asia, Latin America, Africa, the Middle East, and more recently in East Asia.[1] Moreover, it is noteworthy that these recent works are not concerned with state making in itself, but rather with state making as a means to understand the contemporary state. Implicit in these studies is the sense that to understand the modern state in Latin America, Africa, or Asia, we must view the state through a historical lens. We must treat the state as the product of a history of state making.

This is more controversial. There has been little sense customarily that we need to locate the contemporary state in a particular history. Why the need? Why bother, we might ask? Does not political theory teach us that there is only one kind of modern state?[2] The modern state, we are told, is the one characterized in terms of territoriality, unified sovereignty, legitimacy and international recognition, and a monopoly of coercion. The model originated in Europe, and was either inscribed onto the blank canvasses of the South by colonialism, or, more rarely, in the absence of colonial intervention, copied by developing or newly born nations as fast and efficiently as possible, convinced of its obvious superiority over other forms of political organization. To use a Darwinian analogy to the distribution of genotypic and phenotypic properties: let us look for genetic mutations during periods of enhanced competition for scarce resources. Any mutations, such as those that characterize the modern state, that lend even a slight edge in the intraspecies struggle for survival will endow specific organisms with reproductive advantage. Consequently, that feature will tend to disperse throughout the population.[3] In other words, the very presence of the modern European state in the population of polities is determining, regardless of differences in the initial conditions from which the non-European states emerged. More pithily stated, this is what Bayart has termed the 'theory of the radical extraneity of the modern state'.[4] That is to say, it is the claim that the Western state form is an inescapable universal: it was either imposed from outside through colonization or appropriated intact in recognition of its inherent superiority. Every latecomer polity recognizes this, fashions itself according to the now universal principles of territoriality, unified sovereignty, institutional hierarchy and centralization, monopoly and control of violence, presents itself in this form to the international community, and does its best to make domestic circumstances match the claims of the nation-state format.

If we accept this view, there is little need to study state making as a key to unlock understanding of the contemporary state. At best the history of state making will be of interest and utility in laying bare the kind of problems the new state will have in matching fact and form: that is, in manufacturing secular and impersonal loyalties focused upon the state, crafting institutions, establishing territorial integrity, managing its borders, and seeing off its domestic rivals. But ultimately, in this view, the history of state making is redundant. The date of its final redundancy is the same as that upon which these obstacles to the making of the state are overcome. On that day, state making can safely be left to the historians, as the state, emancipated from its history, is left in the hands of political science.

The historicity of the modern state

We take issue with this on several grounds; the first of which targets the historicity of the political entity called the modern state. The parochialism of the dominant theorizations of the state, together with their ignorance of, or indifference to, the historicity of the modern (Western) state, has long been a source of unease for scholars engaged in the study of the vast periphery. The consequently limited utility of, what has come to be seen as, a Eurocentric conception of the state has become central and axiomatic in a body of important works on the states of Asia, Africa, and Latin America.[5] Their core contention is that the analysis of the state is captive to a body of theory and to an analytic lexicon that is exclusively Western. It is not just that the states reflected upon and which have come to serve as the empirical foundations of state theory are Western, it is also that the very terms of analysis are themselves Western. The term 'state' is an inseparable element in a 'secular holy trinity' of terms – 'individual', 'society', and 'state' – that guide analysis. It is inseparable in the sense that its meaning is fixed by reference to the meanings of the other terms, individual and society. In this sense, all three are inseparable, since they are defined in terms of each other. Together, the trinity encapsulates, and is inseparable from, some 200 years of exclusively European experience.[6]

The specific form of the state that empirically and lexically grounds theory even today, that is to say, the state construed by territoriality, citizenship, secularity, and sovereignty, is, of course, the one that evolved in a long-run European history. The story of that evolution is too well known to merit repetition here. It will suffice to note that the features of this specific European state – territoriality, secularism, sovereignty, and nationality – have been conceptualized as the features of *the* modern state. As Finer puts it, '[a]ll these features of the modern state are, without any exception whatsoever, derived from the West'.[7] In the same vein, Weber's conception of the rational-legal authority said to characterize the modern state administration is a reflection of exclusively European experience. More precisely, the centralization, specialization, and hierarchy which Weber identified with formal rationality of the modern state were more a product of Prussia's military and legal institutions and historical experiences than the elements of a universal history.[8]

Of course, to note the historical and geographical particularity of this conception of the modern state is not to dismiss its more general significance. This would be foolish in the extreme; as foolish as arguing that the origins of an invention preclude its adoption elsewhere. However, it is no less unwise to assume that the states of non-European regions were fired in the same crucible and with the same consequences as in Europe. Moreover, state making has been commonplace in many parts of Asia quite independently of, or, in the case of China and Japan, even prior to the processes of state formation in Europe. The historical circumstances of many Asian nations were far removed from those in Europe at their state-making apogee. We can add to this that the emergence of Asian states has been attended by long traditions of indigenous writing and theorizing. Some of these traditions, as in China, were untouched and untroubled by Western conceptions and practices; others, notably in Japan, filtered, interpreted, accommodated, confronted, and even improved upon Western conceptions. These reflections are neither arcane nor exotic; they informed particular understandings of the idea of the state and contributed to the fashioning of its forms and organization. Different histories father different reflections which generate differences in ideas and institutions of enduring and contemporary significance.

Unfortunately, the success of the Western export in modern times, and even more so the apparent universality of its constituent elements, has tended to obscure the differences, practices, meanings, and possibilities behind what has come to be a common nomenclature. This nomenclature, despite its parochialism and indebtedness to culturally and historically specific circumstances, is in general use and is assumed to have the same analytic purchase and relevance in Bangkok, Beijing, Delhi, and Tokyo as in Berlin, London, Paris, and Washington. The nomenclature is the language of the Western state. Its concepts and categories have a self-evident, intuitively persuasive quality in the West precisely because they encapsulate Western history and understandings derived from its study. Take the familiar distinction between state and civil society: for all that this is complex and intensely debated, undoubtedly, the distinction was made upon the basis of the historical experience of Western Europe. At its sharpest, it captures the clash between the nascent bourgeois that seeks elbow room from a state reluctant to grant it. The divide is significant because of the history – it is real and raw and echoes down the years in laws, language, and texts. But imagine a society (Japan) in which there was no such clash; one in which a weakly articulated state indistinctly demarcated from a society – a notion so unfamiliar that there was no word for it – sponsored the rise of the modern economy, sought out and promoted a bourgeoisie? Then the distinction loses its force; the dividing line is scarcely even that and certainly no Rubicon. Here the language of the Western state reaches its limit and its pertinence fades. Understanding is not enhanced by stretching beyond the limit by misconstruing realities so as to fit disciplinary categories.

The projection of a single conception of the modern state onto Asia and elsewhere is objectionable too, precisely because it results in a failure to discriminate between different political entities or 'states'. Political science has long and lazily contented itself with an 'outrageously'[9] undifferentiated usage of the state. We noted above the assumption of a general relevance for the language of the Western state that is the root cause of this failure. We remind ourselves here that the definition of the modern state, often the Weberian definition, derived from this nomenclature, is expected to hold in its embrace Germany and Kenya, Chile and Japan; it requires us to identify Sweden with India and Iran with China. Bayart rejects as fantasy the theory of the radical extraneity of the modern state based on the model of Western bureaucracy on the African continent.[10] What then of those societies that were never colonized? The universalizing essentialism of much contemporary state theory simply does not allow us to do justice to the distinction between a Malaysia which knew a transformative colonial experience and a Japan which was never colonized.

The poverty of state theory

It would be wrong to say that the historicist critique has been entirely ignored. Yet it in no sense commands the heights of the discipline. Historians sensitive to the particularity of Europe and of European politics speak of ours as 'an age that sees itself as moving beyond modernity', and note that 'the ground has shifted under the various grand narratives of its European origins'.[11] However those grand narratives of which the historian speaks are not the stuff of political analysis. Indeed, many political scientists take what might seem a perverse pride in rejecting historical approaches and, overwhelmingly, eschew the notion of narrative. In the process, of course, they disguise the historicity of their own project. The core conceptions of the discipline, the conceptions that structure the political data are themselves encapsulations of these grand narratives.

We may lament this but it need not surprise us. Not only is the tradition Western but so also is the discipline that studies it. By any head count of university practitioners, any tally of the journals and 'research' output, any consideration of the content of university training programs within and outside of the West, political science is a Western profession – in both the occupational and oratorical senses of the word. The parochial-turned-universal nomenclature is replicated by political science which sins doubly by overgeneralizing Western experiences and misconstruing non-Western histories.

The 'bringing the state back' movement in the 1980s is a case in point. The movement treats the state as an organizational entity, and, with the curtest of nods to Weber, asserts a basic and unproblematic distinction between state and society. It becomes possible then to treat the state as an autonomous entity whose actions are neither reducible to nor determined by forces in society. This autonomous organizational entity is said to assume the role of a promoter of collective goals and the 'general interest'. The actions of the autonomous state are said to explain social outcomes. Despite the claim to bring back the state, the movement does not analyze or problematize the state itself. The state is treated as a given, abstracted from the Western tradition. The form and idea of the state and the nature of its authority are not subjects of research. There is no need, since the state is the 'independent variable' in the equation. The states of Germany, South Korea, or Argentina have identical status as the independent variable. What differs is the strength, or capacity, of the state in realizing its policy goals. Typically, this strength is measured in terms of the extent of political autonomy the state enjoys *vis-à-vis* society rather than in terms of the properties of the state.

In an Asian context, 'bringing the state back in' assumes the guise of the developmental state theory. Pioneered by Johnson in his study of Japan,[12] the theory explains the impressive growth of a number of Asian economies in terms of the role played by the state. In other words, the basic concern, the object of analysis, is the capacity of the state to steer economic development, the goal is to explain economic growth in Asia and not the state in Asia. The story is well known. In brief, the theory associates economic development with the capacity of the state to achieve macroeconomic coordination. The general assumption is that latecomers to development require a more central-ized mechanism for capital mobilization, industrial promotion, and techno-logical upgrading. This centralized function is assumed by a developmental state which possesses institutional qualities such as political autonomy, technocratic insulation, social embeddedness, and a development-oriented bureaucracy. The theory has been applied to other East Asian countries including Korea, Taiwan, and Singapore, and has been further extended to other rapidly growing economies including Malaysia and even China. So familiar and habitual is the association that the developmental state has now come to be seen as a characteristic form of the state in many Asian countries.

This is problematic if our concern is to explain the state rather than to explain growth.[13] In the developmentalist account of the state, attention cen-ters on the instrumentality of state in economic development. The questions asked concern what the state has done in promoting growth and how it did so. The state, we have noted, figures as a simplistic, one-dimensional universal. It is seen, much as in the original bringing-back-the-state movement, as a machinery of decision/policy making. If it varies, it does so in relation to its functionality for growth. The point is neatly exemplified in Evans's well-known classification in which states are defined as developmental, midwifery, and predatory, depending on how they use and abuse the national economy.[14]

This is highly misleading in several regards. Firstly, it takes a theory of how economies grow for a theory of the state. As such, it displaces research atten-tion from the political to the economic. Although it is undeniable that eco-nomic development is an important aspect of state making, one needs to be reminded that it is but one aspect. When viewed through other facets of the state-making project, the state revealed and the problems raised are different. Secondly, the state is presented as an accomplished fact. Not only is there no place in the analysis for state particularity but neither is there place for the state understood as an ongoing process of state making. This is problematic even within the limits of the Western state nomenclature since it means that much of the struggle among Asian nations over their territorial boundaries, over the fact and extent of sovereign authority, and over the nature and possibility of nationhood – in other words, the fundamental Hobbesian concerns – is simply ignored. The legitimation of political authority is seen as almost congruent with the needs of economic development. Thirdly, and at the risk of tedious repetition, the state is assumed to have a universal form and to manifest a single state idea. The reference point is the rise of the rational, administrative state – a historical development of the West smuggled into the analysis of Asia.

For all its extraordinary influence the state-as-independent-variable approach in its neo-Weberian guise has been widely criticized.[15] Of particular relevance to our concerns are two criticisms, in addition to those mentioned above. The first is that the approach is one-sided in that it focuses on state and party politics at the expense of political forces outside and beyond the state. In particular, it seems to substitute politicians for social formations (such as class or gender or race), elite for mass politics, and political conflict for social struggle.[16] This is fraught with consequences: not least, the approach reduces the state to an institutional kernel of rationality by definitional fiat as irrationality is hived off behind a largely imaginary dividing line that separates off the state from society, the public from the private and, we might add, the 'modern' from the 'traditional'. The exercise would be transparently mistaken were it not for the repeated citation in support of Weber to legitimize an apolitical account of the state that matches the rhetoric rather than the reality of Western state managers. That there are other readings of Weber within and without his own writing is largely ignored.[17] Equally marginalized is any careful, descriptively thick, account of policy making and policy implementation. Instead, the complexities and ambiguities of bureaucratic politics are quickly displaced by the unilinear certainties of a monochromatic account of the policy process, overconfident of its subject, object, intentionality, and rationality, and ignorant of the fuzziness, indeterminacy, and unpredictability of the 'garbage can' and other more compelling accounts of policy making.[18] To exacerbate matters, the realm of the irrational, demarcated from the state by the state/society dividing line, subsumes the political which is seen as a site of Manichaean intrusion into the orderly, apolitical, rational, technocratic world of the state and the professional bureaucrat. Analytic attention shifts accordingly to the mechanisms of insulation which create and sustain what Mitchell has termed the 'state effect' – the political myth of state autonomy and of the state as a site of technocratic rationality.[19]

A second criticism is particularly germane to our current concerns. The state-as-independent-variable approach, we have noted, takes a cross-section of the polity, treats this as a horizontal plane, and marks it off into two parts: the one state, the other society; the one rational, the other irrational; the one technocratic, scientific, and efficient, the other political, self-serving, and interest-driven. More remarkably, the exercise cuts the state off from its own history, the history of its own making, as comprehensively as it cuts the state off from society. The state theoretically imagined in this way has no past, no personality, and no politics. The rupture between the state and its history is glossed and justified in the distinction between 'state formation' and the 'state achieved'. This might be convenient but it is not persuasive. The argument requires a moment in time which does not exist: a moment at which the job is done, the business is finished, institutionalization is complete, the state is made, and henceforth escapes time. From then on there is only 'policy', not state making. It is as if the state emerges, fully fledged, at the end of an irreversible evolution. History and culture find themselves on the wrong side of the line that separates state from society, condemned to an existence amongst the analytically undeserving and disregarded poor.

This does not stand close scrutiny. Finality of this order is possible only by virtue of the preferences or shortcomings of academic disciplines – it is a finality which exists in the eye of the beholder and is produced by means of the device of *ceteris paribus*, 'assuming all else is held constant' – an analytic convenience but not something that holds true in the real world. Fixity is different. It is a possibility in the real world. But fixity of this order is possible and explicable only in terms of power and political triumphs. These are mostly short-lived and inescapably of limited term. There has not been, nor readily can be imagined, a once-and-for-all pursuit and exercise of political power. Such fixity is always contestable and to be renewed. It is intensely historical. In other words, the task of state making is never finished. There will always be flags to be waved, anthems to be sung, allegiances to be secured, armies to be paid, civil servants to be knighted, businesses to be promoted, missions to be stated, achievements to be celebrated, enemies to be vilified, and memories to be stirred. Historians know this, and by and large, political scientists seem not to. Moreover, since political science abhors a vacuum almost as much as nature itself, the house teleology of the liberal democratic state wells up to fill the historical gap. In other words, there is little need to consider the foundations of the state, to deal with the process of state making if the end product is the same – the modern Western state.

State making reconsidered

We have argued the need to reconnect the state to the dynamics of its making on the grounds that failure to do so results in the loss of understanding of the rich variety and possibilities of contemporary political order. At a minimum, the states of Asia, individually particular in their own right, are hybrids borne of the accommodation of Western forms and conceptions to Asian forms. As such, they are elusive to understandings grounded in expectations of how those forms work in the West. If we are to grasp the meaning and workings of the states we must emancipate their experience from the tight embrace of Western projections and see it as the outcome of a history in which Western examples are but one element. The corollary is an enhanced understanding of state making in the West as the particularity and localism of the Western political order is revealed. If the particularity of states is to be recovered it is essential, we argue, that we reconnect states with their histories; that we elide the distinction between state making and the state achieved; that we go beyond the pretence that history in this respect is to be understood exclusively as either obstacles to state making or the habitually ignored context of state making; that there is some magical moment when the state emerges butterfly perfect from its historical chrysalis, state making ends and policy begins in a permanent present.

Ironically, research prior to the bringing back of the state and the developmental state movements has been more sensitive to the variety of state forms and to state making as a process. The once dominant modernization school of inquiry was well acquainted with the variety of state forms and the complexities and challenges of state making. Scholars concerned with the making of the modern world, stimulated by the surge of newly independent nations after the Second World War, set out to study and shape the formation of these new polities in an exercise brave and bold in many respects. Recognizing that state forms varied tremendously across nations, some modernization theorists even gave up the concept of the state entirely. Unfortunately, abandoning the analysis of the state proved neither liberating nor helpful. It certainly did not result in a less parochial, less ethnocentric understanding of politics. Just the opposite. Loewenstein's estimate of the state problematique speaks volumes.[20] In his view, comparative politics needs to relinquish its narrow concern with the study of the state in order to become 'a conscious instrument of social engineering'.[21] Such an instrument could be used for 'imparting our experience to other nations and . . . integrating scientifically their institutions into a universal pattern of government.'[22] Here the state is displaced by pure instrumentality in service of a vision in which the systems of the West became the exclusive criteria for measuring the modernity of governmental forms in the world. The particular trajectory of historical change that led to the emergence of these Western systems is taken to be the only route for the passage to modernity. Binder sets out the terms of this great narrative:

> The rational culture of modernity is the rational culture of individuals, and the antirational culture which is the contemporary antithesis is the culture of subjectivity. . . . The political path to modernity involves critical changes of identity from the religious to the ethnic and from the parochial to the societal. It involves critical changes in legitimacy from transcendental to immanent sources. It involves critical changes in political participation from elite to mass and from family to group. It involves critical changes of distribution from status and privilege to ability, achievement, and the control and management of capital. And it involves critical changes in the degree of administrative and legal penetration into social structure and out to the remote regions of the country.[23]

From here it is but a short step to the corresponding idea of modern politics with its Western state predicate as a proper politics for moderns. In the words of Coleman, 'the Anglo-American polities most closely approximate the model of a modern political system'.[24]

Subsequent awareness in social science of the dangers, political as much as epistemological, of this kind of sentiment, awareness of its Eurocentricity and teleology, led to a rejection of much of the modernization school project. In part this is to be regretted – the part in question is the early sensitivity of the school to the variety and particularity of state forms, a sensitivity which obtained notwithstanding the conviction of the modernization school that these differences would be erased in the transition to the modern. More troubling here is that for all our certainty that the rejection of the teleology and Eurocentricity of the approach was justified, the fact is that 20 or 30 years after the demise of the modernization school, political modernity is couched and expressed exclusively in the language of democratic constitutionalism. The couplet of the modern liberal state plus democratic constitutionalism is verse and refrain in the discourse on political authority in a modern state in Asia every bit as much as in Europe. Does this mean that there is, after all, only one modern and only one route to the modern and, as a result, a single text from which the politics of the world might be read and that, contrary to our own argument, the nomenclature of the Western state is of universal relevance?[25] We doubt this. Certainly this kind of thinking has deep roots in the nineteenth century and characterized the approach of the masters who shaped much of our understanding of the modern state. One of its predicates is that the autochthonous politics of Asia is at best a flawed or degraded variant of the Western template to which it must inevitably approximate over time. Rudolph notes and rejects the view with force and eloquence:

> Hegel, Marx, and Weber, have understood Asian social, economic and political systems as flawed or degraded performances in a historical race in which all competitors run toward the same finish line – whether the finish line is nation-state, bourgeois capitalism, or universal rationalization. Whereas for Hegel, Marx and Weber there appeared to be but one race, and the West had strung the tape at the finish line for others to break, for us it has become apparent that there are multiple races and many finish lines, and the tapes are manufactured also in Tokyo and Beijing.[26]

In short, while we must recognize the pre-eminence of a republican discourse in the competition for authority, we must not take the word for the fact. We mean this in two different ways: on the one hand, the 'text' upon which the republican discourse is written has proved so loosely worded, so little prescriptive, so expansive and generous in its interpretative possibilities, that we might better speak of the liberal republican discourse as the site and provenance of the nomenclature within which the contemporary state represents itself to itself and to others, than as the text from which it might be read. As anywhere else in the 'political thickets', the nomenclature is to be deciphered; and associated practices have to be discovered and decoded. More concretely put, 'it is not self-evident that the parliaments of Morocco and Egypt or the finance ministries of Iraq and Iran operate exactly the way their American counterparts do, nor is it clear what those differences might mean for the study of elections in the abstract or capital markets in general.'[27] These are matters for investigation. Neither must we confuse the ubiquity of the discourse with the fact of a single political modernity. Emphatically, we must not assume that the liberal democratic, administrative, rational state is a global finish line. We compromise understanding if we disregard the race itself (that is, the state-making process) on the presumption that Asian state making must have been a more or less flawed and degraded facsimile of the process that led to the emergence of the state in the West, a facsimile upgraded and corrected by colonialism and/or self-conscious modeling from the periphery of the institutional norms and values of the modern state. It is, we stress, fundamentally inimical to understanding of the state. Again, if we are to understand the nature of the states of Asia we must reconnect them to their histories of state making.

Why Asia?

Asia is rich ground on which to explore the dynamics of state making. We say this for several reasons. First and foremost, Asia is a challenge to some of the core assumptions of state theory. In so saying, we do not suggest that there is a distinctive Asian state. Our concern is rather with what Whitehead terms the standard assumptions about 'stateness' that are built into prevailing social science discourse (especially that expressed in the English language), and above all with how adequately these capture the essence of order and domination in the diverse states of Asia.[28] The standard assumptions about the nature of the modern state can be summarized as follows. From the outset, the modern state is identified with a specific territorial area as an integral unit. The state claims proprietary jurisdiction over this territorial area, including its space, resources, and inhabitants. Within this specific territorial area, the state is an association of abstracted individuals – citizens – who are the sole bearers of rights and obligations. The state represents an inalienable authority within such a commonwealth of citizens. This authority is embodied in the principle of sovereignty. As the sovereign power, the authority of the state is singular, legal, indivisible, non-negotiable, and impersonal. It is the source of all legal authorities; it speaks on behalf of the commonwealth; and it is recognized by other commonwealths as the sole representative and authority of a particular commonwealth. The state assumes the organizational form of a set of centralized coercion-wielding institutions that exercise priority over all other organizations within a territorial boundary. It is managed professionally by a bureaucratic hierarchy of trained personnel. The organizational understanding of the state is supplemented by a functional understanding of the state as that set of institutions responsible for maintaining social order, revenue extraction, and the distribution of resources.

Problems attend each of the stylized properties of the modern state when these are viewed from within Asia. The notion of an indivisible sovereignty, arguably the indispensable underpinning of contemporary conceptions of the state, is a fairly recent arrival in India, where the conception and practice of sovereignty has argued the multiple rights of multiple groups and entrenched what Eisenstadt speaks of as 'fractured sovereignty', a norm that precluded the development of 'a conception of statehood as a distinct, absolutist, ontological entity'.[29] Problems no less attend the (legitimate) monopoly of the exercise of force. Let us take China as an example. Scholars have long insisted upon a millennial continuity in China's political order in which the Communist regime is to be understood as a manifestation of continuity rather than as a break in continuity.[30] However, there is no evidence of a parallel continuity in the monopoly and exercise of force. The great body of reflection and comment on rule in China makes no claim for the centrality of force. Rather, the axis of the political order, it is often said, is not force but what we might term 'culture' – a notion conspicuous by its absence from any definition of the modern state.[31] The exercise of force has been repeatedly challenged, interrupted, and broken by invasion and usurpation. Argument and evidence of the Sinification reflex by means of which invading powers are accommodated to long-run patterns of rule are themselves testimony to the pre-eminence of culture in the construction of the Chinese political order. In a similar vein, the idea of a monopoly of force is problematic in India as well as in China.[32]

Were we to disregard these reservations, the question of legitimacy would remain a stumbling block. Notable works on the foundations of state power in China explicitly reject the notion of legitimacy as peculiar to the Western state founded in the rule of law.[33] Law in China has ever been an instrument of the state and rarely its master. The same applies to Japan.[34] It is thus more accurate to speak of law as an instrument of rule than of the rule of law. This was as true in 1947 and thereafter as in 1868 Japan.[35] How adequately the current conventions of social science regarding the definition of the state permit us to address the problem of legitimacy will be discussed below.

The territorial dimension of the state in Asia is no simple matter either. Nor for that matter can territoriality be assumed, *without historical examination*, to have the same meaning as that attributed to it in current social science usage. An axiom of the literature on state making in Europe speaks of the role of war between its emergent proto-states as the driving force behind the generation of a tax-gathering apparatus and warranty offices, their centralization and hierarchy. No less axiomatic is war as a demarcator of state boundaries and so as midwife to a territorial conception of political organization. What could more dramatically distinguish between this state and that state, between us and them, than borders drawn in blood and paid for in money? What then, *in these historical circumstances*, could be more obvious than the emergence over time of an understanding of political organization in terms of the representation of space? To be sure, war delineated the territories of the European states as it triggered the formation of the apparatus that would pay for and prosecute war. As such, territory as the fundament of political organization burnt deep in the Western consciousness. None of this is in doubt. But matters were otherwise in Asia. Japan is a case in point. Early state formation was completed in Japan before its entry upon a world stage and in the absence of boundary-defining enemies.[36] The same holds for China.[37] War was not a factor in the definition of a territorial entity to subsume political organization. Japan is, of course, an island; and it might be thought that state boundaries were given in nature so that the need for war to define them was avoided. It was never so. A core notion of the realm – *tenka*, or 'under heaven' – had no territorial reference. The territorial boundaries of the state are necessarily elastic and without sacerdotal meaning since there is no limit to heavenly authority. Conversely there can be no territorial limit and no unconquerable shore. Consequently, Japan might claim 'legitimately' to invade a Korean neighbor. The Japanese state is not a territorial political expression.[38] The same is true of China. The territorial scope of the empire ebbed and flowed over vast expanses – on a scale all but unimaginable to Europeans. The gains and losses amounted sometimes to Europe or its states. The mastery of territory meant little in terms of conceptions of the political: territory was won or lost without incidence for conceptions of rule and authority. Boundaries were not defined by war. Territory did not figure in a movement in which, delimited and sanctified by war and defense, it comes to demarcate the privileged space within which to fashion or represent a political persona. The idea of such a territory and of an associated political persona is deeply engraved in Western social theory. It is significantly less important in Asia.

The ability to construe a political persona from a territory and, conversely, for an extant political power to claim to represent a territory is crucially dependent in the West upon the intervening variable the 'nation'. Indeed, for all that the nation has a troubled and problematic history even in the European heartland of the state, the nation-state is the norm and archetype of Western political organization. And so we come to the second reason that makes Asia not just an important but, arguably, the indispensable site upon which to investigate the variety of contemporary 'states' and to do so by treating them as a product of the history of their making. The nation-state has not been the archetypical organizational form in Asia; that privilege is reserved for the transethnic empire or continental polity. The implications of this for notions such as unified sovereignty and political monopoly, notions indispensable to our conception of the modern state, are so profound that we can for the first time begin to wonder at the possibility of quite different state forms in Asia. Here we can only applaud the acuity of Rudolph's assessment again:

One reason the conventions of comparison developed in a European context serve us ill is that the European polities around which they developed became nation-states whereas the Asian polities did not. The European polities approximate what we in Asia would call regional kingdoms. Asian polities reached for a far greater comprehensiveness; except in South East Asia they were continental polities, transethnic empires. This distinction is so overwhelming and so obvious that it has to be the starting point of all comparative exercises. It suggests to begin with, why the idea of a unified sovereignty, the idea of a political monopoly so crucial to European definitions of the state, cannot be our starting point. A nation-state is a restricted territory in which there is a presumption or at least an aspiration of congruence between the state and a nation or people. By contrast, an empire is an extended territory comprising a group of states or peoples under the control or at least the suzerainty of a dominant power.[39]

It is remarkable that the familiar checklist of the characteristics of the modern state does not include the nation. The Weberian definition of the state, so widely adopted in comparative politics, drops the term altogether. Yet for Weber the nation was without a doubt the privileged site of the modern state. 'Time and again,' he writes, 'we find that the concept "nation" directs us to political power. Hence the concept seems to refer – if it refers at all to a uniform phenomenon – to a specific kind of pathos which is linked to the idea of a powerful political community of people who share a common language, or religion, or common customs, or political memories; such a state may already exist or it may be desired. The more power is emphasized, the closer appears to be the link between nation and state.'[40] He speaks too, of the nation-state and the state based on common language as 'conceptually identical'. We have noted that nation, in reality, has been intensely problematic, and even at the highest point of the classic nation-state, in the first half of the twentieth century, the state was typically far from approaching a pure nation-state form. The problem of creating a nation for the new states reached insurmountable proportions in post-colonial Africa and Asia, to such an extent that often the expression 'nation-state' proved to be a misnomer. Is it this, perhaps, that explains the popularity of the truncated Weberian definition of the state? Where by truncated we mean that the definition cuts out any reference to the nation as an indispensable element of the modern state? An explicit and formal insistence upon the 'nation' as a condition for statehood would greatly reduce the scope of application and so the utility of the term. Dropping the word 'nation' altogether makes it possible to circumnavigate the problem and to re-establish the commonality, as 'modern states', of Western nation-states and newer states that are not the political expression of the nation. Whether the definition of the state left after this exercise would do justice to Weber's understanding of the modern Western state we rather doubt.

The popularity of the abbreviated Weberian definition prompts a second question, namely, does the truncated Weberian definition of the state, by dropping the nation from its list of properties, enable us to emancipate the conventions of comparison from their European bias? Here, to start with, one cannot help but wonder what Weber would have made of such a statement as that we used above, namely, 'creating a nation for the new state'. If this is not non-sense then it is certainly the opposite of the logic he perceived. He writes, 'Whatever the "nation" means beyond a mere "language group" can be found in the specific objective of its social action, and this can only be the *autonomous polity*.'[41] These words of Weber suggest that for him the meaning and significance of 'nation' is precisely the ambition of a group demarcated by language to carve out for itself political autonomy. Nation is the subject, not the object, of the political exercise. Reverse this and the nation disappears and a mere language group is left. The state accordingly is understood as the political expression of the nation and the state is legitimate in so far as it satisfies the national sense of the right to rule.[42] If we make a sharp distinction, as is now customarily done, between state as the body that claims a monopoly of the legitimate use of violence and the nation as a community of sentiment,[43] we encounter formidable problems in grounding the legitimacy principle of the modern state, in answering the question 'legitimate to whom?' Legitimacy, that is to say the feeling among the population that it is normatively correct to comply as well as in one's interest, is an integral feature of the modern state in the absence of which systems of taxation, for example, would be ruinously difficult to police. Many of Weber's most important writings concern precisely the sources of the feeling that one should obey authority: those sources are famously identified in his tripartite schema of rational-legal, traditional-personalistic, and charismatic authority. Legitimacy is no less indispensable to the definition of the state, since without it we cannot distinguish order from oppression, government from repression, the republic from despotism and tyranny. However, it cannot easily be sustained – even at the definitional level – without specification of its grounding. In practice the echo of the nation-state couplet lingers in the truncated definition and its answer to the question, 'legitimate to whom?' is audible to all but the deafest: it is legitimate to the citizen, to the nation, to the people understood as a community of sentiment.[44] The nation-state remains the concealed subject of theorizing, the archetype that underpins the conventions of comparison between West and East.

A third factor which underlines Asia's importance in our inquiry is the rich variety of state-making experiences within the region. In contrast to the countries of Africa and Latin America, which were all profoundly shaped by colonial experiences, the countries of Asia have widely differing histories. Some of the Asian histories included colonization; others avoided it. Self-evidently, colonial intervention is a major influence upon the political institutions and the political practice of the newly independent nations, to the extent that it has been used widely as the basis upon which to argue the generalization of the modern European state form. And yet, we must remind ourselves that even here history is not obliterated, not even in the most vulnerable reaches of Africa.[45] The homogenizing effects of colonialism are themselves offset and particularized in accordance with the particularities of the colonial experience, its timing and character. The response of those colonized is not a given but a task for historical inquiry. As Kaviraj puts it, the imitation of colonial rulers might be pure and thoroughgoing, it could 'equally and elsewhere be perfunctory or absent, limited to externalities like accents, manners, dress codes, a taste for cricket and Shakespeare'.[46]

The argument that Western expansion neither obliterates history nor erases all trace of earlier political development applies with even greater force in countries that escaped colonial intervention. There is a great gulf in political experience between the situation of a country such as Indonesia or India that was colonized and Japan or Thailand that was not. This is not to suggest that the latter got off entirely free from Western influence. But the impact was much less, changes were more self-directed rather than imposed, and choices were selective. In Japan, independence was retained, and it was Japan's elite rather than colonial administrators who managed change. Ito Hirobumi, the principal architect of Japan's modernization project in the latter part of the nineteenth century, enjoyed a luxury denied to Jawaharlal Nehru more than half a century later, in that he was free to see Japan's 'feudal legacies' of ideas, values, and institutions as a repertoire to be drawn on. It was an enormous historical opportunity for Hirobumi whereas Nehru was prisoner to a 'powerful, prior Orientalizing of pre-colonial Indian culture by the British' and was constrained to hunt out 'evidence of modernity in Indian tradition'.[47] In other words, autochthonous political development makes available to the Japanese elite a repertoire of institutional and discursive resources simply unavailable to others. It can hardly be imagined that in such circumstances of stark difference (even allowing for an extremely important element of borrowing and modeling), that elites and masses in Indonesia, India, Japan, and Thailand would craft out the same state.

Japan is not alone in its enjoyment of its own politics. Other nations of Asia, most notably but not exclusively China, have long histories of autochthonous political development. They have their own legacies of institutions, understandings, and demarcations (crudely, for instance: inside and outside, high and low, rather than public and private). Autochthonous development prompted centuries-long reflection by local intellectuals and officials on the nature of government, rule, and administration. These reflections were born in historical circumstances touching war, trade, religion, and philosophy far removed from those of Europe in the seventeenth to nineteenth centuries. As such these reflections bear little relation to the elements of Western state theory, namely, the secular holy trinity of individual, society, and the state. The central references, conceptual, textual, lexical, and historic narratives, are also different. To illustrate the point, in the late nineteenth century a Japanese translator of J. S. Mill's *On Liberty* imaginatively came up with no fewer than 273 alternatives in his efforts to render a conception of place between the person and the state – the missing link 'society' could only be imagined by the translator as a variant of the state itself. The gulf that separates these universes of understanding and argument is immense. It prompts Eisenstadt to argue that the politics and economics of East Asia as much as those of the West are specific to that particular civilization and can only be understood within the context of that civilization.[48] This is an approach that has proved highly persuasive to political scientists in the region itself.

The hybridism of Asian states

In sum, we take issue with the extension to Asia of a reading of the Western tradition as the very model of the modern state. Instead, we problematize the state itself, that is to say we treat it as something to be described and explained rather than as a 'given'. The key to its explanation is to be found in the history of its making. We see the making of the state in Asia as historic and continuing, contentious and problematic processes in which indigenous understandings and institutions can clash, mesh with, and subvert the Western model. As we trace the making of the state viewed in this way, it becomes apparent that the problem of the state in Asia is not just that of maintaining autonomy or of enhancing a capacity to shape economic development, but more fundamentally is compounded with questions of territoriality, citizenship, sovereignty, and nationhood. Problems of this nature were once dismissed by modernization theorists as remnants of premodern forms of rule or as transitional phenomenon during the modernization process, a dismissal predicated upon the assumed universality of the trajectory of the modern state. This is mistaken; what is at issue is not so much the overcoming of the past as the emergence of hybrid forms of the modern state. 'Hybrid forms' is something of a catch-all notion since the range of state-making experiences is considerable: it may be that some or all of territoriality, citizenship, sovereignty, and nationhood are problematic, a consequence of inherent, deep-seated, and enduring tensions in a struggle to incorporate Western forms and indigenous practices; it may be, equally, that some or all of this are 'settled' and in this sense nonproblematic, save for the critical fact that their meaning and significance cannot be read from a standard account of the modern state predicated upon the Western model. The full gamut of intermediary possibilities also exists and can only be gauged by historical and empirical investigation. It is to this that attention now turns.

Our arguments rest upon a comparative study of three major Asian cases: Japan, China, and Malaysia. The three countries have had very different experiences of contact with the West. They have known very different possibilities and ambitions in respect of the adoption and mobilization of Western state forms. They have brought to bear on the state-making process very different historical experiences, ideational, and institutional legacies. In retrospect, they represent three distinct state-making trajectories. Japan envisaged a marriage of indigenous political practices and the Western state form,[49] shorn of its republican features, as the means to a guided industrial and military development that would secure the place of a modernized and invigorated Japan in a world of states. In short the creation of the modern Japanese state owed much to the ambition of a political elite, nothing to bourgeois revolution, and little to war making.

China, more vast, more complex, vulnerable, and subject to interruption, contained a plurality of elites that envisaged and sought to execute quite different visions of the political future. War making had an impact on the Nationalists and their republican vision no less marked than on the Communists and their dramatically different vision. Even so, it is exceedingly unlikely that the final victory of the one rather than the other would have produced the same state – in short state making owed much to the complex interplay of millennial tradition, both as burden and resource, and the aspirations of elites in an equation in which war making was far from determining. Not the least of the interruptions to these endeavors are those that have left China plagued by competing claims to sovereignty and disputes over territoriality.

Malaysia's understanding of the modern state and the resources brought to bear in its state-making project was deeply marked by the British colonial legacy. The political boundary left by the British was so at variance with the social, cultural, and ethnic foundations of a modern state as to be fundamentally inimical to state making on the Western pattern. In consequence the Malaysian state-making project has been sharply characterized, pace Weber, by the search for the nation as the state seeks to invent its foundations. The heterogeneity of Malaysian society with the variety of potential nations is such that the legitimacy of the state is always likely to remain fundamentally in question. In sum, the comparison of the three cases highlights the hybridism of modern state forms in Asia; a hybridism borne out of the clash of Western norms and indigenous traditions, the political and ideological struggles over territoriality, sovereignty, and citizenship, and the problems of ethnicity and religion in defining the cultural and political boundaries of the state.

The Western state model has been transplanted to Asia through colonization, imitation, and selective adaptation. There are good reasons for Asian countries to embrace the Western state form. In the first place, the principle of territorial sovereignty is a powerful principle for postcolonial countries (such as Malaysia), or countries which once suffered from foreign invasion (such as China), to assert independence. The idea that the home state can claim sole jurisdiction over space, resources, and inhabitants within its territory has been an attractive notion to Asian elites eager to consolidate their claim to rule.

Second, since the adoption of the Western state form is a prerequisite for admission to the international community of states, this status is much in demand by Asian elites since it secures their legitimacy and acceptance in global society and has a parallel utility in securing their domestic legitimacy. It is the exclusive means of access to positions of eminence, prestige, and influence in international councils and no less to the goods and services (distributed by the World Bank, the IMF, and so on) available to members of the world community of nation-states.

In the third place, the institutions of the Western state form, particularly in the spare and muscular shape of the colonial state, have proven to be powerful machineries of rule, war making, and later of economic growth – facts that have not escaped the attention of Asian elites. The attractions as a means to rule of a rational administration with specialized functionaries, routinized practices, and well-defined hierarchy of orders that provides a stable framework for collective action, one in *permanent readiness* cannot easily be overestimated. The structures and practices of the state (as is well known) are not put together in a provisional or *ad hoc* manner in response to exigencies of flood or famine. Rather they exist as a 'permanent' edifice, capable of responding instantly to arising needs, disciplining social behavior, and even learning and improving themselves in the constant bid for greater effectiveness and efficiency. This aspect of the state is described in different ways. Whitehead, later in this volume, refers to it as a 'specialized structure of administration' and alternatively as a 'state apparatus', others speak of the machinery of state. What runs through and links these expressions is one aspect of the state that we will refer to as the 'institutionalized agency' of the state – the highly visible means by which the modern state gets things done. Not surprisingly, these properties of structural permanence and institutionalized agency have been the target of imitation throughout Asia. Right across the board, states in Asia have looked to fashion sets of institutions with familiar names: legislature, presidency, cabinet, armed forces, judiciary, planning agencies, and so on. Even Communist China endorsed these 'bourgeois' institutions. It established isomorphic organizations such as the National People's Congress, the State Council, the Supreme People's Court, and the People's Liberation Army.[50] It hardly needs saying, however, that whatever a legislature might do and be in China, it was never likely to be fully identical to a legislature in the modern Western polity, and the same applies with equal force to other institutions with familiar names such as the supreme court and the judiciary not only in China but also in other Asian states not grounded in the rule of law.

More urgently in need of saying is that the ease with which the institutionalized agency of the modern state might be reproduced in Asia should not be allowed to obscure the fact that, once to hand, it could be used not only in pursuit of different goals (it is argued that the institutional legacy of the Japanese colonial state lent itself admirably to the task of economic development in post-independent Korea and Taiwan), but equally to craft different states. We are already familiar with this possibility when states are understood in terms of their functions and priorities – hence our talk of developmental states, welfare states, security states, and so on – but now we speak of something else, that is differences in states consonant with different understandings of rule, of law, of society than those characteristic of, say, the Anglo-Saxon polities. This last observation is lost if we conflate the institutionalized agency of the modern state with the modern state *in toto* – something that occurs only too often in social science where 'bureaucracy' and state are used synonymously and interchangeably.

The imbrication of institutionalized, hierarchic, and centralized agency in broader structures and principles are secured in the Western state model by means of highly particular understandings of space, of collective identity, and of the meaning and locus of the right to rule. These understandings are so familiar as to have lost any sense of their particularity. They are territoriality, secularism, nationality, and sovereignty. We have noted (*ad nauseam* we fear) that these principles took several centuries to develop and consolidate in the unique circumstances of Europe and emerged in the same process that contained the development of the agency principle itself. The inseparability of these elements, the conjoined and mutually fashioning nature of their development in one region of the world, at one (long) moment of time, warrants a degree of caution before we argue that the matrix of the state within which the institutionalized agency of Asia is implicated is the same as in the West. Indeed, it our anticipation of quite fundamental differences in this regard that encourages us to speak of hybrid forms of the modern state.

In the cases of China, Japan, and Malaysia, hybridism is manifested in several aspects. Firstly, state institutions have meshed with local practices of governance to produce the appearance of seemingly universal institutions but which are actually endowed with local meanings.[51] This is not, of course, peculiar to Asia. As Hawthorn has noted, politics in most developing countries enshrines a set of ideas and practices which are more idiosyncratic and various than the common ends, or the constitutional rules, with which the ends are pursued and with which the institutions in the constitutions are actually made to work.[52] Our discussion of the Japanese bureaucracy below will demonstrate the point. Secondly, the case studies underline the eagerness of Asian states to embrace the principle of territorial sovereignty in an attempt to assert independence and yet states like China-Taiwan-Tibet are obliged to wrestle with problems of unresolved – or like Malaysia with a weakly construed – territoriality and overlapping sovereignty. Even more problematic is the modern Japanese state, which, for more than half of its life, has been reluctant to accept any territorial limit to the reach of (imperial) sovereignty. Thirdly, the Asian cases reveal the difficulty and elusiveness of the idea of citizenship, which has become one of the pillars of the Western understanding of the modern state tradition. Asia knows a real variety in the language and conception of political membership. Translating this into a concept of citizenship that sees the state as an association of abstracted individuals – citizens – who enjoy uniform rights and obligations, creates enormous conflict and contention. Rival projects that aim to accommodate indigenous ideas of political membership with the idea of citizenship will illustrate the point. Finally, the cases will be used to show how competing state projects seek to create a sufficient basis of common identity, or nationhood, that is to say, how they endeavor to construct a grounding identity by matching cultural boundaries to political boundaries. The range of projects investigated include the evoking of traditional cultural practices, defining new identities for the people, reinventing the historical past, manipulating ethnicity, or forging the hegemonic dominance of a particular social segment.

Western norms and indigenous traditions

The case of Japan shows how one of the oldest Asian nations took great pains to copy Western political and economic models during the Meiji period. It is an outstanding example of the modern state in Asia as the product of imitation, indigenous traditions, and invention. Moreover, the Japanese case neatly illustrates Meyer's point that the isomorphism of state institutions across the world is not rooted exclusively in efficiency, rationality, or the efficacy of the Western models – the attraction of which we noted above.[53] Instead, Japanese state-making effort was driven by the desire to conform to the dominant state system in the global society of nation-states. State making as such was both an internal and external process: internally, the Meiji state created new rituals and customs for its human subjects; externally, it created a modern state as a subject in an international community.

Detailed case studies of the Japanese reform in economic and political systems examined by Ravina in Chapter 2 of this volume shows the extent these reforms were shaped by the desire to conform to the Western standard. Specifically, the *bakumatsu* fiscal and monetary system which based on fiat money was replaced by gold standard in order to link the Japanese economy to the global economy, even though the *bakumatsu* system was more 'modern' and economically more 'advanced' than the gold standard. In the same vein, constitutional government based on a separation of powers was hailed as the inevitable trend of the times, so it was argued that Japan should follow the institutional norm. The goal was to avoid subjugation by the Western imperialist powers. The means to this goal involved conformity to Western norms that bound the great powers themselves.

Although Western-type state institutions were successfully implanted in the Japanese polity, their actual functioning corresponded less to Weberian principles than to the legacies of indigenous state tradition. This applies no less to such a seemingly universal institution of the modern state as the bureaucracy; this too is heavily endowed with local meanings. It follows that one cannot deduce the actual behavior of the institution, nor its meaning, in the larger matrix of the Japanese state from its familiar label and its 'Weberian' cloak. This is demonstrated in Chapter 3 by Boyd, who examines two distinctive characteristics of modern Japanese politics: bureaucratic sectionalism and bureaucratic transcendence. The latter is the very antithesis of the public service role of the state bureaucracy anticipated by the 'republican' aspect of the modern state. The former means that different organs of the state routinely mistake parochial interests for those of the nation. They exercise a sense of autonomy in which all are pitted against all and 'all' constantly jockey for power in present-day Japan. The entrenched sectionalism of the Japanese bureaucracy originated in the cabinet system constituted in 1885 in terms of which ministerial leaders were not bound by any principle of collective accountability as a cabinet. Over time, this led to a *de facto* right of veto by individual ministries over cabinet decisions. Successive reforms resulted not in the curbing of sectional power, but on the contrary created new bureaucratic amalgams in which the section retained its priority. So central is the fact in the life of Japanese society that for each bureaucratic section there is a ruling Liberal Democratic Party subdivision and an associated tendency for private interests to organize themselves on the same basis.

Sectionalism is complemented by a practice of transcendent administration which also runs counter to the 'public service' conception of the bureaucracy. The chapter carefully documents how the Japanese state tradition supports an understanding of the bureaucratic role readily compatible with the notion of transcendence. It concludes that the peculiar institutional and procedural configuration of the bureaucracy has to be understood in the broader framework of the traditions and practices of the Japanese state as these traditions and practices suborn apparently familiar institutions.

The struggle over territoriality, sovereignty, and citizenship

The experience of China must loom large in any discussion of the particularity of the state outside of the West. We have noted above the conceptual stretch and strain that is entailed in characterizing the Chinese state in terms of territoriality and legitimacy. We have spoken of the 'mismatch', definitionally speaking, of a persistent and uninterrupted 'acceptance' of the state and an interrupted monopoly of coercion. We have suggested too, that long prior to the codification of the European experience of statehood, China's millennial autochthonous political development had prompted sophisticated reflection and debate that led to an extensive corpus of writings. These cover a wide range of political questions from the nature and limits of authority, to the terms and limits of the exercise of official powers and the proper conduct of what political science terms 'civil–military relations'. Their practical influence and importance in Asia was considerable and contributed to the fashioning of the politics of Japan, Korea, Vietnam, and Thailand. Their interest and theoretical importance to social science is considerable for two weighty reasons. The first of these is that the Chinese invention of political order anticipates that of the West by centuries. This is not to suggest that we are either in a race or a social science beauty contest, the point is rather that the political development of China, that is to say the identification and characterization of problems roughly analogous to the Western 'political', the search for their solution and the debate of the merits of these, was uninfluenced by the Western equivalent because this came later. The second reason is no less weighty. We have noted that the conceptual foundations of the analysis of the modern state are, we would say, inextricably caught up in the European history of the sixteenth to the nineteenth centuries. That those conceptual foundations are themselves articulated in a political lexicon made in Greece would hardly need reiteration were it not for the fact that the codification of the Chinese 'political' was not lexically captive to ancient Greece.

This is a point of great importance, particularly in view of the renewal of interest in Karl Jasper's notion of the axial civilization.[54] China is an axial civilization. It fashioned its 'politics' in response to a vision of a transcendent moral order different to that of ancient Greece, and as such it affords us a unique vantage point from which to view the limits and particularity of the political logos of the West. Rather than recognize the distinctiveness of these two monumental political achievements, that of the West and that of China, the conventions of comparison, we have argued, lodge the nation-state in their premises and so skew comparison.

In Chapter 4, Wong deals directly with precisely these: nation and citizenry as the predicate of the Chinese state. Wong is persuaded that the Chinese political past is of abiding contemporary political relevance, and seeks specifically to demonstrate the ways in which citizenship and nation have evolved in twentieth-century China out of earlier practices and beliefs, as well as ideas and institutions brought in from the West. In short, he deals with a critical facet of the state-making process – one that is at the heart of this volume. He does so in a manner broadly suggestive of that process in Asia overall, a process marked in different degrees by selective borrowing, adoption, adaptation, and accommodation of the indigenous and the autochthonous, a process far removed from that caricatured in the theory of the 'radical extraneity' of the Western state. Wong sketches the development of the ideas of nation and citizen from the Qing period to the present day. The treatment is complex and multifaceted, we can do no more here than touch upon themes and conclusions that exemplify some of the points raised in this introduction. From the Qing period, we learn, the quest for the nation was a strategy of rule, a top-down exercise that targeted the creation of 'a set of cultural [Confucian] practices deemed the foundation of proper personal behavior' that would straddle multiregional, multiethnic, multilinguistic differences. With the fall of the imperial order, Confucian teachings came to be seen as conservative and backward, and a new national identity to underpin the state was fashioned in a movement which remained top-down, despite regime change. Now, and even after the Communist takeover, national identity was defined in contradistinction to external enemies as the fight against foreign aggression became the privileged means for the forging of identities. The top-down crafting of national identities proved problematic in a later period, when the attractions of a 'more modern' state founded upon a common-wealth of citizens presented themselves. An associational model predicated upon the citizen understood as bearer of rights and as partner in a negotiated relationship with the state had precious little historical support, and was not easily reconcilable to one that turned upon the politically correct and appropriate attitude and behavior of the people as determined in a one-way exercise by the Communist Party. Indeed, the chapter demonstrates the near impossibility of developing in China a concept of the state based on that of the citizen and his/her republic. Intriguingly, whereas the political aspirations of nation unstitched empire in the West, the converse is true in China. Here, as recently as the 1980s and 1990s, regional and ethnic claims were presented in accordance with the 'top-down' imperative, that is to say, not as a particu-laristic claim that could only be satisfied by unraveling the more general and overarching claims of empire and finally by parceling up the imperial terri-tory into smaller autonomous nation-states but as a substitute for the general claim in total. In consequence, their effect is to preserve rather than fragment the Chinese state/empire.

The Taiwanese case neatly illustrates the entrenched 'top-down' reflex, identified by Wong, to contest the content of the nation, to represent a par-ticular as the general, rather than to claim the particular as the proper unit of government and administration, and so to target the subdivision of the larger political entity China. Even after the retreat of the KMT to Taiwan, the regime insisted upon its sovereignty over the mainland, and organized the representation in its legislature of all regions of the Chinese state as if the whole of the nation could be held within the shores of the island. The case raises interesting questions also when viewed through the conventional apparatus of state analysis – not least with reference to the notion of terri-torial sovereignty. The Republic of China was until the 1970s recognized by the international community as representing the commonwealth 'China', but it had only *de facto* political control of Taiwan and the adjacent isles and had no control of the mainland. The great majority of the world nations now recognize the rival People's Republic of China as representing the whole of China, including Taiwan and Tibet. Yet there are still some two dozen coun-tries in the world which maintain diplomatic ties with the Republic of China. The People's Republic has never been able to extend its political control to Taiwan even though it claims itself to be the sole sovereign state of China.

Wang explores in Chapter 5 how this struggle over sovereignty shaped state making in Taiwan. From 1949 to 1971, sovereignty of the Republic of China was not based upon actual territorial control but on international recognition that owed much to the anticommunist ideology then dominant in the West, complemented by authoritarian control of the populace. This was a state that substituted international for domestic legitimacy. The strug-gle over the transformation of a Chinese state into a Taiwanese state began in earnest in the 1980s, when the ethnic liberation movement of the Taiwanese majority, excluded by and opposed to the mainlander regime, fused with the democratic movement. Rapid political change swept through the island from the early 1990s, creating a *de facto* Taiwan state that corresponds more closely to the territorial realities. The new state has re-established internal popular support and so has secured the bases of domestic legitimacy but remains unrecognized externally as a legitimate state.

An excursion to the Tibetan diaspora completes our exploration of the complex issues of territoriality, sovereignty, and citizenship that attend the Chinese state. The case is fascinating: a study of not so much as a 'state', but rather of an 'anticipation of the state', actualized in some respects and obviously not in others. It suggests the cultural limitations of the Western model of the state, the multifariousness and plasticity of notions of sovereignty and citizenship, and serves as a powerful reminder of the place of historical contingency in state making. Tibet is itself not an independent state. Tibetan exiles in camp in Nepal are even less a state, or so at least it might seem. This is not, however, the perspective of the camp. As Frechette argues in Chapter 6, although the Tibetan exiles lack an exclusive sovereign claim to any territory, they have been able to construct the basic institutions characteristic of modern statehood. The Tibetan refugee camp as a whole is understood by its occupants as a state complete with governing institutions and a claim to sovereign authority, decoupled from territorial control. The chapter explores how the Tibetan exiles manipulate the idea of territorial sovereignty to craft out their own imaginary space for political membership. It shows, too, how the Tibetans have developed their own language and categories to describe political membership, a language different in many respects to the modern republican discourse about individuals and citizenship. Even so, the now familiar practice of modeling and adaptation of Western political forms is here too very much in evidence as the chapter shows how the Tibetan exiles struggle to accommodate their own ideas to the Western concepts of liberty, equality, private property, and the legal persona associated with the idea of citizenship.

Fragmented nations and competing state projects

The Malaysian state, much more than that of China or Japan, is the product of European colonialism. To say this, however, is to speak of the state in the very restrictive sense used above when we spoke of the 'agency principle' of the state. Here, beyond a doubt, the colonial institutional legacy was a determining influence in the making of the post-independence state apparatus. International recognition came hard on the heels of independence to herald the birth of a new state. This left unresolved the problems of that broader matrix of institutions, identities, and relationships which contextualize and give meaning to the state apparatus. Not least the construction of the state as a modern commonwealth remains not only incomplete, in the absence of a community of sentiment and identity coextensive with the territory and reach of the state apparatus, but also precarious and contested, as problems of marrying the newer state forms with indigenous traditions and institutions of public power remain unresolved.

The trajectory of Malaysian state making shows that even though state institutions expanded and consolidated to assume the appearance of the modern state on the Western model, the relationship between the ruling authorities, the human subjects, and the territorial boundary was not settled and has proved highly problematic. The attractions of a settlement along the lines of secularism and citizenship are considerable in a multiethnic, religiously plural society, the prospects of its realization commensurately less. And in fact a relationship undergirded by principles of citizenship has proved elusive. The principle of secularism seems hardly applicable to the Malaysian state. The alternatives are fraught with their own dangers. The formation of a unified nationhood and a uniform citizenry predicated upon a favored ethnicity has proved unsuccessful and subject to opposition from other ethnic groups. Each ethnic group has its elite and their positions and practices of power are often imperfectly and inconsistently accommodated to the formal structures of rule. They dispute persistently, if not surprisingly, the terms upon which the commonwealth is to be constructed. In short, there are competing projects to create the nation which will ground the state. The intensity of the competition to define the nation-making project reflects the high value of the prize at stake. This is nothing less than the state itself. Because the way in which Malaysia answers the question: 'what is the nation?' will closely condition answers to the question, 'what is the nature and purposes of the state?' The question is not only academic. The way in which it is answered will determine the real world, the brute facticity of the state. It provokes us to refer back to our earlier discussion of the truncated or abbreviated Weberian definition of the state. We question again the utility of a definition which purports to define the state without reference to the nature and terms of the community of sentiment that not only sustains the state but also contributes concretely and fundamentally to its making and shaping. For the moment, it has been recognized by the ruling elites that, although Malaysia is a modernizing state, it is not yet a nation-state. A united Malaysian nation is yet to be born.

In Chapter 7, Shamsul and Daud go to the heart of these questions in their analysis of a new project which aims to create a united Malaysian nation-state, a *Bangsa Malaysia*, by the year 2020. The project envisages the adoption of *bumiputera* (son of the soil) culture as the core of the Malaysian national identity. The vision has been challenged by the non-*bumiputera*, led by the Chinese, as well as by the non-Muslim *bumiputera* group and the radical Islamic *bumiputera* group, as each attempts to register its own interests behind a preferred conception of what should constitute the national principle. The non-*bumiputera* argue for a more plural culture that recognizes the equal status of other non-*bumiputera* ethnic groups. The non-Muslim *bumiputera*, in contrast, accept the domination of *bumiputera* but demand that Christianity and native religions be accorded equal status to that of

Islam. On the other hand, the radical Muslim *bumiputera*, represented by the Parti Islam, argue for a 'purer' religious principle and advocate the idea of an Islamic state. In other words, while the governing elites want an ethnic-dominated state, based on unequal citizen rights, and institutionalized along racial lines, the radical Muslim party demands much the same kind of state but instead founded on religious lines.

The differences do not end here. The project Vision 2020 reflects the preferences of the peninsula-based elites. The *bumiputera* of Sarawak and Sabah have their own ideas, and their undertow of vested interests, of what should be the national principle. The rise of Kadazan and Iban nationalism therefore, presents another challenge to the grand vision of a *bumiputera*-based Malaysia. Ethnicity and territoriality are entwined in claims about nation geared to the advancement of particular interests and their espousal by the state – an espousal replete with consequences for the state itself.

The states of Asia and the possibilities of theory

We have argued that modern states in contemporary Asia are not well understood from within the social sciences and that they differ in significant ways from 'standard assumptions about stateness'. We have gone further to suggest that some of the benchmark scratchings in theory habitually in use as the measure of the state, such as territoriality, legitimacy, and coercion, might not be the best markers of political order and domination in Asia. Some of this is as unremarkable to a student of the region as it is, conceivably, objectionable to a reader persuaded of the universality of Western political categories. Whitehead seeks to identify the middle ground in the concluding chapter that assesses the claims of the different chapters and addresses their implications for social science. He is sensitive to the geographical and temporal limits of the universe that inspired theorizing about the state. He is equally persuaded of the need not to dichotomize theory on the grounds of an uncovered Asian exceptionalism but to rebalance state theory: that is, to ensure its responsiveness to Asian as well as to European political experience. His specification of an analytic grid that might sustain comparison while enabling a systematic interrogation of difference demands careful attention. All modern states display the shared morphological characteristics of complexity, temporal continuity, and multi-facetedness. Multifacetedness lends itself to analysis respecting the state as an idea, the state as an organization, and the state as a social formation. These can be further specified as the basis for comparison. Thus at the organizational level we can examine 'the interconnected dimensions of the state as a structure: its territorial control; its command over resources; and its capacity for administration of its subjects'. This is a significant advance. Moreover, it facilitates the clarification and comparison of differences in states not only between Europe and Asia, but also within and across each of these regions.

Conclusion

The title of the volume speaks of the making of the state in Asia. Indeed, both the inspiration for the book, that is to say the widespread renewal of interest in Asian studies in the history of state making and also our principal conclusion, namely that the modern state in contemporary Asia can only be understood by dint of a careful historical analysis of the dimensions of state making identified in the closing chapter, address this theme of state making. The argument proceeds from the conviction that current state theory cannot adequately account for the modern state in contemporary Asia and from the desire to draw a line under any lingering and mistaken belief that the state in Asia is as depictions of the modern state in Europe would have it be.

The grounds for dissatisfaction with state theory are twofold. The historicity of conceptions of the modern state is problematic and limiting. By the 'historicity' of concepts, we mean that conceptions of the modern state are abstractions from and encapsulations of one period of history in one region of the world. Problems arise when, to borrow Whitehead's words, 'concepts abstracted from one small portion of the history of humanity are stretched, transferred, and naturalized by contemporary social scientists until it is taken for granted that they also apply (or ought to apply) in other settings'. The presumed existence in contemporary Asia of modern states on the Western pattern is an instance of this 'taken-for-grantedness'. More brutally, it is the presumption that Asian states are or should be the same as European/Western states. It is to be hoped that enough has been said above to disturb the comfort with which this presumption is made. We have spoken of problems borne of the poverty of state theory. We in no sense disdain the stalwart efforts of scholars to theorize the state in Europe and elsewhere. Much of this theorizing is rich and suggestive; our target is rather the use made of state theory in much of the comparative work that embraces Asia. The state that figures in the state-as-independent-variable approach to the analysis of Asia has no past, no personality, and no politics. It is, to be blunt, ahistorical, apolitical or even anti-political, crude, essentialist, overgeneralized, reductionist, taken for granted, and unexamined. This is unacceptable even when it is not the state but the growth of the Asian economies that is the object of inquiry, since the explanation in this second case returns precisely to the unspecified, untheorized, and little-understood 'state'. These shortcomings are even more pressing and urgent when the state itself is the object of our inquiries.

If we are to overcome these shortcomings, then we must recognize that economic development is but one function of the state and that different functions of the state do not necessarily come together in a harmonious and mutually reinforcing way. We should be skeptical in face of claims that the state is unchanged by its engagement in the economy and by its performance of other functions, such as security, the promotion of welfare, and the satisfaction of sectional interests.[55] We should be skeptical above all about the claims the state makes for its own goals and actions.[56] We must greet with caution and circumspection the claim that states in contemporary Asia are much as the modern state in Europe, and that accordingly concepts evolved in Europe are naturally applicable. The concepts of modern social sciences in general, and the concept of the state in particular, encapsulate an ontology of the social world in abbreviated form. We cannot assume the universality of that ontology, we must interrogate it. We have to establish the nature, purpose, and functioning of apparently similar and familiar institutions by empirical investigation rather than by the projection onto Asia of understandings of how similarly labeled institutions work in Europe. An investigation to establish the facts of the matter will benefit immeasurably from the support of a historical inquiry into the making of the modern state. If we draw back the curtains to reveal the actual trajectory of state making in specific Asian countries rather than to conceal this behind theories of radical imposition and so on, it will further clarify the what, how, and the why of the modern state in contemporary Asia. Moreover, such an approach will also encourage us to view the state not as a fixed point outside of politics and time (the indicted reification effect of the state-as-independent-variable approach), but as a process without end, as institutions and relationships embedded in other institutions and relationships, subject to internal dissension, competing pressures, and a gamut of centrifugal forces, and constantly in need of repair, renewal, and reinforcement.

The kind of state-making approach to the analysis of the modern state that we advocate has shown its merits in the study of the European state.[57] However, we argue that Asia is a critically important site for the investigation of state making and its consequences for contemporary states not only as an end in itself but as a means to retheorize the state even in its European form. We will turn to this below. We have seen that we encounter problems across the board when we seek to construe the states of Asia in terms of the characteristic properties of the state. Certainly, the world presents itself politically and administratively as a grid of territorial units, each with its own sovereign power whose authority is underpinned by some sense or claim to identity or community coextensive with the reach of the territory and by external recognition. Whether territoriality, legitimacy, and even sovereignty enjoy a rigorous consistency of meaning across the range of states can be doubted from what we have seen of the Chinese and Japanese cases. Moreover, when we note the problems encountered by a Malaysia in pursuit of an identity to ground its state or the disputes about territory and sovereignty that bedevil the states of China and Taiwan, we cannot dismiss these as a kind of lingering historical untidiness to be cleaned up in due course, neither as incompleteness, nor as obstacles to be overcome in the transition to modernity, without embracing the mistaken idea that there is a single privileged route to a single political model best represented by the modern state in Europe.

The nation-state that developed in Europe is deeply imprinted in the conventions of comparison that attend the study of Europe and Asia. The effect of this is to skew comparison and worse, to smuggle into comparison the inadmissible conception of political history as the trajectory of the nation-state. We are reduced to asking how far Asian political development matches up to that of Europe. We are left treating much of the political experience of Asia as problematic (problems of nationhood, problems of territorial integrity, problems of formal structures poorly accommodated to informal structures, and so on) rather than locating the problems perceived in the categories that govern our perceptions and shape our questions. We cannot center these 'problems' in analysis and cannot (have not) made much sense of concepts such as transethnic empire, continental polity, and regional kingdom in the organization of political domination. We have made even less use of traditions of political thinking and practice couched in terms other than those inherited from ancient Greece. And yet the potential payoff is extraordinarily rich: from an Asian perspective we can hope for a more accurate account of the substance concealed by too familiar labels (we have spoken of hybrid forms), from a European perspective on offer is a vantage point outside of Europe from which to gauge the particularity and limits of Western states and their making. This is not to make a case for Asian exceptionalism, however, as Whitehead emphasizes in Chapter 8. One feature of the state in Asia that must differentiate it from the Western state is that it possesses its own long and separate tradition of self-reflection embedded in the history and language of the major Asian civilizations. Given that the historical reality of state formation is a patrimony of humanity not the exclusive property of any one limited geographical region, so also our theorizing about the nature of the modern state should be drawn equally on Asian as much as on Western experience. In short, it should be informed by a knowledge of both traditions of self-understanding. This is simultaneously a recognition of the importance of invigorating an Asian perspective on state making and no less an encouragement to broaden and deepen comparative research.

Notes

1　Notable contributions include J. P. Arnason, *Social Theory and Japanese Experience*, London: Kegan Paul International, 1997; M. N. Barnett, *Confronting the Costs of War: Military Power, State and Society in Egypt and Israel*, Princeton: Princeton University Press, 1992; S. Heydemann, *Authoritarianism in Syria: Institutions and Social Change, 1946- 70*, Ithaca: Cornell University Press, 1999; S. Heydemann (ed.), *War, Institutions and Social Change in the Middle East*, Berkeley: University of California Press, 2001; C. Young, *The African Colonial State in Comparative Perspective*, New Haven: Yale University Press, 1994; J. Herbst, *States and Power in Africa: Comparative Lessons in Authority and Control*, Princeton: Princeton University Press, 2000; B. Silberman, *Cages of Reason: The Rise of the Rational State in France, Japan, the United States, and Britain*, Chicago: University of Chicago Press, 1993; F. Lopez-Alves, *State Formation and Democracy in Latin America 1810- 1900*, Durham: Duke University Press, 2000; M. A. Centeno, *Blood and Debt: War and the Nation-State in Latin America*, Philadelphia: Pennsylvania State University Press, 2002; M. A. Centeno and F. Lopez-Alves (eds), *The Other Mirror: Grand Theory through the Lens of Latin America*, Princeton: Princeton University Press, 2001; M. Doornbos and S. Kaviraj (eds), *The Dynamics of State Formation: India and Europe Compared*, New Delhi: Sage Publications, 1997; S. Khilnani, *The Idea of India*, New York: Farrah Strauss Giroux, 1997; S. Subrahmanyam, *The Makings of Early Modern Asia: A Polycentric Approach*, Boulder: Westview Press, 1998; S. Subrahmanyam, *Prenumbral Visions: The Making of Polities in Early Modern South India*, Ann Arbor: University of Michigan Press, 2001; and R. B. Wong, *China Transformed: Historical Change and the Limits of European Experience*, Ithaca: Cornell University Press, 1997.

2 All the more so since the fascist and totalitarian forms of the modern state have disappeared from the political landscape.

3 D. Waldner, 'From intra-type variations to the origins of types: recovering the macroanalytics of state building', paper presented for the conference on Asian Political Economy in an Era of Globalization, Dartmouth College, 10–11 May 2002, pp. 57–8.

4 F. Bayart, 'Finishing with the idea of the Third World: the concept of the political trajectory', in J. Manor (ed.), *Rethinking Third World Politics*, New York: Longman, 1991, p. 51.

5 Besides the works cited in note 1, see also D. Chakrabarty, *Provincializing Europe: Postcolonial Thought and Historical Difference*, Princeton: Princeton University Press, 2000; S. H. Rudolph, 'Presidential address: state formation in Asia – prolegomenon to a comparative study', *The Journal of Asian Studies*, 1987, vol. 46, no. 4, 731–46; Manor (ed.), *Rethinking Third World Politics*; and G. Steinmetz (ed.), *State/Culture: State Formation after the Cultural Turn*, Ithaca: Cornell University Press, 1999.

6 Here we seek to build upon and are indebted to a series of observations from Sudipta Kaviraj. See S. Kaviraj, 'On state, society and discourse in India', in Manor (ed.), *Rethinking Third World Politics*, pp. 72–9; and S. Kaviraj, 'The modern state in India', in Doornbos and Kaviraj, *The Dynamics of State Formation*, pp. 225–50.

7 S. E. Finer, *The History of Government from the Earliest Times III: Empires, Monarchies and the Modern State*, Oxford: Oxford University Press, 1997, p. 1475.

8 S. H. Rudolph and L. I. Rudolph, 'Authority and power in bureaucratic and patrimonial administration: a revisionist interpretation of Weber on bureaucracy', *World Politics*, 1979, vol. 31, 218.

9 We share Kaviraj's impatience. See S. Kaviraj, 'In search of civil society', in S. Kaviraj and S. Khilnani (eds), *Civil Society, History and Possibilities*, Cambridge: Cambridge University Press, 2001, pp. 287–323.

10 Bayart, 'Finishing with the idea of the Third World'.

11 See 'Call for papers' for The Historical Society conference, 'Reflections on the Current State of Historical Inquiry', 3–6 June 2004, Boothbay Harbor, Maine.

12 C. Johnson, *MITI and the Japanese Miracle*, Stanford: Stanford University Press, 1982.

13 For a fuller review and critique of the developmentalist account of the states of Asia, see R. Boyd and T. W. Ngo, 'Emancipating the political economy of Asia from the growth paradigm', in R. Boyd and T. W. Ngo (eds), *Asian States: Beyond the Developmental Perspective*, London: RoutledgeCurzon, 2005, pp. 1–18.

14 P. Evans, *Embedded Autonomy: States and Industrial Transformation*, Princeton: Princeton University Press, 1995.

15 For a comprehensive review, see Bob Jessop, 'Bringing the State Back in (Yet Again): Reviews, Revisions, Rejections, and Redirections', paper presented to the International Political Science Association conference, Quebec, 2000, pp. 1–23.

Online. Available http: <www.comp.lancs.ac.uk/sociology/papers/jessop-bringing-the-state-back-in.pdf> (accessed 10 May 2001).

16 L. Gordon, 'The Welfare State: Towards a Socialist-Feminist Perspective', in *Socialist Register*, London: Merlin Press, 1990, p. 181; cited in Jessop, 'Bringing the State Back In', p. 5.

17 See Whitehead this volume; and Rudolph and Rudolph, 'Authority and power in bureaucratic and patrimonial administration'.

18 Not least of the problems relate to the divergence of ostensible or publicly stated goals from the private considerations of government. So, for example, it is widely held that privatization schemes in Japan under Nakasone and in the UK under Thatcher were driven in addition to economic goals by a political concern to weaken public sector unions and so undermine the support and the electoral prospects of opposition parties. Some scholars fundamentally doubt the ability of states to modify their strategies in response to changed circumstances. For one such 'organizational rigidity' theorist, see H. Kitschelt, 'Political opportunity structures and political protest', *British Journal of Political Science*, 1986, vol. 16, 57–86. The garbage can approach argues that supposed 'solutions' to external problems are 'merely streams of internal resolution that coincided with such difficulties' in a process characterized as much by solutions in search of problems as problems in need of solution. See J. March and J. Olsen, *Ambiguity and Choice in Organizations*, Bergen: Universitetsforlaget, 1976. Almost without exception the state intervention school draws a discrete veil over these problems.

19 T. Mitchell, 'Society, economy, and the state effect', in Steinmetz, *State/Culture*, pp. 76–97.

20 K. Loewenstein, 'Report on the research panel on comparative government', *American Political Science Review*, 1944, vol. 38, 541.

21 Ibid., 542.

22 Ibid., 547.

23 L. Binder, 'The crises of political development', in L. Binder, J. S. Coleman, J. LaPalombara, L. W. Pye, S. Verba, and M. Weiner, *Crises and Sequences in Political Development*, Princeton: Princeton University Press, 1971, pp. 49, 53.

24 J. S. Coleman, 'Conclusion: the political systems of the developing areas', in G. A. Almond and J. S. Coleman (eds), *The Politics of Developing Areas*, Princeton: Princeton University Press, 1960, p. 533.

25 This is very much John Dunn's point. He argues the universal applicability of a tradition of thinking about politics that derives from Aristotle. While we are not in complete agreement with Dunn, his superb study obliged us to work hard further to clarify our own thoughts. See J. Dunn, *The Cunning of Unreason: Making Sense of Politics*, London: Harper Collins Publishers, 2000.

26 Rudolph, 'Presidential address', p. 732.

27 L. Anderson, *Pursuing Truth, Exercising Power: Social Science and Public Policy in the Twenty-First Century*, University Seminars/Leonard Hastings Schoff Memorial Lectures, Columbia: Columbia University Press, 2003, p. 80. See also L. Anderson, 'Understanding Our Global Present: International Issues and Area Knowledge', American Council of Learned Societies Annual Meeting May 2003, Philadelphia, pp. 1–8.

28 See Whitehead in this volume.

29 S. N. Eisenstadt, *Japanese Civilization: A Comparative View*, Chicago: University of Chicago Press, 1996, pp. 408–9.

30 R. Wagner, 'Political institutions, discourse and imagination in China at Tiananmen', in Manor (ed.), *Rethinking Third World Politics*, p. 142; G. Jin and Q. Liu, *Kaifang zhong de bianqian* (Changes during openness), Hong Kong: Chinese University Press, 1992.

31 We might note here the sterling efforts of Arnason and others to root the state in

the notion of a civilization. See J. P. Arnason, *Social Theory and Japanese Experience*, London: Kegan Paul International, 1997; Eisenstadt, *Japanese Civilization*. These works are in turn indebted to the pioneering work of N. Elias, *The Civilizing Process: Sociogenetic and Psychogenetic Investigations*, Oxford: Blackwell, 1994.

32 B. Stein, 'Review of Sangam polity', *Indian Economic and Social History Review*, 1968, vol. 5, 109–15; B. Stein, 'The segmentary state in South Indian history', in R. G. Fox (ed.), *Realm and Region in Traditional India*, Durham, NC: Duke University Press, 1977, pp. 3–51; B. Stein, *Peasant State and Society in Medieval South India*, New Delhi: Oxford University Press, 1980.

33 S. Schram (ed.), *Foundations and Limits of State Power in China*, Hong Kong: Chinese University Press, 1987.

34 See J. O. Haley, *Authority without Power: Law and the Japanese Paradox*, Studies in Law and Social Control, Oxford: Oxford University Press, 1991.

35 R. Boyd, 'The rule of law or law as an instrument of rule? Law and the economic development of Japan with particular regard to industrial policy', in Christoph Antons (ed.), *Law and Development in East and South-East Asia*, London: RoutledgeCurzon, 2002, pp. 154–96.

36 Arnason, *Social Theory and Japanese Experience*.

37 See Wong in this volume.

38 This is not to suggest that *tenka* had a single, uncontested, and unchanging meaning. Moreover, Tokugawa Japan developed a significant discourse of politics, geography, the state and the public realm – the implications of which for post-Meiji political meanings have yet to be fully elaborated. We can note at least, for purposes of the present discussion, that there was no hegemonic discursive specification of the territorial limits of 'political' authority and that any discourse of the physical boundaries of authority stood in tense relation to the discourse of the 'international' system of East Asia, central to which was a variety of borderless conceptions of authority. These are tricky matters. For a highly accessible introduction to some of the terms and an indication of the debates and the main English-language references, see Eisenstadt, *Japanese Civilization*, pp. 192–9.

39 Rudolph, 'Presidential address', p. 736.

40 M. Weber, *Economy and Society: An Outline of Interpretive Sociology*, vol. 1, ed. G. Roth and C. Wittich, Berkeley: University of California Press, 1978, p. 398.

41 Ibid., p. 395.

42 This is not to deny the role of cultural and political elites in the construction of nations, not least in the West. Neither is it naively to ignore the role of force and violence in the fashioning of the modern state nor to forget what Foucault has taught us about the 'drilling of the nation'. However, at issue for the moment are definitions and their consequences. See M. Foucault, *Power: Essential Works of Foucault 1954-1984*, vol. 3, New York: The New Press, 2000. On the construction and invention, still highly relevant is E. Hobsbawn, *Nations and Nationalism since 1780*, 2nd revised edn, Cambridge: Cambridge University Press, 1990. For a very interesting account of the role of ongoing state-sanctioned violence and sacrifice in the fashioning of the 'community of sentiment', see C. Marvin, D. W. Ingle, J. C. Alexander, and S. Seidman (eds), *Blood Sacrifice and the Nation: Totem Rituals and the American Flag*, Cambridge: Cambridge University Press, 1999.

43 'Community of sentiment' is the expression used in Weber, *Economy and Society*, 1978.

44 Finer is unequivocal: 'nationality' is an indispensable element of the modern state, the first of a syndrome of characteristics 'worthy of emulation'. See Finer, *The History of Government*, p. 1474.

45 Herbst, *State and Power in Africa*.

46 S. Kaviraj, 'In search of civil society', in Kaviraj and Khilnani (eds), *Civil Society*, p. 310.

47 S. Vlastos, 'Tradition: past/present culture and modern Japanese history', in S. Vlastos (ed.), *Mirror of Modernity: Invented Traditions of Modern Japan*, Berkeley and Los Angeles: University of California Press, 1998, pp. 12–13.
48 Eisentstadt, *Japanese Civilization.*
49 It is well known that the Japanese had a sophisticated sense of the range and possibilities of Western state forms, were well able to 'mix and match' and in no sense reluctant to proceed by trial and error in borrowing, adapting, and transforming political forms from the West.
50 It was only during a brief radical period in the Cultural Revolution when some of these bourgeois institutions were abolished and replaced by revolutionary committees. They have been all restored subsequently.
51 See the discussion in H. Antlöv and T. W. Ngo, 'Politics, culture, and democracy in Asia', in H. Antlöv and T. W. Ngo (eds), *The Cultural Construction of Politics in Asia*, Surrey: Curzon Press, 2000, pp. 1–18.
52 G. Hawthorn, 'Waiting for a text?' in Manor (ed.), *Rethinking Third World Politics*, p. 32.
53 J. W. Meyer, 'The changing cultural content of the nation-state: a world society perspective', in Steinmetz (ed.), *State/Culture*, pp. 123–44.
54 K. Jaspers, *The Origins and Goal of History*, New Haven: Yale University Press, 1953. See also S. N. Eisenstadt, *The Origins and Diversity of Axial Age Civilizations*, Suny Series in Near Eastern Studies, New York: State University of New York Press, 1986.
55 Whitehead (in this volume) puts it well when he suggests that, 'More generally, the state-economy linkage is better understood as an interaction than a one-way flow of causality. Similarly with state-society, and state-ideology and state-political linkages.'
56 One might have thought the point was too obvious to make. We have heard Japanese officials express their astonishment at the reliance political scientists place upon the public version of official documents and reports as evidence, not least because of the care and attention with which these are sanitized prior to publication, and the uncritical ease with which official reassurances about the nature and goals of policy are accepted by scholars.
57 There are clear parallels with the 'Long Arch' approach. See P. Corrigan and D. Sayer, *The Great Arch: English State Formation and Cultural Revolution*, Oxford: Blackwell, 1985.

2 Japanese state making in global context

Mark Ravina

In the 1850s Japanese social and political institutions bore little resemblance to those of the great imperial powers. Japan lacked anything resembling a modern centralized state. It had not one, but two national sovereigns (a shogun and an emperor) and many powers of state were exercised by daimyo, regional lords. There was no national treasury, no national army, and no national navy. There was no national taxation. There was no foreign ministry: the shogunate handled foreign affairs, but it treated Western powers as 'barbarians'. Japan had no banks, no public companies, no bonds, and no stocks. Merchants arranged long-term agreements, but there were no contracts, no contract lawyers, and no national laws for commercial transactions. At the symbolic level, Japan lacked a national flag, a national anthem, and national holidays.

By 1900 most all of this had changed. Dedicated reformers, both in and out of government, had radically transformed Japan's social and political institutions. The emperor was now the sole sovereign of Japan. By law, his rule was constrained by a constitution and by an elected assembly, but this was in concert with European models. In practice, his actions were governed by the advice of senior statesmen, again in concert with European models. Japan had reformed its legal codes to European standards and the great powers had dropped their demand for extraterritoriality. Japan, however, had extracted colonial concessions, including extraterritoriality, from Korea. Japan had national taxation, a national currency, banks, stocks, bonds, and commercial contracts. Japan had a national flag, appropriately patriotic national festivals, and a newly composed national anthem.

How can we explain these radical changes in Japanese institutions? Was this 'Westernization' or 'modernization'? What caused this isomorphism with European institutions? American historians have relied on a variety of theories. Many early accounts of Japanese history assumed the superiority of Western models. In *A History of the Modern World*, Palmer argued that Japan adopted 'Western ways' because of 'an admiration for Western statecraft'. Japan was most impressed by the 'external apparatus of Western civilization ... science, technology, machinery, arms, political and legal organization'. The Japanese adopted these external manifestations as a defense against

Western 'penetration' and in order to protect 'the innermost substance of their culture'. The convergence of Japanese and European institutions was thus based on Japan's acceptance of European superiority.[1] Japan specialists adopted a similar take when they wrote of Perry 'opening' Japan and of Japan's 'Westernization'.

The dominant school of historiography in the 1960s and 1970s was modernization theory. Based on Weber and Parsons, this approach assumed parallel patterns of development in all 'modernizing' societies. Modern society required instrumental rationality, specialization of function, and bureaucratic organization. The most 'modern' societies were those in which these features were most fully developed. The best example of the modernization school approach is Robert Bellah's *Tokugawa Religion*, which examined early modern Japanese religious practices searching for parallels to the Protestant ethic. Japan's successful transition to capitalism and modern society, argued Bellah, was rooted in the similarities between Japanese religious traditions like *shingaku* and Protestantism.[2] Although Japanese historiography is beyond the scope of this chapter, it is worth noting that while modernization theorists were hoping to emplot Japanese history into a Weberian metanarrative, Japanese historians were doing the same with a Marxian metanarrative: searching not for Weberian rationality, but for appropriate markers of class consciousness and class formation. Notably, both schools ignored what has become an important part of recent historiography: ethnicity. Both schools assumed the nation (ethnic homogeneity) and asked merely 'what sort of state?'

More recently, historians have begun to focus on modernity rather than modernization. The concepts of modernity and modernization share a number of features: both focus on issues such as the rationalization of social and economic roles, the emergence of new social and economic positions. But the concept of modernity is centered on the power relations implicit in the new positions, not the functional merits of modern society. Theories of modernity also focus on the reflexive quality of modern society: the concepts used to distinguish modern social life from premodern social life, concepts such as economic efficiency and individuality, are themselves products of modernity and are enmeshed in its system of power relations. An outstanding example here is Fujitani's *Splendid Monarchy*. Drawing on Foucault's theory of governmentality, Fujitani examines the development in Japan of a modern monarchy and a modern nation-state. His concern is with the production of new social and political spaces, new subject positions, and possibilities for political action, not with the increased ambit of instrumental rationality.[3] In a similar vein, a recent study on the invention of tradition in Japan demonstrates how the very concept of tradition is a function of modernity. Japan and Scotland, for example, both invented 'traditional' life as part of the process of industrialization.[4]

World society theory

In this chapter I would like to propose an alternative explanation based on world society theory. World society theorists find that, in the modern world system, nation-states are 'structurally similar in many unexpected dimensions and change in unexpectedly similar ways'. They posit that international systems require a level of uniformity among their members: in order to interact states must have a minimal set of shared institutions and concepts. Increased interaction deepens this global culture and leads to greater isomorphism. Globalization is, therefore, a cause of isomorphism.[5]

World society theorists acknowledge a functional component to isomorphic forces. States in the modern world have similar goals so, quite naturally, they develop similar institutional solutions. From a functionalist perspective (or, in political science parlance, 'realist' perspective), states are rational actors, acting logically to peruse coherent agendas. Nation-states are similar but this is only because they share a common agenda. World society theorists acknowledge this functional aspect of isomorphism, but they counter that states adopt similar institutions even when they have different agendas.[6] The external institutional uniformity between the United States, North Korea, and Iran is far greater than rational planning would suggest: all three states have departments of agriculture, departments of defense. Many of the rituals of statecraft are similar: military parades, national holidays, myopic history texts, flags, etc. States are similar in their external aspect even when their ideologies and levels of development are radically different.

To explain this unexpected isomorphism, world society theorists look to social construction: the existence of nation-states as subjects in a world of nation-states. Meyers, Boli, Thomas, and Ramirez articulate this view through a witty, hypothetical case:

> If an unknown society were 'discovered' on a previously unknown island, it is clear that many changes would occur. A government would soon form, looking like a modern state with many of the usual ministries and agencies. Official recognition by other states and admission to the United Nations would ensure. The society would be analyzed as an economy, with standard types of data, organizations, and policies for domestic and international transactions. Its people would be formally reorganized as citizens with many familiar rights, while certain categories of citizen – children, the elderly, the poor – would be granted special protection. Standard forms of discrimination, especially ethnic and gender based, would be discovered and decried. The population would be counted and classified in ways specified by world census models.[7]

The institutions of the nation-state are thus created less by the society's own needs than by the needs of world society, the society of other nation-states.

Global political culture, like any culture milieu, defines the identities of actors. In a world of nation-states, polities must conform to the rules of nation-states.[8] Or as Giddens has observed, it is simplistic to assume the sovereign state preceeded the interstate system. Rather, the world system was 'the condition, and in substantial degree the very source of the development' of the nation-state.[9] As Duara has suggested, there is a parallel process between the social construction of individuals in civil society and the construction of states in international society.[10] Actors who will not or cannot assume recognized roles within a social order, have no agency. In a republic, an actor who identifies himself a subject of the king is certainly acting inefficiently, but, more importantly, he is acting unintelligibly. In a republic, there are no subjects of the king. The issue is not functional: the problem is not that subjects of the kings vote for a losing political party. The problem is ontological: subjects of the king do not exist as voters. Actors who insist expressly on nonstandard social positions become socially incompetent and incapable. In modern society, an actor who declares his occupation as serf or knight errant is, by definition, mentally disturbed. In the modern world serfdom is a fantasy rather than a social fact. A self-declared serf will therefore likely be deemed mentally incompetent. This process of marginalization occurs in both human society and international society. The most germane international case is Korea's diplomatic stance in the late nineteenth century. As the last defender of the Chinese world order, the kingdom of Korea insisted on its status as an autonomous vassal kingdom of the Chinese empire. Korea was thus deemed a mentally diminished actor in world society, a 'hermit kingdom' in period terminology. Like a hermit in a modern society, Korea needed either to be taught a proper social role (hermit does not appear on either the Department of Labor or IRS tables of occupations) or become a ward of the state. Significantly the Treaty of Kanghwa, imposed on Korea by Japan in 1876, insisted on Korean sovereignty: Japan sought to minimize Chinese influence and advance its own geopolitical agenda by bringing Korea into the modern world order as a sovereign state. When this failed to secure Japanese security interests, Japan fought, successfully, to have Korea redefined as a protectorate. In this rhetoric, widely accepted by the other colonial powers, Korea was an immature state and therefore could manifest its independence only with Japan's aid and protection. Japan, as a fully realized international subject, would take responsibility for raising its fledgling neighbor.[11]

In the context of world society theory, the construction of the Meiji state can be understood as the construction of a legitimate modern subject. The construction of modern subjects was thus both an internal and an external process: internally, the Meiji state created new rituals and customs for its human subjects. Externally it created a modern state-subject, the Japanese nation-state as a new subject in an international community. The two projects were clearly interconnected: Japan was a legitimate international subject (or actor) in part because it mastered the paraphernalia of nationalism (flag, anthems, processions) and used these practices to create, domestically, a nation of Japanese nationals. These domestic changes were part of Japan's 'invention of tradition': the creation of culturally uniform nationals.

A major impetus to invent national traditions was the discourse of state legitimacy. In the modern world order, nation-states exist to speak for and defend discrete cultures. Duara calls this relationship a 'regime of authenticity': states are legitimate because they represent the will of organic, pre-existing nations, and because they protect those nations' traditions, values, and institutions. Since national boundaries are rarely coextensive with cultural borders, this regime of authenticity is often problematic. Many nations are too small to have their own civilizations, and many civilizations overflow national boundaries. More broadly there is an inherent conceptual tension in the regime of authenticity. The defense of a discrete culture legitimizes the state in the world order, but that world order requires a certain isomorphism of national practices. As Duara observes, 'a nation's sovereignty was perceived to derive from two sources: recognition by the evolving system of nation-states and world culture; and in a more immanent conception, inherence in the preconstituted communal body of the nation.' Each nation-state thus needed to represent both a unique, discrete culture and a single instance of global culture.[12] Or, more succinctly, all nations should be identical in their uniqueness. These two faces of the 'regime of authenticity' can be seen in the dual nature of national flags. Flags must represent the distinct national culture of their nation-state, but they must also conform to international standards. In the joint displays of national flags, which became commonplace with the emergence of international expositions in the nineteenth century, each flag must be distinct but all flags must be of common size and shape: the Japanese flag and the Saudi flag appear as national variations on an international theme. This interplay of distinctiveness and isomorphism is a visual manifestation of the modern concept of state sovereignty: all states are equally sovereigns but each represents a unique nation.[13] There is a parallel duality in national anthems, all of which must be of uniform length and structure (there are now fixed-length 'short-form' anthems for Olympic medal ceremonies), yet each of which is, in theory, a manifestation of that nation's unique common culture.

The process of state building in Japan must be understood in terms of this dual nature of sovereignty. Meiji leaders were fascinated by the noncoercive 'rules' for international society, and by the prospect of legitimizing Japan's place in that society. They were not blind to raw power and aggression, but they were also interested in how rules for international conduct both legitimized the international order and its constituent members. But the process of state building also required an invention of tradition: a discovery of unique Japanese cultural forms that could legitimize the state as subject in world society. These dual demands prompted contestations, as statesmen and intellectuals debated how to create a regime that was both essentially Japanese and recognizably global.

The modern world system and Meiji Japan

The duality of nationalist symbols appears with striking clarity in the history of 'Kimigayo', the Japanese national anthem. The first version of the anthem was composed in 1869 for an imperial review of the imperial guard, a new joint military force comprised of troops from Tosa, Satsuma, and Chōshū. Oyama Iwao, an army officer from Satsuma, ordered several army musicians to work with John William Fenton, a British bandmaster stationed in Yokohama. They worked feverishly and completed the composition in less than two weeks. The lyrics to the anthem were drawn from a verse in the Kokinwakashū, a tenth-century imperial poetry anthology, and this became a permanent part of the anthem. The tune, however, adapted from a Satsuma lute melody, became a subject of fierce criticism and was later changed.[14]

A key critic of the music of 'Kimigayo' was Nakamura Suketsune, a navy bandmaster. In 1876 he wrote a memorial to the imperial court arguing for a new composition and his memorial is a distillation of dual meanings of national anthems. Nakamura noted that music had long been used to enhance state authority of the state, and that ancient Chinese emperors had ruled with both laws and odes. More recently, rulers in Europe and America had used the arts both to excite their peoples and to reveal their authority and virtue. Anthems were essential because 'at great state ceremonies, each country plays its own anthem and thereby reveals its glory as an independent and free country and manifests the majesty of its sovereign'. 'Kimigayo', however, was inadequate to this task. The tune, Nakamura complained, was incompatible with the musical sensibilities of the Japanese people and it therefore could neither exalt the emperor nor express his majesty. Nakamura's critique is somewhat disingenuous: since the melody for 'Kimigayo' was pulled from a Satsuma lute ballad it was not un-Japanese. By 'incompatible' Nakamura meant insufficiently national. In 1876 Satsuma and the central government were slowly tilting towards war and Nakamura, as a Satsuma native, was acutely aware of Satsuma's powerful regional identity. Rather than favor any regional style, Nakamura advocated creating a new national musical idiom, under the direction of the imperial court.[15]

The government embraced Nakamura's proposal and in July 1880 it empanelled a four-man committee (including Nakamura) to create a new anthem. The committee looked to *gagku*, the music of the Japanese imperial court, for a national musical tradition. But simply to perform *gagku* would not have served the broader purpose of establishing Japan as a subject in the world of nations: Japan's state music had to conform to world standards. The imperial court had recognized these multiple demands in 1878 when it decided that the Imperial New Year's celebration and the Anniversary of the Emperor Jinmu's Accession would be celebrated with native music (*bugaku* and *kumemai*, respectively) but that the Imperial Birthday should be marked with Western music.[16] Nakamura and the committee thus had 'Kimigayo' orchestrated for Western musical instruments by Franz Eckert, a German composer. Eckert reportedly drew on the harmonies of English church music, but worked with a melodic line from *gagku*. The finished composition was performed on 15 October 1880 and was widely deemed a success. The current version of 'Kimigayo' is essentially unchanged from Eckert's orchestration. The government formally declared 'Kimigayo' its national hymn in 1888 and sent copies abroad for use in diplomatic ceremonies. This international dissemination of 'Kimigayo' to mark Japan as a nation-state preceeded its domestic use to create Japanese nationals and 'Kimigayo' was not well known in Japan until the surge in patriotic ceremonies during the Sino-Japanese and Russo-Japanese Wars. But the perceived need to have Japanese nationals know their own national anthem was an international phenomenon. In 1890 the *Ongaku zasshi* lamented that Japanese did not know how respectfully to sing their own national song. This was especially disturbing since such rituals, they observed, were the same around the world.[17]

In the case of a national anthem, the state resolved the dual demands of national essentialism and international isomorphism by 1880. The second version of 'Kimigayo' was, simultaneously, Japanese and universal. The case of weights and measures shows similar demands, but a more contested and erratic process. Because early modern taxation was largely a local affair, Japan did not have fully standardized weights and measures. There were, for example, regional differences in the size of a *shaku* (the standard measure of length), as well as different types of *shaku*, including, for example, the *kyoku shaku* (bent *shaku*), the *kujira shaku* (whale *shaku*), *tatami shaku* (rush matting *shaku*), and the *gofuku shaku* (clothing *shaku*). The need for uniform nationwide standards in a centralized state was immediately obvious and in 1868, before the shogunate had even surrendered Edo castle, Matsudaira Shungaku wrote on the reform of Japanese metrology. Shungaku, however, addressed the problem like the former daimyo he was: he called for the Shuzui house, the family invested by the Tokugawa as arbiters of weights and measures, to redouble their efforts to enforce national standards.[18]

The debate over weights and measures quickly became enmeshed in the debate over international standards and international society. The early years of the Meiji state coincided with the formal expansion of the metric system: the first international metric convention was held in 1875 and resulted in the establishment of the International Bureau of Weights and Measures. This was a movement towards international norms that Japanese bureaucrats, politicians, or scientists could not ignore. But there was countervailing impulse to re-establish Japanese uniqueness. Japanese nativists (*kokugakusha*) blamed Japan's nineteenth-century crisis on the indiscriminate adoption of Chinese, Indian, and Western practices and believed that the re-establishment of ancient traditions, particularly rites and rituals, would bring about a revival of ancient virtues. These two approaches collided full force in the narrow field of metrology. The first director of the new Division of Metrology Reform (*Doryōkō kaisei gakari*) was Shibusawa Eichi, a central figure in Japanese banking and tax reform and later its most successful modern businessman. Shibusawa was succeeded by Tomomatsu Ujikata, a disciple of Hirata Atsutane, the influential nativist scholar. Tomomatsu was then replaced by Satō Yoshinosuke, a disciple of Katsu Kaishū, the noted naval officer and military reformer.[19]

The struggle between internationalist and nativist perspectives can be discerned in the earliest reform proposals. In 1871 the Division of Metrology Reform, then in the Finance Ministry, proposed setting the new *shaku* equal to 1/120,000,000 of a 'great arc' of the earth. This curious choice of number and physical feature was a means of tacitly promoting conformity with the metric system. The meter, as set by the French Academy in 1791 was 1/10,000,000 the length of a line from the North Pole to the equator, passing of course through Paris. So the new *shaku* would have been exactly 1/3 meters. (This new *shaku* would have been 1.101 *kyoku shaku*.) The independent Bureau of Systems, however, presented two different proposals. The first involved using the old Tenpyō *shaku*, which was only 0.978 *kyoku shaku*, but was established during the Nara era, the heyday of imperial rule. The second proposal argued that the new *shaku* should be 1/360,000 of the circumference of the earth at the equator. This had no historical precedent but directly linked the *shaku* to an objective physical standard. The implicit logic here was the reverse of the Finance Ministry's. Rather than conform to international norms Japan needed either to return to ancient ways, or to develop a unique system directly connected to objective physical phenomena. The *shaku* could be naturalized or historicized, but not internationalized.[20]

These competing proposals were handled with customary efficiency by the Shūgiin, the short-lived parliament of daimyo. The chamber rejected all the proposals in a vote which provided 16 different opinions, such as 'adopt neither proposal but pursue gradual reform', 'implement [a reform] after the minds of the people have being quieted', 'adopt the best of both proposals', 'adopt neither proposal, but use the best of the existing system', and the ever-helpful 'no opinion'.[21] The topic was too politicized for easy resolution, but not so urgent that it required immediate resolution. Indeed, many in the government feared that an abrupt change in the units employed in tax collection would cause widespread public discontent. In this political context, the Finance Ministry opted for an incremental approach. In 1874 the government decreed new nationwide standards for weights and measures and assigned officers in each prefecture to ensure smooth implementation and enforcement. The system included both the *kyoku shaku* and the *kujira shaku* and neither had any clear relationship to the meter.[22]

The international convention on the metric system reopened the question of internationalization and on 8 July 1875, at the prompting of Japan's representatives to France, the council of state requested opinions on the merits of the convention from the Finance Ministry and the Home Ministry. Implicit arguments now became explicit. The Home Ministry argued that 'as measurements are something essential to daily life, each country must have its own system'. Certainly the lack of standardized measures within Japan had been an impediment to trade, but the problem had been resolved by the recent reforms. Any further change should be postponed until the recent reforms were fully implemented. The Finance Ministry disagreed: it wanted a single system of measure for both domestic and international trade and wanted Japan to pursue membership in the new conference. The Finance Ministry argued that the metric system was not only simple and logical, it was part of a world system which encompassed 28 nations and roughly 500,000,000 people. The metric system was currently a Western affair, but because it conferred 'benefits in general international relations' (*udai ippan gaikō eki*) the ministry believed that Asia nations would soon be applying to join.[23] The choice of the term '*gaikō*' bears special attention: narrowly defined it means 'diplomacy' but the Finance Ministry clearly meant the term in the broader sense of 'international relations'. 'Benefits in general international relations' thus corresponded to what Bourdieu, in a different context, would describe as symbolic or social capital: adoption of the metric system would mark Japan as a civilized and fully vested member of an international order.[24]

The government elected to hedge the issue. Japan joined the metric convention in 1885 and formally adopted the metric system in 1891, but maintained the *shaku* as a legally valid system of measurement. Although my focus in this chapter is on the early Meiji era, it is worth noting that metrology continued to track broader political movements. In 1909, near the apex of Anglo-Japanese and Japanese-American amity, Japan adopted the foot and the pound as legal measures. But in 1921, in the context of post-First World War internationalism, the government made plans to abandon both the *shaku* and the foot in favor of the meter. These policies were scrapped during the ultra-nationalist 1930s, although after the Second World War the American occupation meant the *de facto* adoption of the foot and the pound. Only in 1966 did Japan adopt the meter as its sole official measure of length.

World society and its dual demands of essentialism and isomorphism also shaped Meiji discourse on currency. The choice of a currency system is largely arbitrary: cowry shells, copper, or nonconvertible paper are all equally useful as money, so long as they are widely accepted. In an international system what matters is the interoperability of different national systems. An international trading system requires that different currencies be convertible: there must be some shared store of value. Even if a system of currency is fully functional in isolation, it must meet an international standard in order to be integrated into an international system. This need for conformity destroyed the early-modern Japanese currency system. Within months of the start of trade with the Western powers, the shogunal monetary system began to collapse. By the mid-1860s the country was plagued by spiraling inflation. The Meiji reformers agreed that, in order to establish a stable monetary regime, Japan would need to adopt the prevailing world standard, a gold-based convertible currency.

The irony of this process is that the shogunal system was arguably more sophisticated and modern than the Meiji system. The shogunate had, for nearly over 200 years, managed to supply Japan with stable fiat money. Shogunal coins were made of gold and silver, but their face value was much greater than their precious metal value. The coins were fiat money: they were valuable to the degree that they were scarce and this scarcity was assured by shogunal laws against counterfeiting. The shogunate regularly debased its coinage, usually by including more silver in its 'gold' coins, and nineteenth-century critics often cited this reminting as a failure of the system. But debasement had not caused systemic inflation. The reminted coins were clearly marked as new issues and merchants valued them according to scarcity. The debasements increased the money supply, but the Japanese economy was growing, so shogunal policy was sound monetary policy: prices remained stable. The early modern monetary system even included fiat paper money, issued by daimyo domains. Some of these issues were widely accepted, others rapidly depreciated into worthless scrip, but moneychangers managed to assess them all.[25]

The early modern system collapsed not because it was flawed, but because it was different. According to modern economic theory, the *bakumatsu* fiscal system was more 'modern' and 'better' than the gold standard which replaced it. However, since none of the world powers recognized the fiat money, much less the shogunal monetary system, the fiat values of Japanese currency could not be sustained internationally. Japanese money would need to be revalued according to prevailing precious metal standards: gold and silver coins would be assessed by their metallic content at world values. Unfortunately these values bore little relation to the fiat money value of Japanese coins. World-wide an ounce of gold was worth 15 times as much as an ounce of silver, but a Japanese silver *ichibu* coin could buy only five times its weight in gold. Japanese gold was thus available for one-third its world price. Trade with the West meant that Japan would export gold until its monetary system collapsed and its coins corresponded to their specie values. The shogunate tried valiantly to limit the repercussions of this monetary collapse, but the problem was unfixable. Prices began to rise rapidly in 1860, when the shogunate debased its coins to conform to specie values, and began to spiral after 1865, when the survival of the shogunate itself came into question. Significantly, Western observers did not recognize that they were destroying a fiat money system. They were, on the contrary, alarmed by the 'arbitrary' values of gold and silver that the shogunate had 'forced upon the people'.[26]

When the Meiji regime sought to create its own currency it looked at international norms. While reformers sought the most advanced monetary system, they were aware that the 'best' system was the most accepted system. Standard was normal and normal was normative. The decisive voice for adopting the gold standard was Itō Hirobumi. In 1870 he wrote from the United States to inform the government of the results of his study tour. Virtually all economists, Itō wrote, advocate the gold standard as the best monetary standard. Although some major nations, such as Austria and Holland, still maintained a silver standard, 'if a system of coinage were to be newly established by any of these countries, there is no question but that the gold standard would be adopted'. Gold, insisted Itō, was the 'best metal for the standard of value'.[27] Itō was, in this instance, acting like the leader of the hypothetical new nation-state envisioned by Thomas *et al.*: advocating that his new nation adopt the emerging international standard.

Although Itō was searching for the 'best' system he was clearly aware that the best system was the most widely accepted system. Japan, he argued forcefully, needed to adopt metric coinage because this was the emerging world standard. It was, of course, more convenient, but more importantly, it was being adopted in the United States and this would make it a world standard. Itō quoted the chairman of the American Coinage Committee: 'Now that we have adopted this system, the nations of the world will be compelled to adopt it also.'[28]

England, Itō noted, had initially rejected metric coinage, but, he insisted, it would eventually adopt metric coinage 'in light of future trends'. It would be advantageous for Japan, Itō argued, to adopt metric coinage 'in advance of other nations' because then Japanese coinage would 'be exchanged without impediment in all nations'. Itō not only understood 'best' as most common, but also recognized that international standards were evolving and that Japan could adopt a world standard before an advanced power like England. Itō was not advocating that Japan adopt a Western standard, he was suggesting that Japan lend its weight to an emerging world standard.[29]

Finally, I would like to turn to politics in the strictest sense: the debate over the nature of the Japanese polity. A similar sense that conformity to world standards was, in itself, a powerful legitimizing force can be found in the Japanese debate over constitutional government. A central text in this regard is Katō Hiroyuki's 1862 essay *Saishinron*, literally 'Newest Theses'.[30] The essay is arguably the first discussion in Japanese of modern Western law. Katō (1836–1916), a samurai from Tajima domain, was sent in 1860 to Edo to study at the Bansho torishirabejo, the shogunate's institute for the study of 'barbarian' books. There he learned German and began the study of Western law. He wrote and circulated *Saishinron* in secret: the study of foreign political systems was controversial and technically beyond the charter of the Bansho torishirabejo, which focused on military science. Katō's essay is especially important because of his later career and intellectual development. In the 1860s and 1870s, Katō emerged as a leading political philosopher and prominent advocate of natural rights theory. He was active in the Meirokusha, a prominent group of progressive intellectuals. In the late 1870s he began a turn towards Social Darwinism and German political theory and in 1881 banned further publication of his earlier political writings. He was rewarded by the government with the presidency of Tokyo University. He later served in the House Peers, the Privy Council, and the Genrōin. Katō's understanding of natural law and human rights has been widely examined, as has his rightward turn in the late 1870s. Here, I wish to examine the theme of global standards in Katō's writings.

Saishinron takes the traditional form of a dialogue between a student and a teacher over political systems. The context is the decline of China and the rise of the European powers. What, asks the student, should Japan do now? And why did China fail? The student and teacher agree that China failed to appreciate European advances in science. In their arrogance, the student observes, China failed to grasp Europe's great scientific advances. That is indeed true, replies the teacher, but the problem with China goes beyond merely adopting Western arms. China lacks the spirit to deploy Western arms. This weakness of spirit, the teacher declares, is an external aspect of a deeper problem: China lacks military might because it lacks national harmony.[31]

China, the teacher notes, did not always suffer from spiritual weakness. Ah yes, the student replies, China needs to return to its ancient ways: it needs a benevolent and virtuous ruler. The teacher agrees in part. Certainly, the ancient sage kings of China ruled with impartial justice (*kōmei seidai*), but later, lesser rulers were not as virtuous and thus China declined. There is, however, a political structure that can assure benevolent and just rule even under a benighted ruler. Teacher then begins an explication of the 'political systems of the countries of the world'.

This discourse has an explicitly functional goal. Teacher and student wish to find the political system that will help Japan hold its ground against the Western powers. Having located China's failure in spiritual weakness and lack of unity, teacher then explains which systems encourage spiritual vigor and national solidarity. It is here that Katō makes his singular contribution to Japanese political discourse: because autocracies enervate their subjects, weaker governments can produce stronger states. Republics work, he notes, because the division of power produces greater not lesser unity.[32]

The explicit goal of strengthening Japan is a major force in Katō's argument. But throughout the essay we can also find the subsidiary force of isomorphism. Not only is a division of powers better for Japan, it is the emerging global standard. The move towards division of power, argues teacher, is a global trend, literally 'an inevitable trend of the times' (*jisei no kanarazu shikarazaru o ezaru tokoro nari*). Teacher cites the promulgation of a constitution in Prussia in 1848 as a part of this trend and points to three late-developing powers: Russia, Austria, and Turkey. These are still absolute monarchies, he notes, but this will change. Within decades they will adopt constitutional division of power. In the more distant future all the nations of the world will become either republics or constitutional monarchies. (Katō, in an authorial gloss, asserts then, within a hundred years, all the countries of the world will be republics.) The reason for this global convergence of political systems is, in part, functional: the division of powers matches 'popular sentiment (*yojō*)'. But the trend is also 'natural' and based in 'the will of heaven'. The development of the constitutional division of powers as a global standard is a trend with its own ineluctable force, and this inevitability is, in itself, a reason for a constitutional regime. Since all states will eventually adopt a division of powers, why should Japan delay? The force here is more cultural and ontological than practical. Since all states will eventually become republics, resistance is nonsensical. Absolutist regimes are not just inefficient; they are disappearing as actors in global society. In the emerging global culture, an absolutist regime will be as marginal and incomprehensible as a feudal squire in a republic. Practically, these regimes will disappear because they will lose wars. Culturally and ontologically, they will disappear because they have no subjectivity in the emerging global society.

This idea, that certain political forms are 'global' and that Japan must conform to global trends, appears independently in other important political works, such as Sakamoto Ryōma's eight-point program from 1867. Unlike Katō's essay, Sakamoto's brief draft was not a work of political theory, but a hastily drafted proposal. Sakamoto, a samurai from Tosa domain, was active in organizing the coalition of anti-shogunal forces that founded the Meiji state in 1868. His own lord, however, favored a negotiated settlement with the shogunate rather than a violent confrontation. Sakamoto's program, drafted on a ship en route from Nagasaki to Hyōgō, was designed to secure the surrender of the shogunate. Under Sakamoto's plan, the last shogun, Hitotsubashi Keiki (Tokugawa Yoshinobu), would resign his title of shogun and become president of the upper house of a new legislature. In eight short articles, Sakamoto outlined his vision of a new state: the restoration of the emperor as monarch, a bicameral legislature, military expansion, and thorough domestic legal reform. This prescient plan collapsed because Keiki refused to surrender shogunal land along with his title and in January 1868 anti-shogunal forces launched a coup.[33]

Like Katō's essay, Sakamoto's program assumed a trend towards institutional isomorphism. It was essential to announce this program 'to the nations of the world (*udai bankoku*)', and there was no other way to address the present crisis'. If Japan adopts this system it will 'stand equal with the nations of the world'. Sakamoto does not explain how a new political system will advance Japanese interests, but this silence itself is important. Presumably the constitutional division of powers is better, but Sakamoto does not develop this reasoning. Conformity with global standards is, by itself, a reason for political reform. Japan must adapt to the 'world situation' and the 'nations of the world'.[34]

Even when philosophers saw adopting a constitution as instrumental, there is a great emphasis on international norms. In 1867 Tsuda Mamachi, for example, advocated a constitutional government with a bicameral legislature with the following logic. If Japan adopts 'the so-called republican form of the Westerners, then no nation and none of the great powers will be able to discriminate against us'.[35] Clearly, there is something both normative and instrumental about Tsuda's argument. The immediate goal is to avoid subjugation at the hands of the imperialist powers. But the means to this goal involves conforming to global norms that bind the great powers themselves. This is very different from the functionalist advantages of superior military technology. These global norms, like all social norms, are constructed. Tsuda, by advocating that Japan conform to these norms, is helping to reproduce these norms and is thereby helping to create the very global culture to which Japan must conform.

World culture had a pronounced impact on radical political thought, but it also shaped conservative political practice. We can find clear reference to the importance of international norms, for example in the writings of Saigō Takamori. Born into a low-ranking Satsuma samurai house, Saigō rose to national prominence and, with Okubo Toshimichi and Komatsu Tatewaki, negotiated the Satsuma-Chōshū alliance to overthrow the shogunate. In the early years of the Meiji era, Saigō, Okubo, and Kido Kōin were the three most powerful politicians in Japan and were the principal architects of the Meiji state. But Saigō is famous also as a rebel: the leader of the Satsuma Rebellion of 1877, the largest military challenge to the Meiji government. Saigō believed in a strong central state, but he could not quite accept that such a state would collide with the traditional autonomy of Satsuma. Saigō died leading a rebellion against a state he helped to found, fighting an army he helped to create. Saigō was, in essence, the most reluctant partner in the creation of the modern, centralized, Japanese state – but that makes his understanding of that such a state especially important. Saigō was not a Westernizing radical – rather he made radical reform possible by giving it conservative support.

Saigō grew up thinking of Satsuma, a Japanese daimyo domain, as his state (*kokka*) and his country (*kuni*) and he only slowly came to support a nation-state. Imperial loyalism had a powerful, but limited impact on his thinking. Saigō used 'state' in the modern sense, to refer to Japan, immediately after meeting Fujita Tōko, the imperial loyalist scholar. Writing on 29 July, 1854 of his meetings with Fujita in Edo, Saigō reported that, although he felt unworthy, Fujita had taken him on as a disciple: he was thus delighted to be serving the 'state'. Since Saigō was from Satsuma and Tōko was from Mito, 'state' in this context meant Japan: clearly the Mitogaku idea of imperial sovereignty had influenced Saigō's vocabulary.[36]

This was, however, an extremely short-lived change. Only a few days later, Saigō was again using a more traditional vocabulary. In a letter of 2 August 1854 Saigō wrote that he wanted to 'remove the calamities that plague the state'. Here he was referring to his domain of Satsuma – and the 'calamity' was a bloody succession struggle within the lord's house. This was an extremely traditional sense of 'state' – what I have elsewhere called the 'patrimonial' aspect of politics: the 'state' was the lord's family.[37]

Saigō was thus a firm believer in early-modern multivalent politics. Until 1867 he continued to support the *kōbu gattai* formula in Japanese politics: a union of the imperial court and the warrior houses. Japan, thought Saigō, could best be governed by a council of daimyo and the shogun, invested and legitimized by the emperor. Several factors eroded Saigō's faith in *kōbu gattai*. Saigō deeply distrusted Hitotsubashi Keiki, the last Tokugawa shogun. Saigō thought Keiki was devious, dangerous, and immoral. Since he could not envision cooperating with Keiki, Saigō began to consider destroying the shogunate itself.

But another critical factor was Saigō's understanding of the global scene. Saigō was deeply interested in English views of Japan and he related, in great detail, his conversations with the English consul general, Harry Parkes, and the consul's translator, Ernest Satow. A constant theme in Saigō's accounts was world political standards: Japan needed a polity commensurate with other states. In his meeting with Parkes in July 1866, for example, Saigō spoke of Japan's desire for 'normal international treaties (*bankoku futsū no jōyaku*)', his way of describing revision of the unequal treaties. Parkes responded that Japan's polity was, by world standards, abnormal. It had two sovereigns, a shogun and an emperor, and its laws did not conform to world standards. If Japan wanted 'normal' treaties, it would have to have a 'normal' polity. Saigō took these comments to heart. Months later, when advising his daimyo on national policy, he described conformity with global norms as an essential part of political reform: 'if we deal with foreigners on the basis of the laws of the nations of the world there will be no dissent in the realm and in the future the realm will recover its fortunes.' Saigō was a devout imperial loyalist, but he now understood that the essence of political reform was making the Japanese monarchy conform to world standards. This idea surfaced again in Saigō's conversations with Ernest Satow in July 1877. Saigō and Satow agreed that the 'Japanese king would take political power, make the daimyo subordinate to him, and establish a national polity (*kokutai*) equal to the nations of the world (*bankoku*).' Then Japan would have a 'solid political system' that could have regular and normal relations with the 'nations of the world' (*bankoku*).[38]

Saigō restated this understanding of global norms after the Restoration in a November 1871 opinion paper (*ikensho*). 'The goal of the national polity of the imperial nation,' Saigō declared, should be a return to central position of the emperor as in ancient days, with 'extensive consideration of various nations, even the Western lands'. Saigō here uses a curious phrase: '*seido seiyō no kakkoku made mo*,' literally 'even as far as the Western lands to the West.' He uses both the term '*seido*', which can include both India and China, and '*seiyō*', which commonly means only Europe and America. When discussing military reform in the next paragraph, however, Saigō refers merely to the 'consideration of various Western nations' (*seiyō no kakkoku*). There is a subtle but important shift here. On pragmatic matters like military reform, the West is clearly the standard. But on political reform, Japan must situate its ancient tradition of state sovereignty in a global rather than merely Western context.[39] Or, to return to the sociological metaphor, Japan needed a subjectivity, a persona, appropriate to international society.

This subtle shift in language points to what I consider a major difference between the concept of importing Western models and conforming to global standards. The former assumes that the West is better. Therefore, since Japan needs to import the best it will import the West. The latter concept assumes that global standards are decentered: the West must conform to these norms as well. Although Western nations may be the most successful in modern politics, modern international political society is not, in itself, Western. The norms of world society are socially determined, even new and weaker members of society can affect these norms. Global norms are 'better' only because they are norms: commonly accepted ways of being and ways of behaving.

It is important to understand Saigō's thought as part of the framing metaphor of Meiji politics. Saigō was not a progressive, but he understood that Japan needed a legitimate subjectivity in international society. Since Saigō was a conservative, not a progressive, his acceptance of this idea meant that Meiji political discourse was about how Japan should establish its international persona, not whether Japan should do so. The breadth of consensus on this issue was remarkable: even Tokugawa Yoshinobu, the last shogun, alluded to it in his 1867/10/14 letter of resignation. 'Now, as intercourse with foreign countries grows daily more extensive, unless the imperial court is made the sole authority, it will be difficult to maintain law and order.' If, however, the Japanese polity is properly reformed then Japan will 'rank with the nations of the world'.[40]

Conclusion

The emergence of Japan as a nation-state was thus part of a much broader process: the emergence of the modern world system. To argue that Japan adopted 'Western' forms of government is to miss a broader point. Japanese statesmen were interested in Western political forms because they held the promise of international legitimacy and Japan's adoption of these forms gave the system of nation-states a newly international dimension. The transformation of Japanese institutions in the 1870s and 1880s reflected the dual demands of world society. Japanese institutions needed to be both uniquely Japanese and recognizably Western. I do not here wish to argue that world society can, in isolation, explain the remarkable transformation of Japanese state and society in the late 1800s. The force of world society coexisted with the logic of capitalist development and modernity: historians should not consider world society theory as an exclusive concept. World society theory, however, highlights the ways in which Japan's adoption of 'Western' models was an early instance of the current phenomenon of globalization.

Notes

1 R. R. Palmer, *A History of the Modern World*, New York: Knopf, 1952, p. 563.
2 R. N. Bellah, *Tokugawa Religion: The Values of Pre-industrial Japan*, Glencoe, Ill.: Free Press, 1957.
3 T. Fujitani, *Splendid Monarchy: Power and Pageantry in Modern Japan*, Berkeley and Los Angeles: University of California Press, 1996.
4 S. Vlastos (ed.), *Mirror of Modernity: Invented Traditions of Modern Japan*, Berkeley: University of California Press, 1998.

5 J. W. Meyer, J. Boli, and G. M. Thomas, 'World society and the nation-state', *American Journal of Sociology*, 1997, vol. 103, no. 1, 145.
6 J. W. Meyer, 'The changing cultural content of the nation-state: a world society perspective', in G. Steinmetz (ed.), *State/Culture: State Formation after the Cultural Turn*, Ithaca, NY: Cornell University Press, 1999, pp. 123–8.
7 Meyer *et al.*, 'World society and the nation-state', pp. 145–6.
8 J. W. Meyer, J. Boli, and G. M. Thomas, 'Ontology and rationalization in the Western cultural account', in G. M. Thomas (ed.), *Institutional Structure: Constituting State, Society, and the Individual*, Newbury Park, Calif.: Sage Publications, 1987, pp. 11–37; J. W. Meyer, 'The world polity and the authority of the nation-state', in Thomas (ed.), *Institutional Structure*, pp. 41–70.
9 A. Giddens, *The Nation-State and Violence: Volume Two of a Contemporary Critique of Historical Materialism*, Berkeley and Los Angeles: University of California Press, 1985, pp. 112, 281.
10 P. Duara, 'Civilizations and nations in a globalizing world', in D. Sachsenmaier and S. N. Eisenstadt (eds), *Reflections on Multiple Modernities: European, Chinese, and Other Interpretations*, Leiden: Brill, 2002, pp. 90–1.
11 For an imaginative discussion of this issue, see A. D. Eastwood, 'International Terms: Japan's Engagement in Colonial Control', PhD, University of Chicago, 1998, esp. pp. 1–85, 139–41; and P. Duara, *Rescuing History from the Nation: Questioning Narratives of Modern China*, Chicago: University of Chicago Press, 1995, pp. 22–3.
12 Duara, 'Civilizations and nations', pp. 80–97.
13 On the link between sovereignty and equality of states, see Giddens, *The Nation-State and Violence*, pp. 281–2.
14 K. Shigeshita and T. Sato (eds), *Kimigayo shiryō shūsei*, 5 vols, Tokyo: Kyoeki shōsha shoten, 1991; vol. 5, pp. 38–44.
15 N. Odagiri, *Kokka Kimigayo kōwa*, in Shigeshita and Sato (eds), ibid., vol. 5, pp. 30–5. Reprinted in *Kimigayo shiryō shūsei*, vol. 3.
16 Y. Tsukahara, 'Meiji no kyūchū gyōji saihen to gagakuka (reijin) no seiyō ongaku kenshū', in H. Matsushita (ed.), *Ibunka kōryū to kindaika* (Cultural encounters in the development of modern East Asia), Tachikawa-shi: 'Ibunka kōryū to kindaika' Kyōto kokusai seminā, 1996, soshiki iinkai, 1998, pp. 214–21.
17 Shigeshita and Satao (eds), *Kimigayo shiryō shūsei*, vol. 1, p. 2.
18 Nihon keiryō kyōkai (ed.), *Keiryō hyakunen shi*, Tokyo: Nihon keiryō kyōkai, 1978, p. 6.
19 Ibid., pp. 6–7.
20 Ibid., pp. 7–11.
21 Ibid., pp. 10–11.
22 Ibid., pp. 11–18.
23 Ibid., p. 79.
24 P. Bourdieu, *Practical Reason*, Stanford: Stanford University Press, 1998.
25 P. Frost, *The Bakumatsu Currency Crisis*, Harvard East Asian Monographs No. 36, Cambridge: East Asian Research Center, Harvard University, 1970.
26 Ibid., p. 15. For a sympathetic contemporary account, see R. Alcock, *The Capital of the Tycoon: A Narrative of a Three Years' Residence in Japan*, 2 vols, New York: The Bradley Company, 1863; vol. 2, pp. 345–62.
27 M. Masayoshi, *Report on the Adoption of the Gold Standard in Japan*, New York: Arno Press Inc., 1979 (reprint), p. 5.
28 Ibid.
29 M. Nakamura, K. Ishii, and Y. Kasuga (eds), *Nihon Kindai Shisō Taikei 8*, Tokyo: Iwanami shoten, 1988, pp. 6–13.
30 This essay is also known as Tonarigusa, translated variously as 'Neighboring grasses' and 'Essays on a neighboring land'. See W. Davis, *The Moral and Political*

Naturalism of Baron Katō Hiroyuki, Berkeley, Calif.: Institute of East Asian Studies, University of California, Berkeley, 1996, pp. 469–92. I rely here on the annotated text in E. Emura, *Nihon kindai shisō taikei 9: Kenpō kōsō, Nihon kindai shisō taikei 9*, Tokyo: Iwanami shoten, 1989, pp. 2–25.

31 Wakabayashi argues that the more substantive meaning of 'harmony' (*jinwa*) is 'popular unity and integration'. See B. T. Wakabayashi, 'Kato Hiroyuki and Confucian Natural Rights', pp. 471–2.

32 Emura, *Nihon kindai shisō taikei 9: Kenpō kōsō*, p. 24.

33 M. B. Jansen, *Sakamoto Ryōma and the Meiji Restoration*, Princeton: Princeton University Press, 1961, pp. 294–311.

34 Emura, *Nihon kindai shisō taikei 9: Kenpō kōsō*, pp. 32–3.

35 Ibid., p. 23.

36 Saigō Takamori zenshū henshū iinkai (ed.), *Saigō Takamori zenshū*, 6 vols, Tokyo: Yamato shobō, 1976–80; vol. 1, pp. 31–3.

37 M. Ravina, *Land and Lordship in Early Modern Japan*, Stanford: Stanford University Press, 1999.

38 Saigō Takamori zenshū henshū iinkai (ed.), *Saigō Takamori zenshū*, vol. 2, pp. 233–6.

39 Ibid., vol. 3, pp. 78–9. A variant copy of Saigō's opinion paper makes the same point in different language. Rather than the odd term '*seidō*', Saigō explicitly referred to Asia. Clearly Saigō meant to contrast the 'West' and the 'world'. See M. Yui and S. Obinata (eds), *Nihon kindai shisō taikei 3: kanryōsei keisatsu*, Tokyo: Iwanami shoten, 1990, pp. 39–40.

40 E. Shibusawa and Nihon shiseki kyōka (eds), *Tokugawa Yoshinobu kō den shiryō hen*, 3 vols, Tokyo: Tōkyō daigaku shuppankai, 1975 (reprint); vol. 3, pp. 183–4. There is an approximate translation in W. W. McLaren (ed.), *Japanese Government Documents*, 2 vols, Washington, DC: University Publications of America, 1979; vol. 1, pp. 1–2.

3   The making of state–bureaucracy relations in Japan

Richard Boyd

The current practice of political science encourages a generalized and universalizing account of the term 'the state', which has as its predicate the modern Western (liberal democratic) state. This hinges in turn upon the assumption that there is only one route from the 'traditional' to the politically modern and that the modern polity finds its ultimate expression in the Western state. In other words, the more developed a polity is, the closer it will come to reflect the chief characteristics of the modern Western state. From here it is but a short step to the view that the institutions of states worldwide will or should function much as they are thought to in the Western state. The current practice of which we speak has come under increasingly close and critical scrutiny in the last decade – indeed its essential inaccuracy is an axiom of much scholarship on the state in Asia, Africa, and Latin America.[1] We too take issue with the customary approach in respect of Japan where to read off actual political practice from the familiar account is to risk serious misunderstanding: since the 'familiar landmarks of parties, elections, parliaments, and ministries may all be on display, but how they really operate is not so evident' (see Whitehead in this volume). Here we follow Veyne and seek to explore his penetrating observation that, 'even if comparative analyses show that human societies manifest a certain number of shared, universal structures and behaviors, the meaning of some of these seeming universals is an extremely variable, contingent, and local construction, which it is a task of empirical and historical analysis and interpretation to reconstruct.'[2]

The field for our examination is the Japanese state, more specifically the Japanese bureaucracy and the relationship between the two. We take this as the site for our investigation since our sense is that the workings of the Japanese bureaucracy, although much written about, have been misunderstood in some rather important respects.[3] Moreover, this misunderstanding is rooted in the projection onto Japan of notions of what the bureaucracy is, of how it functions, and of how it relates to the state of which it is one element, which owe rather more to an estimate of how these things are in the Western state than to a careful historical and empirical investigation of the actual facts of the matter in Japan.[4]

The misunderstanding is borne of two errors in comparative analysis. We note both but it is the second of these that we will address in this chapter. The first is the failure to recognize that seemingly comparable institutions in different societies may serve quite different functions. As Grew puts it, to juxtapose institutions that carry the same name can amount to little more than mistranslation. It is essential to move, comparatively speaking, from consideration of formal purposes to the analysis and comparison of institutions as social practices. The injunction has extra force in Japan since here we have to hand a large body of research to show that for all the adroitness with which Japan adjusted to the demands of the contemporary world, selecting, adapting, and transforming a multitude of Western institutions along the way, tradition remained a force to be reckoned with. There is no less a weight of research to demonstrate the plasticity and even the novelty of tradition in Japan. In the process we have become so accustomed to the 'fact of multiple combinations within Japanese society of old customs, values and rites with new forms of social organization (that this) requires no special explanation.'[5] Given how familiar and well established this conclusion is in respect of a whole raft of Japanese institutions, we might even *expect* Japanese bureaucracy to be different and so embrace Veyne's call for careful empirical and historical analysis to elucidate its meaning.

The problem is exacerbated in the Japanese case owing to the fact that the state has not been a central object of political inquiry in Japan. Other questions have presented themselves and seemed to be more urgent; so in the immediate aftermath of the Pacific War the fate of the constitution commanded attention. Then at precisely the moment that attention turned to the political process in Japan, political science lost confidence and interest in the concept of the state. By the time the state was back in the analytic toolbox, attention had shifted to the explanation of growth and the state was seen as explanation rather than explanandum.

There is a second comparative error. The misunderstanding of the bureaucracy is rooted in a conflation of the state and the bureaucracy in much contemporary writing; that is to say the bureaucracy is treated as if it is the state *in toto*. The state occluded in the process is unexamined and assumed to afford the bureaucracy the same kind of context and meaning as it does in the West. Conversely, it is assumed that the bureaucracy relates to the broader state in Japan much as it does to the state in the West and so that it has much the same function and meaning as its Western counterparts. There is usually no attempt to justify these assumptions – they are borne of the habit of mind we spoke of at the outset that which presents the political trajectory of the West as that of the world *in toto*. Concealed in its premises is a Weberian conception of history as a process of rationalization in which the state figures as the epitome of rationality and the bureaucracy looms as the privileged bearer and agent of state rationality. So engrained is this habit of mind that it is difficult even to speak of 'the bureaucracy' without tacitly endorsing this world view and succumbing to the attendant danger of overgeneralizing the

Western experience of political modernization. The danger is real since we will argue that the state context of the Japanese bureaucracy is different, state-bureaucracy relations are different in Japan, and that this has significant consequences for the behavior of the bureaucracy.

The question arises as to how best to capture and explain that difference. Here we are confident that the problem cannot adequately be addressed in the habitually favored terms of the Weberian state analysis. There are two reasons for this. The Weberian definition of the state postulates a human community that successfully makes certain claims. It is indifferent (in the definition at least) to the particular form and nature of the body that makes the claim. We will argue that it is precisely the particularities of the state form in Japan that fashion and condition the meaning and function of bureaucracy in that country. The definitional shortcoming is readily explicable: Weber is persuaded that the administration of all nation-states would eventually converge in one form characterized by rationality and legal authority. Consequently, the question of particular state forms might have seemed only of marginal significance. Silberman, a pioneer of Western study of Japan's bureaucracy is sensitive not only to the need to distinguish state and bureaucracy but also to the diversity of bureaucratic roles and organizational structures worldwide. In particular, he distinguishes between two types: professional and organizational. Both types are a product of bureaucratic rationalization – to this extent he shares common ground with Weber. Where he departs from Weber is in the argument that the process of administrative rationalization took, in fact, two courses. Permeable organizational boundaries and the allocation of information characterize one path by 'professionals'. The other path leads to an organization stamped by well-defined boundaries and the allocation of information by organizational rules. The choice of path is historically determined; levels of uncertainty about leadership succession being the prime cause.[6]

Our focus is somewhat different. We are less concerned with the local unfolding of a universal history of bureaucratic rationalization than we are with the rootedness of states in the particular history of their making and the consequences of this both for the fashioning of a particular style and pattern of administration and for its replication and reproduction over time. To this extent and in this context we line up with the 'splitters' – those who note particularity at the periphery (and by 'periphery' we mean all those countries remote from the European heartlands of the social sciences), and we line up against the 'lumpers' (that is to say, those who believe that the concepts and theories of the social sciences which are predicated upon, encapsulate and reflect an exclusively European history are a sufficient measure which can do justice to the experiences of the 'periphery'). In terms of the immediate discussion of state and bureaucracy in Japan, this means that we do not wish to sweep up the Japanese state in an overgenerous Weberian embrace which will conceal more than it will reveal. Nor do we wish to blend and dilute our understanding of long-standing and enduring Japanese practices of rule and administration and their conceptualization so as to accommodate the claim to universal validity of Weberian social science. The upshot of our debate is of less significance for the facts of the matter than it is for how we weigh the facts. No student of Japan's governance will dispute the facts: the entrenched and ineradicable sectionalism of its bureaucracy and the elitism, hauteur, 'proactiveness,' power and prestige, transcendence even, of its officials. For some observers these behaviors are to be downplayed because they occur at the margin of, cannot easily be accommodated to, and even subsist in defiance of universal historical processes. We do not see these as the negative consequences, the local coloration, the unfortunate side-effects of otherwise universal processes of administrative rationalization. In fact, two defining characteristics of the Japanese bureaucracy are its entrenched sectionalism and its cult of transcendence. These are of the first importance for the conduct of the bureaucrat's business in Japan. They owe nothing to the rationalization of administration, more often they suggest the very opposite. The Japanese bureaucracy was shaped and fashioned to function in the late nineteenth–early twentieth century in a state-making process which institutionalized understandings of the loyalty and identity, the moral authority, and the material utility of the relationship between the official and his section. The section and its officials came to understand it and their role in terms of the relationship between a strongly articulated state and a weakly articulated society; a relationship which first stimulated and later sustained an activist and interventionist, a leadership and shepherding conception of the bureaucratic role in Japan. Over time, these understandings enjoyed a long-run and more or less uninterrupted history of replication and reinforcement sanctioned by habit and familiarity. We speak to the present of a state which daily permits and elicits from its officials behaviors which owe little to long-run process of rationalization and in which sectionallism and administrative transcendence are renewed daily. To make sense systematically of these behaviors, we must clarify the relationship between the bureaucracy and the state rather than seek to clarify the state/society relationship.

This requires that we resurrect the distinction between the state and the bureaucracy. In respect of the former, it is customary to rely upon the Weberian definition that is to say the state is to be understood as a human community that (successfully) claims the monopoly of the legitimate use of physical force within a given territory.[7] We have noted the problematic nature of Weber's relative silence on the nature and organization of this unspecified human community. The definitional problem is exacerbated in the present context by the close association of the Weberian definition of the modern state with his no less famous account of the bureaucracy. The strength of this association is such as to prompt us to embrace the Japanese state in familiar terms and to assume too easily a ready fit between the Japanese bureaucracy and the conventional notions of rationality, formality, hierarchy, instrumentality, and service. Since it is precisely the status of these conventional judgements that is at issue in this chapter, it is strategically unwise to adopt a definitional approach that hypostatizes these attributes.

In short what is required is a definition of the state that does not anticipate and prejudge the nature of its constitutive elements, their functioning, and their role but that leaves these open to and subject to revelation by historical and empirical investigation. Finer[8] suggests that the modern state has three characteristics:

1   They are territorially defined populations each recognizing a common paramount organ of government.
2   This organ is served by specialized personnel: a civil service, to carry out decisions and a military service to back these by force where necessary and to protect the association from similarly constituted associations.
3   The state so characterized is recognized by other similarly constituted states as independent in its action on its territorially defined – and hence confined – population, that is on its subjects.

Finer's definition is eminently serviceable for present purposes. It distinguishes the bureaucracy from the state; it reminds us that the bureaucracy is but one element in the state and above all it draws attention to a relationship critical to our understanding of the state that is to say *the relationship between the paramount organ of government and the 'specialized personnel' that serves it.* This relationship is neither a given nor is it to be read from conventional wisdom regarding the Western state. It is critical to what we will have to say about the Japanese case specifically. The terms of the relationship between the paramount organ of government and the specialized personnel have massively reinforced the tendency, already visible in other bureaucracies, for administrative units to act independently, as laws unto themselves and to act with scant concern for formal hierarchies. We speak of this as sectionalism.

Whitehead refines the definition in his specification of the minimum conditions implied by the modern state.[9] His approach is not restrictive, prejudicial, or anticipatory – that is to say, it does not assume the universality of Western forms nor anticipate the uniformity of their parts by projection from Western models. It healthily allows for particularity and difference (and not only between Asia and Europe but no less within and across these regions) without detriment to the possibility of comparison – indeed a matrix of comparative possibilities is suggested. One facet of Whitehead's definition, missed by Finer, is of immediate utility. Whitehead speaks of the multifacetedness of the state and suggests that this multifacetedness has at least three key analytical dimensions: the state as an idea, the state as an organization, and the state as a social formation. The Weberian definition makes no reference to the idea and end of the state, and yet this is of great importance for the political practice of the state – even in the West, a point persuasively made by Dyson in his excellent and woefully neglected account of the state tradition in Europe.[10] We take *the state as an idea* to be an indispensable point of comparison between the Japanese and other states. It remains a critical means of explaining the behavior of the bureaucracy that serves the state idea in Japan. The organization and conduct of the Japanese state in its modern or post-Meiji guise is comprehensible only in so far as we acknowledge that its grounding idea was not the mastery of territory, a task accomplished with relative ease and speed, but the transformation of a society so as to meet the challenge of an encroaching and armed Western modernity. The founding principle of the Japanese state is active, dynamic, and transformational. This too has consequences for how the bureaucracy came to see its role and to understand its relation to society, in fact to the birth of a conception of the bureaucratic role that owes little to public service notions and much to the administration's sense of its 'transcendence' over society and public. We shall first consider more fully the facts of the matter in respect of these two characteristics of the Japanese bureaucracy – its sectionalism and transcendence – before proceeding to an explanation of the relationships that brought them into being.

Sectionalism: the thesis

> The principles of office hierarchy and of levels of graded authority mean a firmly ordered system of super- and subordination in which there is a supervision of the lower offices by the higher ones.[11]

It is said of the developmentalist account of the state that this notoriously underestimates the universality of bureaucratic politics, the turf wars, interagency rivalries, and squabbling that characterizes much of administration in the modern state, and which tends to deform policy making and so to call into question technocratic, instrumental, and rationalist accounts of decision making. The states of East Asia are no exception to the rule. Recent scholarship confirms that in Japan, Korea, and Taiwan bureaucratic decision making is riven by bureaucratic politics.[12] The sectionalism of which we speak is not all of a piece with, nor is it reducible to an otherwise ubiquitous bureaucratic politics although it undoubtedly exacerbates these. The sectionalism of the Japanese bureaucracy is systematic and structural – the thing itself – that is to say, we should not see ministries and other agencies as administrative units threatened by subordinate intraagency loyalties and other centrifugal forces but rather we should recognize that it is the intraministerial section that is the fundamental politico-administrative unity. The section commands the loyalty of its members; it is in many respects a world and a law unto itself. It is deeply, extraordinarily entrenched. Sectionalism which has had competing agencies kidnap potential recruits,[13] conspire to abolish each other,[14] sabotage Japanese participation in international trade talks[15] rather than compromise sectional interests, sabotage each other's programs, replicate each other's programs, and more for nigh on a century. The sections govern; respecting matters that fall within their jurisdiction their competence and *de facto* authority are all but inviolable. They make policy. They unmake policy. Notwithstanding constitutional and legal pretensions to the contrary they initiate policy. As Kyōgoku, a leading analyst of Japan's politics writing in 1983 puts it: only those policy proposals that originate endogenously within it are viewed as 'authentic' or 'legitimate'; policy proposals emanating from other agencies or sections or from the public are ignored by the agency that claims jurisdiction.[16]

In short it is not enough to reiterate the (well-intentioned) platitude that states are not monoliths nor for that matter that ministries are not monolithic, and that accordingly both must be unpacked and disaggregated. The fact is that, 'the locus of formal competence and the locus of actual decision making power do not coincide' in Japan.[17] The administrative sectionalism of Japan stands in sharp contrast to Weber's characterization of bureaucratic administration in terms of strict hierarchic supervision, of disciplined, specified, and authoritative relations of superordination and subordination in which the locus of responsibility is clearly indicated. It owes nothing to the long-run processes of rationalization that are so often equated with processes of modernization. Indeed some authors see it as timeless; the manifestation in administration of a distinctive and characteristic system of rule in Japan which is to say, 'the tendency in different ways but at almost every period of Japanese history for effective rule to devolve to levels below, sometimes well below, those in titular authority.'[18]

Sectionalism: the evidence

It is acknowledged that entrenched bureaucratic sectionalism is as old as the modern Japanese state: thus post-1905, 'The Naimusho, the Army, the Navy, the Ministry of Foreign Affairs, the Ministry of Finance, the Privy Council and other vital institutions of state were all led by men who identified with these institutions rather than with the center of power they were supposed to represent. They were often not even on speaking terms with each other.'[19] And as time went on, 'the different organs of the state, mistaking parochial interests for that of the nation, began to develop a sense of autonomy resembling that of the abolished fiefs of the Tokugawa period . . . jockeying for power. [They] were vigorously pulling the country in different directions.'[20]

Things did not improve in wartime: 'The cabinet remained a federation of ministries and agencies, each scrupulously guarding its privileges and autonomy. The Prime Minister could neither dictate to the other ministers nor change them at will: replacing a minister was a complicated task which required both pressure and persuasion.' Indeed the ability of agencies, above all the Army and the Navy, to decide themselves who was and who was not acceptable as their minister came in time to constitute a veto over the entire cabinet-making process.[21]

And after World War II it was much the same. 'Excessive sectionalism and bureaucratic infighting' remained the norm. Examples are legion. Writing of sectionalism in the 1960s Chalmers Johnson details the defeat of public initiatives to find solutions to the problems of traffic jams, pollution, and the high cost of taxi services in the cities. These foundered on an entrenched sectionalism that ignited jurisdictional rivalries and pitted against each other with deadly effect agencies with relevant responsibilities: the Ministry of Transport (taxis), the police agency (traffic), the Ministry of International Trade and Industry (automobile manufacturers), the Ministry of Construction (roads), and the public safety commissions (under the influence of the police agency).[22]

Decades of 'reform' changed little. In the late 1970s, Ministry of International Trade and Industry officials explained to their minister that although it was the case that post-oil crisis 'structural depression' was a multisectoral phenomenon, and much as a policy was a desperate political necessity (an electoral crisis was in prospect – it was 1977, and business was reluctant to fund the Liberal Democratic Party (LDP) in the absence of policy to assist the process of adjustment), the fact was that legislation that touched sectors supervised by agencies outside of the Ministry of International Trade and Industry (for example, the shipbuilding industry under the supervision of the Ministry of Transport) was simply not workable. It could not be done. The minister, in view of the imperative political circumstances, insisted. Ministry of Transport officials from the Ship Bureau were uninterested, they had their own legislation. Senior individuals from the Ministry of International Trade and Industry were reduced to pleading with their counterparts in the Ministry of Transport 'to join in' so as to salvage at least the appearance of a comprehensive law for dealing with depressed industries.[23] Later still, the 1980s and much of the 1990s have been a period when 'the Ministry of Finance, for example, in the name of fiscal restraint has blocked virtually all policies aimed at expanding domestic demand, even though many Liberal Democratic Party politicians (the LDP was elected government of the day) believe that reflation of the economy would have brought in more revenue and might have made taxpayers less hostile to a tax increase. Similarly, the Ministry of Agriculture, Forestry, and Fisheries has become a virtual kamikaze squad protecting the farmers from any form of competition. And the Ministry of International Trade and Industry fights with everybody in the government to keep or put high technology industries under the jurisdiction of its industrial policy.'[24]

Sectionalism does not only pit ministry against ministry. It pits intraministerial agencies, bureaus, sections, and divisions against each other. And it places sections within a ministry off limits not only to the minister but also to senior civil servants within the ministry. Let us stay with the Ministry of Transport within which the Maritime Technology and Safety Bureau, the Maritime Safety Agency, the Marine Accidents Inquiry Agency, and the Meteorological Agency are all independent kingdoms, technical monopolies, jealous of their particular legacy of operating procedures, and 'anthologies of legal and written precedents', impervious, impenetrable, and deaf to the appeals of the law and economic generalists at senior levels as they are to the

Minister of Transport himself. Ports and Harbors are happy to defy its minister to the extent of challenging the US administration.[25] It recruits its own staff (its Directory General has 22 directors; one of these is a career official, 21 are technical specialists directly recruited by Ports and Harbors), it has its own budget, its own revenue flows (hypothecated shipping charges), and its budget and its accounts are off-limits to the ministry's accounts department. Ports and Harbors makes its own policy. Within the same ministry, the Engineering and Safety Department also makes its own policy. The latter, with a clientele of automobile inspection and tune-up businesses and a payroll of 380,000 private-sector employees, has repeatedly defeated the earnest wishes and the best and repeated efforts of the Ministry of Transport hierarchy to reform the vehicle inspection system. These are regularly and invariably defeated or compromised.[26]

Sectionalism has proved refractory to reform efforts. Reform efforts have been in vain. Reflecting on all but two decades (1948–1972) of administrative reform initiatives, retired Ministry of International Trade and Industry vice-minister Sahashi Shigeru voiced the view that sectionalism is so entrenched as to be refractory to organizational reform, that in fact the latter – the (re)combination of ministries into new organizations – simply triggers new turf wars and so serves to reinforce sectionalism and interagency competition.[27]

Often section boundaries, jealously guarded by officers of the section ever alert to the possibility of their expansion are protected, *inter alia*, by regulatory thickets which are impenetrable to senior civil servants, ministers, and Prime Ministers, including the most ardent and vigorous reformer of them all Nakasone. He set up the Transport Policy Bureau (1982) within the Ministry of Transport to transform the latter 'from a licensing agency to a policy-making agency'. The Transport Policy Bureau is extant and powerless in face of sectional regulatory walls and license powers – in 1991 the Ministry of Transport issued 1,996 licenses out of the total of 10,710 issued by all agencies. A pervasive and impenetrable sectionalism means that a ministry such as transport is in no real sense a public agency with an effective and integral responsibility for a multifaceted task of transport but is better understood as a convenient calculus to imply order, a simple addition without a meaningful total of individual agencies with their own recruitment, information, jurisdiction, functions, clientele, and regulatory walls.[28] This is in all probability even more so following the government 'reforms' and the creation of the National Land and Transportation Ministry successor to the MOT as the increase in the number of sections in the new organizational combination exacerbates the problem of sectional government.

Sectionalism means that officials even at the level of division chief must be as much politicians as bureaucrats skilled in the art of government. The division chief must manage as he cannot master the section chiefs who monopolize the formulation of policy within his division. The informal discussions of the division chiefs determine which policies will be blocked and which will be advanced. Coordination mechanisms are weak or absent. Consensus is by no means a rule of the game. Unbending defense of sectional/ divisional interests is. Compromise is not welcome, and even more rarely volunteered. It could not be otherwise since it is a direct challenge to the territorial imperative of the section and so of the division. The language that expresses the ruling norm of the game is colorful and changes little with the years: know the turf (*nawabari ishiki*), defend the turf (*kakkyo-shugi*), guard the foxhole (*takotsubo-shiki gyōsei*). If compromise happens it is likely to have been imposed, most likely by the Liberal Democratic Party and even then it will take the form of 'add two sectional/divisional interests and divide by two', so that each gets half. The compromise measure goes back to both agencies where its obvious transgression of the rules of the sectional game means that it may well languish there unless public outcry and the clamor of the mass media in the wake of an accident or a scandal demands action. Sectionalism within the division and the attendant downwards displacement of the power to decide means that what is required higher up the line, of ministers (elected politicians), vice-ministers (career bureaucrats), and bureau chiefs (career bureaucrats) is 'the art of governing that rests on mutual adjustment of division chiefs' that stands in turn on a bedrock of stubbornly independent sections.[29]

Let us repeat, the reform of sectionalism has become a means to the reproduction of sectionalism. Prime Minister Miyazawa called the Third Provisional Council on Administrative Reform to work in 1992. The disarticulation of Japan's intensely sectionalized, vertical administration was again a priority for administrative reform. The announcement was greeted with little public enthusiasm and considerable bureaucratic maneuvering as it became apparent that while the call for reform could no longer be resisted, it might prove to be a chance to extend existing bureaucratic empires. The result was even more intense interagency rivalry and competition. The waters of Kasumigaseki swirled and boiled faster and faster as the sharks (Ministry of Finance, Ministry of International Trade and Industry, Ministry of Construction, Ministry of Home Affairs, Ministry of Health and Welfare, and the National Police Agency) circled to bear down on their prey. The Ministry of International Trade and Industry (at one point rumored to be a target itself) had the Ministry of Post and Telecommunications in its sights. The Ministry of Construction pursued the breakup of the Ministry of Transport. The Environment Agency and National Land Agency were said to be easy game. The newspapers spoke of an unholy alliance of the Ministry of International Trade and Industry, the Ministry of Construction, and the Ministry of Home Affairs which targeted variously against the Ministry of Foreign Affairs, the Ministry of Transport, and the Ministry of Post and Telecommunications. A feeding frenzy was in prospect.

The Ministry of Construction was the big winner following passage of the Central Ministries and Agencies Reform Basic Law on 9 June 1998. The National Land and Transportation Ministry now, having devoured the

Ministry of Transport, National Land Agency, and the Hokkaido had become a ministerial behemoth with 13 bureaus, 145 sections, 680,000 officials, and an allotment of 80 per cent of the current public works budget. This was not what the Administrative Reform Council (*Gyōsei Kaikaku Kaigi*) established by then Prime Minister Hashimoto Ryūtarō and which issued its final report on 3 December 1997 had initially envisaged. These foundered on the refusal of the bureaucracies and the sections within them to cede jurisdiction or to merge. The upshot was that reform could only proceed by means of the transfer *in toto* of the functions of current ministries and agencies to new agencies. There was not a single case in which the reforms led to the division of the functions of a single bureau.[30]

In sum, the sectionalism of Japan's administration has been widely noted. But beyond that there is little recognition that sectionalism is a defining characteristic of the Japanese state with wide-ranging implications for the conduct of policy and the possibility of reform and that sectionalism is a consequence of the state-making process itself but now deeply imprinted and self-replicating in the musculature of the modern state. More often than not the discussion of sectionalism has been normative and evaluative rather than analytic and theoretic. Sometimes the approach has been dismissive; talk of sectionalism in Japan is 'old hat' and further discussion is greeted with impatience since sectionalism is said to happen everywhere. This kind of dismissal is no longer acceptable as scholars look increasingly to differentiate between state forms, to specify and to classify the ideational and institutional variety and meaning of the modern state so as to escape the embrace of a simple-minded Weberianism.[31]

Administrative transcendence: the thesis

> As a naval officer, *a bureaucrat* and a politician, I had always been on the side of the rulers and had not been accustomed to take account of the feelings of the ruled.[32]

Nakasone's candid identification of bureaucracy and rule is revealing of how a Japanese bureaucrat understands his role and how greatly this differs from the 'public service' conception of the bureaucratic role. Democratic norms require of bureaucracy a subordinate and instrumental quality and anticipate a conception of the bureaucratic role in terms of public service. Weber famously anticipated how problematic this requirement would prove to be and argued that in the modern state the bureaucracy would rule, that it must inescapably rule. He writes, 'In a modern state the actual ruler is necessarily and unavoidably the bureaucracy, since power is exercised neither through parliamentary speeches nor monarchical enunciation but through the routines of administration.'[33] The problem has been exacerbated by the loss of accountability, that is to say the 'bureaucratic problem' is due not merely to the fact of hierarchically organized institutions performing specialized functions, but from the exercise of unauthorized political and governmental power by administrative bodies. The problem presents itself in acute form in Japan where we have seen that an entrenched sectionalism enables the machinery of Japanese government to escape formal controls.[34]

The problem is exacerbated by a second characteristic of the Japanese bureaucracy that we can speak of as 'administrative transcendence'. By this, we mean something other than the ubiquitous sense of a creeping accretion of powers to the bureaucracy and the conclusion that ours is the age of bureaucracy. Indeed, our view is that there is rather something inherent in the concept of the bureaucratic role – hinted at by Nakasone, that distinguishes Japanese officialdom. Certainly in the Anglo-Saxon democracies there is a significant normative underpinning of the bureaucracy as public service. Reflecting on the problem of the administrative state in the United States, Belz usefully comments upon what he terms the 'configurative effect' of American constitutionalism. He argues that constitutionalism shapes political life directly in so far as constitutional principles 'become matters of commitment and belief possessing intrinsic value that motivate political action' and also indirectly in that,

> Constitutionalism has a configurative effect also in providing the forms, rhetoric, and symbols by which politics is carried on. Political groups and individuals ordinarily try to choose courses of action that are consistent with or required by the Constitution. They do so not because they are in each instance committed to the constitutional principle or value at issue; in different circumstances they may employ an alternative or conflicting principle. Rather political and governmental actors adhere to constitutional standards because they know that the public takes the Constitution seriously, believing that it embodies fundamental values and formal procedures that are the touchstone of political legitimacy. In American politics the Constitution is a justifying concept, and groups that invoke constitutional arguments do so, from their own perspectives perhaps and in an immediate sense, instrumentally. Considered from an external and long-range view in relation to the polity as a whole, however, reliance on constitutional principles and rules is normative and noninstrumental. In this way constitutionalism shapes political events.[35]

We should not exaggerate the significance of these constraints but neither should we lightly dismiss the importance of a public service idiom in the constitutional democracies – even including those in Europe.

The situation in Japan is different; at a minimum the public service code is rivaled by a preexisting and deeply entrenched code of administrative transcendence, the principal term of which, brutally stated, is bureaucratic rule in the name of the emperor in consequence of which the bureaucracy is elevated above the public. This definition we will clarify and qualify below and also suggest in what form it persists in Japan in the postwar period. Administrative transcendence has been widely remarked upon but the remarks have tended to be descriptive, and the phenomenon has been neither carefully specified nor theorized. There are two unfortunate consequences to this. It has obscured the particularity of the Japanese bureaucracy, a problem of considerable importance when this is held to be a model of the Weberian ideal, *and so* of great utility in the promotion of economic development. Indeed we will suggest below that it is where the Japanese bureaucracy is least 'Weberian' that its utility for economic or other kinds of social transformation is greatest. It has also obscured how much the characteristics and capacities of a bureaucracy owe to the particular processes of state making in the country in question as opposed to a universal process of rationalization.

To repeat, the phenomenon of bureaucratic transcendence has not gone unnoticed. In one account, transcendence 'depict(s) the guardians of . . . (the) state, the elite bureaucrats, as occupying a firmly autonomous space above the rest of the society'. It should be noted that although the author of the quote agrees that 'a case can be made for transcendence', his own work is distinguished by a sensitivity to the extent to which the bureaucracy has partners and works with, through, and even for social actors.[36] Johnson concedes that 'the bureaucracy does not rule in a vacuum in Japan, but it does hold an ascendant position'.[37] On the other hand, if administrative transcendence is to be understood exclusively in terms of power then opinions are sharply divided, even diametrically opposed. For McVeigh, 'compared with Euro-American polities, the Japanese bureaucracy . . . possesses considerable power',[38] while for Haley, 'Little evidence . . . supports the common view that the Japanese bureaucracy is any more influential in formulating public policy than the bureaucracies in at least half a dozen different European states, including France, Germany, and the United Kingdom.'[39] At worst the analysis of administrative transcendence in terms of power has degenerated into a sterile exchange about, 'who was more powerful bureaucrats or politicians' with scant regard to what was at issue, nor to the adequacy of this kind of dichotomized account of the political game and its conceptual undergirding – a zero-sum account of power.[40]

Administrative transcendence is also said to be a matter of image, social prestige, and the popular representation of the cosmology of power. According to journalist Takahide Ikuta, the familiar term '*amakudari*' best encapsulates this aspect of administrative transcendence. Literally meaning 'descent from heaven', the word suggests a metaphor with origins in Japanese mythology of the descent from heaven by deities to create and to inhabit the Japanese archipelago. It refers now to the postretirement movement of officials into jobs in the private and public sector. 'This practice perhaps became known as *amakudari* because bureaucrats consider their jobs to be the most prestigious of all; the government agencies are 'heaven', and all other employees inhabit lesser worlds below.[41] A less familiar word '*amagaari*' (literally ascending to heaven) is used currently to denote the reverse flow, that is to say, for example, the transfer or loan of bank employees to the Economic

Planning Agency.[42] The flows might be reversed but the principle points in the cosmology are preserved. Okada Tadao writes of the '(deeply ingrained) habit of exalting the government official at the expense of the ordinary citizen' even after nearly two decades from the promulgation of the 'new' constitution.[43] Dower speaks of the 'continuing tradition of bureaucratic hauteur'.[44]

Administrative transcendence is also understood in the more restricted sense of the lack of accountability of the bureaucracy to the public. In this sense it has been a target for the reform efforts of the Administrative Reform Commission since 1964 whose recommendations regarding the introduction of an Administrative Procedure Law were defeated by the resistance of the bureuacracy aided and abetted by the Liberal Democratic Party. Thirty years later the bureaucracy tarnished by scandal and under external pressure (*gaiatsu*) in the wake of the Structural Impediments Initiative could not block the passage of an Administrative Procedure Law in November 1993, which took effect in October 1994, whose goal was to make the conduct of the Japanese state bureaucracy more transparent and the bureaucracy itself more accountable. By requiring automatic and timely processing by the bureaucracy of applications, notifications, and other requests for action on the part of private citizens, groups, and corporations, the law, Carlile tells us, makes the activities of the bureaucracy more visible to those outside the system. Plainly, the fact that the law was passed at all is of some significance but commentators have been alive to its weaknesses, loopholes, escape clauses, and loosely phrased obligations that all in all enable the bureaucracy to circumvent the law with little prospect that the courts will subsequently impose sanctions on bureaucrats who disregard the law. Moreover, areas of especial interest and sensitivity to the bureaucracy were succesfully ruled off-limits.[45] Carlile further notes that,

> No less interesting is what was left out of the law, largely as a consequence of resistance from the bureaucracy. Provisions for a special chapter in the law that would deal with two areas that have in the past been critical to economic development strategy and which have also been areas of extensive public criticism of bureaucratic procedures – land use planning and public works – were dropped early on. Stipulations that would alter the process of rule making and planning inside the bureaucracy – by, for instance, provisions that would mandate citizen participation in bureaucratic planning – were also put forward in committee and commission discussions but were dropped entirely from the final bill.[46]

The Information Disclosure Law (*Jōhō Kōkai Hō*), which was passed by the Diet in May 1999, to take effect in April 2001, was developed in tandem with the Administrative Procedure Law and much as the latter is the result of forty years of struggle with the bureaucracy. The motivation here were the struggles of pollution victims and other protest movements to get information they needed out of the Japanese ministries. And much as with the Administrative Procedure Law, 'the Information Disclosure Law is marked by various loopholes, namely in the area of defense, foreign policy, police affairs, and instances where the identity of an individual citizen might be revealed. At the same time, however, the law also sets up general principles that require the ministries to respond to requests for information in a timely manner and at an affordable cost.'[47]

Most strikingly, as Carlile points out in regard to the Information Disclosure Law, 'the point most vehemently (and ultimately successfully) resisted by the bureaucrats was the characterization of the citizen access to bureaucratic information as a *"right* to know" ... this meant in effect that the bureaucracy was granted relief from the definition of access to information as a right that might substantially limit discretion in internal bureaucratic decision-making.'[48]

Important as these aspects of bureaucratic power, bureaucratic image, and formal accountability are, they do not exhaust the notion of administrative transcendence. At least if not more important in our view and little remarked in the literature is how the transcendence code encourages the bureaucracy to conceive its function in activist, interventionist, and transformational terms in which the leadership and guidance of society is more pronounced than notions of instrumentality, execution, and subordination. The code is informal but also deeply embedded and configurative of political and administrative action in much the same way that constitutionalism is in the USA. In short the issue is not exclusively one of power, nor image, nor even of democratic accountability but also of the bureaucratic conception of its role. Here the notion of transcendence speaks to a conception of the bureaucratic role quite at odds with notions of instrumentality and subordination, of institutionalized, asymmetric relations between a principal and his agent.[49] What is at issue in Japan, and encapsulated in the notion of a transcendent administration, is the institutional and ideational embodiment of agency in the absence of a principal (or 'a paramount organ of government').

Administrative transcendence: the evidence

Bureaucratic activism in the economic field

Administrative transcendence understood in terms of a particular conception of the bureaucrats' role is well evidenced in the story of Japan's economic development in the twentieth century. Please note we are emphatically not discussing here how the Japanese economy grew or how far economic growth is attributable to the efforts of the state. For present purposes, the critical point is that whatever we might think is the explanation of economic growth, whether or not we accept that Japanese bureaucrats caused the growth of the economy, there is no doubting how generations of bureaucrats have understood their role in relation to the economy. This was activist, interventionist, and transformational. Johnson's classic study[50] is ostensibly the study of an institution, the Ministry of International Trade and Industry of course, but its pages are full of the stories of officials, of men who are personally identified with the initiation and promotion of policy initiatives, the definition of problems, and the identification of opportunities. There is not so much as a hint here of executive subordination. The men who fill these pages are explorers, 'politicians,' and decision makers. They sniff the air and scout the horizon, they journey abroad to find out what problems confront their competitors, to investigate the solutions others have found in other countries to problems held in common. They return and organize clubs and drinking sessions in which to brain storm, to stimulate, to enthuse, and to engage junior colleagues. They encourage the same juniors to go abroad on voyages of discovery and exploration. They contact and cajole their alma mater to ensure a flow of the like-minded and the highly able into their offices, they connive with cunning to ensure the promotion of themselves and their followers, and they fight like dogs to defeat their political and bureaucratic rivals.

It is no surprise then that Johnson lists the principal protagonists in the making of industrial policy and the fashioning of economic growth. He lists all of the political and administrative heads of the trade and industry bureau from 1925 – and we meet them one after another in the pages of his study – the pages of which teem with their initiatives, their sobriquets, the policies they championed, the reputations they earned, the measures they secured, the laws they had passed. Ishiguro Tadaatsu who in his young thirties in the Agricultural Policy Section of the Agricultural Affairs Bureau in the Ministry of Agriculture and Commerce 'imbued the ministry with a sense of mission to protect the small tenant farmer';[51] a young Yoshino Shinji who as chief of the Documents Section pushed to improve the quality of recruits to the commerce and industry division of the Ministry of Agriculture and Commerce, and was aided and abetted in this by an even younger assistant in the same section Kishi Nobusuke, the pair who are later, jointly, to invent Japan's industrial policy; Hayashi Shintarō, infamously dismissed in a political squabble but no less 'famous for developing the postwar Japanese sewing machine industry into a thriving business';[52] Murase Naokai whose endeavors as chief of the Commercial Affairs Bureau caused him to come to be known as 'the champion of the small businessman,'[53] and then a great raft of officials who tested their metal in the fraught and uncertain circumstances of Manchuria, who honed their skills and tested their industrial promotion initiatives under the watchful eye of the Japanese army (arguably an even more exacting examiner than the market).

It is not for nothing that Manchuria has been termed 'the great proving ground' for Japanese industrial policy. Men such as Shiina Etsusaburō, Uemura Kōgorō, Kogane Yoshiteru, Hashii Makoto, Minobe Yōji, Wada Hirō, Sakomizu Hisatsune, Aoki Kazuo, and Hoshino Naoki, 'bureaucrats' who took upon themselves a personal responsibility for the definition of industrial strategies for Japan in the war years. Exacting were the war years – unquestionably so. But the 'political economy of war' was in no sense the sufficient cause for the emergence of this bureaucratic mind-set; this was something that had long predated war and Manchuria and which was to endure in the very different and substantially more 'secure' circumstances of the postwar period and of the American nuclear umbrella.[54] Even before then there emerged a new generation of bureaucrats who understood their task still in pioneering and transformational terms but now in respect of the challenge of peace not war and all of whom, brought into the General Affairs Bureau by Shiina Etsusaburō, subsequently became leaders of industrial policy during the era of high-speed growth in the postwar period, and most of whom went on to become Ministry of International Trade and Industry vice-ministers – they include Yamamoto Takayuki, Hirai Tomisaburō, Ueno Kōshichi, Tamaki Keizō, Yoshida Teijirō, Ishihara Takeo, and Tokunaga Hisatsugu.[55] The list of names would be incomplete without that of Sahashi Shigeru, not least because he is the living and breathing encapsulation of the administrative transcendence code, a bureaucrat who as chief of the Enterprises Bureau within the Ministry of International Trade and Industry and later as vice-minister presided over the ministry's and so Japan's initial response to economic liberalization, and whose policies are said to have laid the groundwork for the extremely rapid industrial growth of the late 1960s, and whose vocal, opinionated, combative, decisive, and innovative style made him the exemplar in chief of the transcendent bureaucrat – a 'samurai among samurai.'[56]

The list of policies and laws initiated and championed by these men is voluminous. To repeat an earlier point we do not need to concern ourselves with the merits, or even the success and impact of these policies and laws to be persuaded of the fact of bureaucratic activism in the economic field. These are not men that Weber might recognize as mere officials. Beyond a doubt the capacity for leadership, innovation, and decision of those of whom we speak cannot be read off from a conventional account of a classic, meritocratic, career bureaucracy. Conversely, countries that adopt the recommendations of the World Bank and other international agencies to develop a meritocratic achievement-oriented career bureaucracy should not anticipate that having done so they will benefit from the presence, approach, and achievements of the kind of men of whom we have spoken. They are – we will argue – a product of the particular circumstances of state building in Japan and emphatically not of any putatively universal process of administrative rationalization.[57]

Bureaucratic activism in the social field

We have said that the very heart of our conception of administrative transcendence is the bureaucratic understanding that it has a privileged and leading role in the management of society, a role that requires of it decision, initiative, and intervention. This role cannot readily be described in terms of the execution of decisions taken elsewhere, even of decisions taken within a policy or legislative framework fixed elsewhere (that is, as is the case with some forms of delegated decision making). Nor is it compatible with notions of instrumentality. We add now that this understanding and the terrain upon which it is exercised are not confined to the economy. The Japanese bureaucracy understands the whole of society to be its field of operation. In consequence, extensive intervention in 'society' is as much a feature and a manifestation of administrative transcendence as is intervention in the economy. Here too our concern is not with the merits or success of such interventions but the fact of them. Much as Johnson speaks of elite economic bureaucrats as *the Economic General Staff*, so Garon in his path-breaking study of social management speaks of the elite bureaucrats in the Home Ministry as *the General Staff for Domestic Regulation*. The parallel is extremely striking, as is the use of the military metaphor with all of its implications of hierarchy, command, discipline, and direction. Home Ministry officials have a different self-description which preserves the ideas of guidance and direction in a gentler more pastoral image – they are the 'shepherds of the people'.[58] They see themselves as responsible for 'society' in much the same way that the elite economic bureaucrats see themselves as the guardians of the economy. It is their task to take the lead, to anticipate crisis, and to design appropriate measures.

The Home Ministry was dissolved at the end of the Pacific War upon the insistence of the Supreme Command of the Allied Powers. This changed but by no means ended the activities of former officials of the Home Ministry nor expunged their understanding of their role in respect of their preferred vision of Japanese society. This remained deeply imprinted in official thinking and in the institutions that assumed the shepherding role in the postwar era. Rather rapidly, obstacles presented by the Occupation reforms – up to and including the constitution – were circumvented and new techniques, most notably the mass media, were harnessed to old understandings.

Garon speaks of this, the relationship between state officials, projects of social transformation, and the Japanese people as 'social management'. Social management is the object of his analysis. For us the phenomenon he describes is of great interest as evidence implicitly of a certain bureaucratic style, of a particular conception of the official's role. We speak of bureaucratic activism to highlight the facts of initiative, leadership, and social guidance in the behavior of the Japanese official and to heighten the contrast with notions of instrumentality and executive subordination to legislatures and the implementation of decisions taken elsewhere that is idealized in some conceptions of the meritocratic, career-based Weberian administration.

While Garon is sympathetic to the notion of administrative transcendence and is satisfied that this is rooted in the particularities of state making in Japan (which following Inoue Kiyoshi he understands as the 'emperor system'[59]), where he takes issue with those who favor the expression 'transcendence', and who speak of the emperor system as its site is that those who use these terms generally portray the state bureaucracy as acting alone and from above in controlling society. He is undoubtedly right in his insistence that Japanese officials work with and through social groups in formulating and implementing projects to manage society to develop and to inculcate desired social behaviors. In this way 'civil society' becomes a means not so much of limiting but of extending bureaucratic reach.

However, (and to repeat) our concern is less with the state-society relationship and more with the ways in which Japanese state making have shaped and stamped the bureaucracy with consequences for its understanding of its role in terms of 'bureaucratic activism'. That is to say our focus is state–bureaucracy relations. In short, we seek to draw from Garon's work evidence of how Home Ministry officials before the Pacific War and their successors in the ministries of education, health and welfare, local government, and so on understand their task and the nature of their role.

From the opening years of the twentieth century, officials from the Home Ministry have understood their role to be to guide and to manage the Japanese people; these officials are not passively attendant upon events, including legislative events, but understand themselves as having a responsibility to be alert to possible problems at home, to chart exhaustively what other countries deem to be problematic and why, to collect information about the policy responses of other countries to problems perceived, to investigate the costs and benefits of these, to gauge whether or not they are appropriate for the Japanese situation, and to search out more cost-effective solutions that draw upon and reinforce resources (said to be) specifically Japanese. A core image has been that of a self-reliant Japanese people who work tirelessly for national prosperity while making minimal demands upon the state. Officials such as Inoue Tomoichi and Tokonomi Takejirō worked in the early years to develop welfare policy on this basis. A second generation of 'social bureaucrats' prioritized legislation which made the critically important industrial workforce something of an exception to the self-reliance philosophy, and championed a raft of policy and legislative initiatives to create labor exchanges (1921), workers health insurance (1922), improved hours for women and children (1923), and retirement and severance pay (1936). Official initiatives touched not only policy and law but also the institutional means for their delivery and implementation, notably a hugely extensive system of local volunteers, 'district commissioners' who operated in all but every municipality by 1942. The district commissioners constituted a multipurpose policy conduit, initially for assistance to the poor and in the war years to enhance social mobilization, to encourage austerity programs, and to implement enforced savings.[60] Bureaucratic activism in the social field was not confined to welfare policy; the nation's religions were actively managed by officials (supported when thought to be conducive to the social management task, outlawed and attacked when thought to constitute a threat to official goals and visions) as was the civic participation of women who were seen much as the district commissioners and as a means of extending the spread and depth of official intervention in society.

The Home Ministry was disbanded in 1947, when 'In one stroke, the Japanese state lost much of its capacity to coordinate policies relating to the police, local government, welfare, new religions, Shintōshrines, prostitution, women's political activities, (and) savings promotion'.[61] And yet bureaucratic activism in the social field, that is to say intervention in society, persisted, albeit in a modified fashion. Garon, our guide in these matters, charts a markedly high degree of continuity of prewar practices of social management through the postwar period in savings drives, social education, and so-called 'new life campaigns'. Some continuity might well have been expected – as proved to be the case in the economic bureaucracy very much the same people were in place after the war as before. In the case of social bureaucratic activism and intervention there were more than 30 former Home Ministry officials elected to the Lower House of the Diet in 1952 available and willing to lend political and legislative support to bureaucratic initiatives in the social field. Not for nothing has it been noted that the early postwar savings campaigns were hardly distinguishable from their predecessors prewar. Nor should it be imagined that this kind of activism in the social field was a kind of immediate postwar residual – soon to disappear, of earlier times and practices. The investigations of John Campbell and of Sheldon Garon reveal how far official initiatives in respect of the 'aging-society crisis' in the period from 1975 conformed to our model of bureaucratic activism, the administrative transcendence mode in the social field.[62] The problem was defined by officialdom, solutions were designed by officials and were predicated much on the same self reliance principle that informed prewar welfare policy and not least relied for its implementation upon the efforts of the local volunteer service of district commissioners, now renamed and reinvigorated. The essential continuity of bureaucratic activism to the present day is apparent in welfare policy as are 'both the limits and resiliency of the long-standing drive to manage society.'[63]

Sectionalism and administrative transcendence: the explanation

We wish initially simply to make the point that fundamental characteristics of the contemporary Japanese bureaucracy are the product of a particular state-making experience. The analytic consequence is that the history of state making in specific countries is to be prioritized over and above accounts of the local unfolding of universal processes of rationalization and modernization.

The institutional explanation of sectionalism is rooted in the tightly knit relationships within an agency in the cabinet government system established in 1885.[64] Constituted then were the key ministries, most of which endure (in one form or another) to the present. The act recognized: the Prime Minister, Imperial Household, Foreign Affairs, Home, Finance, Army, Navy, Justice,

Education, Agriculture and Commerce, and Communications, the ministers of which were said to constitute the cabinet.

The different agencies and their ministerial leaders were not bound by any principle of collective accountability as a 'cabinet'. Each ministry and its minister were individually accountable to the sovereign. The Prime Minister could demonstrate no closer or more substantial nor privileged a linkage to the sovereign than the individual ministry head, and so could not persuasively claim to be the chief executive of the cabinet. The result was that he could be at best *primus inter pares* in a situation in which he could cultivate authority only by orchestrating consensus. This led in turn to a cabinet procedural norm of consensus as a precondition for decision making. This over time led inexorably to a *de facto* right of veto by the individual ministry over cabinet decisions. Early in the twentieth century this meant that when a single minister did not support the Prime Minister the cabinet could fall. It followed that loyalty to the ministry was more rewarding than loyalty to any broader entity, and each ministry came to regard itself as a sovereign kingdom. The only entity that might have corrected this tendency was the Privy Council, which as the highest ranked advisory body to the emperor had the last word on administrative matters and was entrusted with the power to coordinate ministerial action for the benefit of the administration *in toto*. However, the Privy Council was itself composed of former bureaucrats who could not easily interdict a ministry that was individually accountable to the emperor.

Sectionalism in the prewar period was further reinforced by reliance upon policy making through imperial decrees – which in some years greatly outnumbered laws passed by the national legislature and which escaped perusal by both the Privy Council and the Legislation Bureau – since the ministry whose jurisdiction was touched by the contents of the decree had close to a power of veto. In such circumstances the development of an administrative culture and of standard operating procedures conducive to unswerving commitment to the section was unsurprising. Over time, sectional commitment percolated down through the agency and came to color all areas of its life and to be reproduced in sections within sections. Following upon enactment of the Occupation reforms and the establishment of the Diet as Japan's principal law-making body the number of laws increased substantially – there are now more than 1,600 laws on the statute books, more than three times the number on the eve of the Pacific War. This has not, however, had an equally dramatic impact upon (that is to say, a reduction of) the power of the section to make its own law. Such was the reliance within legislative bills upon the delegation of ordinance powers to particular agencies that leading academic authorities in Japan[65] spoke of the persistence in the final quarter of the twentieth century of a legal usage familiar in the last quarter of the nineteenth century that is to say a usage of law as an instrument of administrative rule rather than the rule of law. Given that the jurisdiction of the agency is broad while the extent of its coercive powers is rather less (although we should not take lightly the coercive menace of licensing powers, particularly in the first half of the postwar period), the agency has been obliged to rely upon its ability to persuade and to reward the interests that fall within its jurisdiction, not least by setting high costs on entry and securing rewards or compensation for exit in a process that draws agency and its partners closer together with the consequence of yet a further reinforcement of sectionalism. Close partnerships between bureaucratic agencies and 'private' sector partners are close and persistent consequence, cause, and corollary of entrenched bureaucratic sectionalism.

Notwithstanding the dramatically different terms of the new constitution it is not possible to argue that postwar it has proved possible substantially to master bureaucratic sectionalism, the ministries guard their prerogatives as spiritedly as in the prewar period. Let us briefly consider the Ministry of Finance, the Diet, and the management of public finances. Articles 83–91 of the Constitution specify that the power to administer national finances shall be exercised as the Diet shall determine (Art. 83), no money shall be expended, nor shall the State obligate itself, except as authorized by the Diet (Art. 85), and not least the Cabinet shall prepare and submit to the Diet for its consideration and decision a budget for each fiscal year (Art. 86). The reality is rather different and finance bureaucrats have managed to defeat all attempts to wrest control of the budget away from the Ministry of Finance. Johnson tells us that,

> The longest continuing struggle in the Japanese government, dating from well before the war, has been over the attempt to take control of the budget away from the Ministry of Finance in order to lodge it in the cabinet or some supra ministerial coordinating agency. In 1955 Kōno Ichirō conceived of an independent budget bureau; in 1963 the Temporary Administrative investigation council recommended creation of a system of cabinet assistants to oversee the budget; and in 1970 Kawashima Shōjirō called for the establishment of an Overall Planning Agency (*Sōgō Kikaku-chō*). The Ministry of Finance successfully beat back all these proposals. Regardless of what the constitution says, the coordinating power of the Japanese executive branch is exercised through the three annual budgets (general account, special accounts, and government investment), and control over them is in the hands of the Budget Bureau and the Financial Bureau of the Ministry of Finance.[66]

Wright studying Japan's public finances nearly two decades later takes a more nuanced view. Certainly, 'the influence exercised formally and directly through party (LDP) and governmental structures, and particularly at the time of the "revival" negotiations (that is, after the submission of formal budget requests, at the successive stages of hearing, examination, negotiation, and "revival" conducted by MOF's Budget Bureau) was more apparent than real. The purpose was mainly to demonstrate publicly the party's involvement in budget-making, and its apparent influence.'[67] However, overall negotiated discretion on the basis of equal and informal exchanges between politicians and bureaucrats has become a characteristic of Japanese financial management. The collapse of public confidence in Ministry of Finance officials in the wake of scandals and a popular perception of the ministry's failure to manage economic recession in the 1990s led the way finally to the creation of the Council of Economic and Fiscal Policy, which was to be chaired by the Prime Minister and charged with formal responsibility for determining the budget strategy and compiling the budget.[68]

With their structures and procedures intact and often extended, the ministries and their internal sections continued in the postwar much as in the prewar period. The Ministry of International Trade and Industry promoted its industries in a headlong pursuit of competitive advantage *vis-à-vis* its bureaucratic rivals, jealous of its recruitment, its turf, its ability to come up with new projects and policies, and to oblige the Ministry of Finance to finance them. The latter did exactly the same for much the same reasons and in much the same way to promote banking insurance and securities. The Ministry of Transport was no less diligent in respect of its industries: sea, air, and land transport and shipbuilding; the Ministry of Post and Telecommunications pushed broadcasting and communications; the Ministry of Agriculture, Forestry, and Fisheries focused on agriculture and fisheries and the food industry; and the Ministry of Health and Welfare championed the pharmaceutical industries. 'All these industries undertook their pet projects independently without any national level co-ordination.'[69] Any attempt at 'coordination' and the overcoming of sectionalism was seen as a territorial encroachment and was bitterly resisted.[70] Wright who terms these ministries 'semiautonomous states' puts it neatly:

> the machinery of central government has strong roots in the arrangements made at the time of the Meiji Restoration. MOF, MOFA, MOJ, MOE and the Cabinet Secretariat have an unbroken organizational line from the last quarter of the nineteenth century to the end of the twentieth. . . . the stability and continuity of those organizational arrangements have resulted in the 'collective identities' of individual ministries and agencies becoming deeply embedded. That embeddedness has reinforced organizational inertia by strengthening the 'verticalization' of Japanese bureaucracy, as ministries and agencies sought to protect long-established jurisdictional boundaries . . . change has taken place only gradually: new functions were grafted on to existing responsibilities, or transferred to organizations evolved from existing structures.[71]

The hole at the center was officially recognized as early as 1961 with the establishment of the Provisional Commission for Administrative Reform. In its final report of September 1964 the commission noted that:

> The Prime Minister's position is far stronger under the current system than it was under the constitution of the Empire of Japan. The Prime Minister can co-ordinate and adjust the administrative power of the entire government, however the auxiliary organizations that are intended to aid the Prime Minister in this function are extremely weak. At present, these supplementary organizations of the Cabinet and the Prime Minister are dispersed among the Cabinet Secretariat, the Prime Minister's Office, and their subdivisions; their functions and objectives are not clearly defined. Because of the absence of effective supplementary organizations, the cabinet cannot exercise leadership in budget making, which in effect, amounts to policy making.[72]

The agencies bitterly resisted and defeated or diluted the reform proposals – most particularly those aiming at cabinet responsibility for budget making. (Twenty years later Nakasone managed to create a rather weakened Management Coordination Agency by merging the Administrative Management Agency with part of the Prime Minister's office.) If anything the cabinet has tended to reproduce sectional divides. The minister attends to represent his ministry. 'Ministry' positions are painstakingly established in a protracted process of 'exhaustive delivery'[73] of the policy proposal (*ringi-sho*) to even those sections with marginal connections to the proposal. Each section has a *de facto* power of veto over the proposal. Too often the minister is a prisoner of the final proposal. The ability of the Prime Minister to 'knock heads together' is small. The administrative reform commission discussed as recently as 1998 the Prime Minister's *ability actually to propose agendas to cabinet meetings*.

Having defeated the reform proposals they initiated their own proposals. The solution to the problem was eloquent testimony to the nature of the problem itself. If sectionalism precluded interagency cooperation and if coordinated public private sector activity was only possible within the jurisdiction and on the turf of a single public agency, then the only solution was to create new agencies with exclusive responsibility for the new tasks and their burden of coordination. In short the form of the state governed the policy response. To put it in other words, the solution was to create more sections. The latest reorganization of the Japanese government, as we have seen, has been driven by the selfsame principle namely, given the near impossibility of securing interagency cooperation, the jurisdiction of single agencies must be expanded so as to embrace all interests, resources, and activities implicated in a public policy task. In the process all subsections together with their interlocking jurisdictions, interests, partners, entry rules, and prices must be swept up intact and together.

An explanation of sectionalism by reference to the institutional form of the Japanese state would be incomplete without finally some reference to the relationship between the government and the ruling party – a relationship that echoes some of the conceptual difficulties posed by the party–state relationship in Communist China. As is well known, from 1955 to 1993 the

Liberal Democratic Party has commanded a majority of seats in both houses of Japan's parliament. This has meant that nomination as Prime Minister follows almost as a matter of routine selection or election to the presidency of the Liberal Democratic Party. The ministers themselves hold office by virtue of their position within the Liberal Democratic Party. For all that, cabinet and ruling party remain two separate and discrete institutions. The ruling party has developed its own central organization and there are regular meetings of this and the cabinet – the so-called, Government and Ruling Party Coordination session. The policy positions taken by party representatives emerge from the deliberations (above all) of the Policy Affairs Research Council that consists of committees differentiated by policy areas that precisely match the functional divisions of the government itself. To oversimplify, for each bureaucratic section there is a Policy Affairs Research Council subdivision and, not surprisingly, an associated tendency for 'private' interests to organize themselves on the same basis. The private, the bureaucratic, and the party political policy organization is isomorphic and their interrelations close and intense. The consequence is a further, 'extrabureaucratic' reinforcement of sectionalism. In neither cabinet nor party does the top-level function of intersectional integration exist.

The party–state relationship also tends to undermine the Prime Minister himself and so his ability to command the center and offset sectionalism. The Prime Minister's own team – the Cabinet – and the party's top officials are not necessarily loyal to the Prime Minister and his policies. There is a long-standing convention that the ruling party and the government are equal and separate. The government has first to clear its legislation with the Liberal Democratic Party's Executive Council before submitting this to the Diet. The effect of the arrangement is to increase the party's power *vis-à-vis* its own leader, the Prime Minister. It is not unusual for the party's top officials, the head of the Executive Council or the Policy Affairs Research Council to openly criticize the Prime Minister's policies and his cabinet appointments. The current efforts of Prime Minister Koizumi to reform public administration as part of a general structural reform of Japan have been stubbornly opposed by party leaders.[74]

Toward the comparative analysis of state–bureaucracy relations in Japan

Sectionalism and administrative transcendence are two distinct characteristics of the Japanese bureaucracy. They are a product of the particularities of state making in Japan but they are sustained, renewed, and reinvigorated daily by the forms and values of the state made in the Meiji period and reformed after the Pacific War. Two measures that permit the comparison of states are important here. The first of these concerns the nature of the 'paramount organ' of the state and of the relationship between this organ and its 'service personnel' – in this case, the Japanese bureaucracy, the second of these deals with the 'idea of the state'.

The bureaucracy and the paramount organ of the state in imperial and postwar Japan

Reflecting on the first 12 years of postwar politics in Japan Tsuji Kiyoaki – the elder statesman of the study of public administration in Japan concluded that the axis of the *tennō* system, that is to say the imperial state had been preserved. He did not mean simply that the imperial institution had survived but rather that as in the prewar period 'the structure of a state bureaucracy unconstrained by either the cabinet or the Diet' had survived.[75] To put this in somewhat different language, the issue here in terms of an institutional conception of the state is the relationship of the bureaucracy to what Finer has usefully termed the 'paramount organ' of the state. He speaks of two characteristics of the contemporary state: (i) they are territorially defined populations, each recognizing a common paramount organ of government, and (ii) this organ is served by specialized personnel – a civil service to carry out decisions and a military service to back these by force where necessary and to protect the association from similarly constituted associations.

This theoretically is precisely the ground upon which Weber centered some of his anxieties. 'In view of the growing indispensability of the state bureaucracy and its corresponding increase in power, how can there be any guarantee that powers will remain which can check and effectively control the tremendous influence of this stratum?'[76] If, as in imperial Japan, it is left to a monarch to serve as counterforce to the bureaucracy the prospects are bleak. 'In the modern state the monarch can never and nowhere be a counterforce against the pervasive power of the professional bureaucrats. He cannot supervise the administration, for it is a professionally trained apparatus and the modern monarch is never an expert, with the possible exception of military matters. Above all, the monarch is never a politician who received his training within the machinery of the parties or of diplomacy ... and the struggle for power is not his natural milieu.' Indeed, 'He does not experience the harsh realities of party life by descending into the political arena, rather he is removed from them through his privilege.' Not only is transcendence then to be anticipated rather than explained so also is sectionalism particularly should the monarch attempt to govern. Then, 'If there is no powerful parliament, the monarch is today dependent upon the reports of officials for the supervision of the work of other officials. This is a vicious circle. A natural consequence of such allegedly "monarchic" government, which is without a responsible political leader is the continuous war of the various ministries against one another.'[77]

There was never any intention that the Emperor Meiji would serve as a governing monarch in Japan. Indeed the possibility was precluded by the nature of his authority that required him 'to be transcendent of actual historical and political processes.' Indeed the institutional arrangement in which it was stipulated that all ministers of state countersign and assume responsibility for cabinet-level decisions and by which sectionalism was greatly reinforced flowed directly from the conception of imperial authority, and accordingly was designed legally to remove the emperor from the realm of political action.[78]

Equally there was never any intention that the imperial parliament should emerge as the paramount organ which would have as its instrument a civil service whether or not it had this potential. The principal concern was the consolidation of the new state in a sequence that ran from the defeat of the enemies of the new order (this was not achieved until 1878; from 1873 to 1878 more than 30 rebellions were attempted), the consolidation of a bureaucratic state apparatus prior to the promulgation of the constitution (when the constitution was finally promulgated in 1989 a decade after its announcement a cabinet had been in operation for five years as the executive head of government, ministries had been fashioned to monopolize taxes and tax collection, foreign and internal affairs, defense, and a channel of recruitment through the University of Tokyo had been carved), and as the last act in the consolidation of the state the adoption of a constitution positively to sanction the new order.

The goal of the constitution was not to institutionalize asymmetrical relations between a sovereign (Finer's paramount organ) and his agents. There was to be no differentiation of decision and execution. Bureaucracy was to unite in itself both aspects of rule (both the 'political' and the 'administrative' both the decision and its implementation) and to do so in the name of the emperor. Najita captures the relationship of the constitution to bureaucratic rule perfectly when he comments upon the motives of its drafter: 'Itō's astuteness lay in his perception of the role of the constitution in confirming and legitimating an operative bureaucratic order: its function was to "absolutize" political constructs after questions of power had been settled and not to create new competitive power relations.'[79] The quintessential requirement was a code (kempō), an authoritative text (charter, rescript, oath – the magic of the confirmatory text) to afford actual ruling arrangements sanction confirmation and approval. The constitution was to be the logos of bureaucratic rule not a text critically to be revisited.

The transcendence of the bureaucracy in the imperial state owed much to the absence of a paramount organ to which the bureaucracy was not only symbolically but also operationally and procedurally subservient in a regular and systematic fashion. To borrow the language of Schaffer, the asymmetry of paramount organ and of bureaucratic agency had not been established and institutionalized.[80] Indeed, the paradox of bureaucracy in the imperial period was the use made of the paramount organ to permit and to facilitate claims to transcendent leadership by both the civil and more successfully the military bureaucracy.

The key question in the postwar period concerns inevitably the success of the Diet. Did the new Diet develop as the paramount organ of government? The constitutional answer is unequivocal: the preamble speaks eloquently of popular sovereignty. Article 41 states that the Diet shall be the highest organ of the state power and shall be the sole law-making organ of the state. Article 66 legislates the subordination of the executive to the Diet. These are without a shadow of doubt great changes. And, yet, as we have seen one seasoned observer writing 12 years after the promulgation of the Constitution concluded that the prewar system of rule remained substantially intact. Perhaps we should not be surprised at the persistence of prewar patterns of administration since these are remarkably resilient and enduring. Ernest Barker in his study of the development of public administration in Europe makes a distinction between England, which 'would not follow the lines of an administrative absolutism . . . but would be governed by the King in Parliament at Westminster, aided – or sometimes thwarted – by the local justices of the peace' and France and Germany, which 'have followed the lines of an administrative absolutism and have maintained these lines basically intact in spite of the revolutions and reforms they have undergone'.[81] Certainly much recent scholarship has emphasized transwar continuities in political and administrative life and it is taken as a given that much of the procedural and organizational furniture of the postwar economy was fashioned in the 1940s. Critically there was no popular democratic revolution. There was only a qualified espousal of the notion of popular sovereignty, and so the Diet lacked the final stamp and seal of legitimacy that might have substantiated its constitutional position.[82] Our view is that the balance of changes and continuity obliges one to speak of at best a qualified success of the Diet qua paramount organ of the state.

A complex of other factors push us to this conclusion. The story is complex and it has been told elsewhere[83] and need not detain us. The Japanese bureaucracy was left substantially intact (or at worst temporarily detained) by the purges. Its powers were greatly extended. Its military and political rivals were removed at a critical juncture. The constitutional draft was a shock, far removed from the draft of the Japanese government and quite at variance with their wishes. For all this, the expectation was that it was the Japanese elite who would oversee the introduction and nurturing of democratic postinstitutions and arrangements. Yoshida Shigeru was both the most influential postsurrender Prime Minister and no less the champion of imperial bureaucratic autocracy and almost as much the architect of postsurrender Japan as the Supreme Command of the Allied Powers itself. Flanked by ranks of former officials of the old imperial bureaucracy who staffed the ministries and parastatal agencies of the postsurrender polity, Yoshida, much as any prewar 'shepherd of the people' had his own views of the legitimate public. This did not include organized labor. There was an important continuity and, even more importantly, an operational and recruiting osmosis in the personnel that staffed what under the new constitutional dispensation might be distinguished as political and administrative institutions but which under the old dispensation were not so readily distinguishable. Whether one sat in the Diet or the Ministry of Labor or the Ministry of Justice or Education or Finance, the distance socially, ideologically, normatively, and a myriad other ways was rather short. The osmosis was institutionalized in 1955 with the creation of the Liberal Democratic Party and later the successive election of ex-bureaucrats as Prime Minister. The watershed was the struggle over the Security Treaty. The solution – the officially orchestrated displacement of popular energies into the pursuit of material well-being, a spectacular instance of bureaucratic activism, the income doubling plan was a clever exploitation of prewar statecraft but damning of prospects for the emancipation of a public independent of official constructions. The Cold War made it all the easier to present in favorable terms to both domestic and to international publics the retreat from democracy. In this perspective, the question 'Why did the attempt to impose a paramount organ above the bureaucracy fail?' is something of a nonquestion.

The bureaucracy and the idea of the state in imperial and postwar Japan: the imperial ideal and the chaos principle

We turn now to the explanation of sectionalism and administrative transcendence in terms of the idea of the state. There are two aspects of this that merit attention: the imperial ideal and the chaos principle. The first of these is rather well documented, famously so by Maruyama[84] and so rather well known. The second has received rather less attention but it is the critical undergirding of the activism element in administrative transcendence. Maruyama has demonstrated how deeply implicated these characteristics (sectionalism and administrative transcendence) were in the imperial ideal of the prewar Japanese state. The authority that underpins administrative transcendence is a function of the proximity of the bureaucracy to the imperial sovereign – in short, it is the presence as much as the absence of the sovereign that undergirds and potentiates prewar bureaucratic transcendence. Proximity is critical since there are no norms, no absolute values *outside* of the Emperor – these are embodied in the person of the Emperor, 'the eternal culmination of the True, the Good, the Beautiful throughout all ages and in all places.'[85] Worth is measured not by law, not by conceptions of the public and of public service but in terms of distance from the Emperor. Transcendence is constituted by the same measure since 'the consciousness of being separated from the humble people increased in proportion with the sense of being near the ultimate value, that is the Emperor.' The corollary (that is to say, the subordination of the people, the public, or society) is of course equally true since the gulf that separates the people from the Emperor separates the people from virtue and worth. Proximity to the Emperor also sustains 'sectionalism'. Maruyama tells us 'Japanese sectionalism, . . . derived from a system according to which every element in society was judged according to its respective connection, in a direct vertical line, with the ultimate entity. This involved a constant impulse to unite oneself with that entity, and the resultant sectionalism was of a more active and "aggressive" type than that associated with feudalism.'[86]

It would be wrong to say that the imperial ideal has been completely expunged from the postwar idea of the state and yet plainly it has been so diluted that Maruyama's argument can account for the birth of these practices but not for their persistence in the postwar period. Moreover, even in the prewar period the imperial ideal was more significant as a source of authority than it ever was as an operational code, a lodestone, or some other kind of guide to action. This was provided by the chaos principle.

Inoguchi[87] and Ooms argue that the norms that characterize the modern Japanese state date from Tokugawa times and are grounded in Tokugawa ideology. Ooms speaks of an 'obsession with order', the 'threat of disruptive forces', and concludes that 'To this day, those in power in Japan have not lost an acute anxiety about an integrated whole without fissures.'[88] This is to say that the threat of disorder and a consequent drive to order is the lodestone of Japanese statecraft. Kyōgoku argues that this fundamental idea of the state changed somewhat in the Meiji period, but remains to the present, a guiding principle of Japanese statecraft. He insists in a scintillating analysis of politics in Japan today (1983) upon the struggle against chaos as the deep principle of both political and administrative life in Japan.[89] His argument is subtle, but closely laps that of Ooms. At its core is a persistent sense of threat to domestic order that prompts constant vigilance in the monitoring of events. Since the Meiji period the chaos principle has located the world outside of Japan as the likely source of threat – so 'the search is directed to the outside, especially the Western world. Field trips abroad, foreign study, correspondents abroad, dispatching study groups';[90] 'when something new takes place . . . a new definition of world trends becomes necessary.' It demands a new definition of reality, this must be encapsulated and communicated, officially sanctioned, and an 'appropriate' policy response must be found. An appropriate policy response is one that cajoles, persuades, tweaks, and teases or in extremis adjusts or reconstitutes the order of the domestic whole so as to ensure its compatibility with the new reality. Only in this way the collapse into chaos can be avoided.

The chaos principle is at the heart of Japanese statecraft – it is an elemental, constitutive idea of the state. The operational sequence it demands is urgent and imperative. There are always crises and new developments abroad. The sequence implicates the bureaucracy at every stage: the library research and trips abroad to monitor 'the new,' the coining of phrases to capture the new reality (brain-storming sessions in the favored watering hole of a senior official facilitated by the institutional osmosis that facilitates easy movement between officials, journalists, and politicians), the official sanctioning of the new reality ('the new image of reality is adopted and sanctioned by official documents and government pronouncements in such forms as statements, speeches, and orders'[91]), the search for policy, and the endeavor to implement it.

The chaos principle survived the defeat in war and the passage of political reforms. Indeed, defeat in war and the agonies of surrender, Hiroshima and

Nagasaki reinforced the sense of threat, of imminent collapse into chaos, and the consequent need for official vigilance in the urgent pursuit of order attuned to the realities of the world situation. It is a sensitive reflex in Japanese statecraft memorably tripped by the Oil Shock and the Hanshin Earthquake (when officialdom was roundly condemned for its 'failure' to respond speedily to a critical 'new situation').

We might well ask at this point how does talk of the chaos principle at work in Japanese statecraft contribute to our understanding and explanation of sectionalism and of administrative transcendence? The answer is that the chaos principle is the cause and reinforcement of bureaucratic activism. Elite bureaucrats schooled in Japanese statecraft come to have an activist conception of their role as they scan the (policy) horizon, work to name the object in the viewfinder, to capture the phrase, to sanction the reality, to discover the policy, to design the laws, to shape the institutions, to fashion the ideologies that form model citizens, and to implement the disciplines that regulate behavior that preserve order and so postpone the collapse into chaos.[92]

Conclusion

There has been a tendency in the social sciences to read all states from a simple, undifferentiated account of the modern Western state – a practice that does scant justice even to difference amongst the states of the West and which borders on obscurantist when extended to non-Western worlds. There has been a no less marked tendency to conflate the state and the bureaucracy and to use these terms synonymously and interchangeably. Problems are compounded and misunderstandings are multiplied when the resultant amalgam is read off from a readers' digest of Weber. A vast gulf in understanding arises then between the all but common-sensical accounts of politics and administration, and of state and bureaucracy in countries of the periphery and the bowdlerized accounts of these that return to the center.

The topics touched upon in this chapter are a case in point. The postwar study of Japan has thrown up only one concept that has fed back into the mainstream social science literature – that is the development state. The coiner of the phrase was acutely aware of the particularities of the bureaucracy in Japan and of their importance in the fashioning and practices of the 'development state'. As the phrase passed into more general usage awareness of these quintessential particularities has been lost. The Japanese bureaucracy has come to be presented as a prime exemplar of a Weberian bureaucracy. There are two problems with this. We are in danger of losing sight of the fact that the characteristics of rationality and instrumentality, of perfect hierarchies, of elegant structures of super and subordination, of objective and scientific management, of institutions and officials without interests and indifferent to power politics are the stuff of norms and ideal types rather than of brute day-to-day realities and actual administrations. To characterize any bureaucracy in this way is more than somewhat fanciful. A second set of normative yardsticks is also in play. These are liberal democratic and include the idea of the bureaucracy as public service or even more benignly, as 'civil' service. This too is as much if not more a matter of hope than fact in respect of any public administration any where on earth. And yet the stylized fact that returns to the center allows us to believe that Japan has somehow squared the circle and has come to satisfy both sets of norms.

We are not champions of 'Japanese exceptionalism' but rather, confident that it is possible simultaneously to do justice to the particularity of Japan while engaging in a systematic comparative theoretical exercise. To this end, we have argued the need analytically to distinguish between the state and the bureaucracy – neither of which is to be read from projections from Western models, both of which are to be investigated historically and empirically. Further, we have said that it is a mistake to assume how state making has fashioned the bureaucracy and to make assumptions about the state context in which contemporaneously the bureaucracy operates. So much for particularity. Given our concern to return Japan to the theoretical mainstream (we too desire an 'Other Mirror' to reflect light from the East Asian periphery alongside that proposed by Centeno and Lopes Alvez),[93] it is essential that we identify comparative yardsticks that permit us to measure the particularity of Japan but to link it directly to the experience of other state-bureaucracy ensembles. Here we borrowed from Sammy Finer's notion of the relationship between the 'paramount organ' of the state and its specialized service personnel and from Dyson the 'idea of the state' – these being terms of both heuristic and comparative value. We argued that 'administrative transcendence' and sectionalism are enduring aspects of Japan's bureaucracy of great practical and contemporary significance and that these are rooted in the state-making process and are directly a product of the nature of imperial sovereignty (its effective absence) and the consequent terms upon which the relationship between the sovereign and his agents was institutionalized. These arrangements were buttressed and reinforced by the imperial ideal in the 'idea of the state', that is to say, by the imperial monopoly of morality in consequence of which the moral authority of his agents (our bureaucracy) depended upon their nearness to him and the associated eagerness of others to immerse themselves in the sectional link in the chain that led to the emperor. These understandings, together with the behaviors, values, procedures, and institutions they gave rise to were embedded and substantially unchallenged for the best part of five decades.

We asked how far defeat in war and the imposition of reforms cut across these arrangements and we came up with a qualified response. Change there certainly was. The constitutional elevation of the paramount organ together with the constitutional subordination of the bureaucracy was unequivocal. But the impulse from outside to change cooled with the outbreak of the Cold War while domestically a legitimizing principle predicated upon popular sovereignty did not fully and effectively replace the imperial ideal. Change was further offset by the return to position in the Diet and in the administrative structures that emerged from the debris of the Home Ministry and in a reconstituted Ministry of International Trade and Industry of officials well versed in the statecraft of the prewar period and steeped in its codes, procedures, and habits of mind. The imperial ideal was attenuated (if not eclipsed) but the operational code, the chaos principle, embodied in the idea of the state not only persisted but was reinvigorated. Japan experienced calamity on a scale unknown in the previous history of the state; Hiroshima and Nagasaki were an unimaginable embodiment of chaos, the threat of disorder and disruption.

And so to our conclusions. Sectionalism has not only proved ineradicable it has been reconstituted on a massive scale – the postadministrative reform agencies of the twenty-first century are huge lumbering beasts, semiautonomous states within a weak state struggling with issues of centralization. Administrative transcendence is a different story. For all the uncertainties and limits we have charted, undoubtedly the new paramount organ, the Diet is an immanent sovereign in ways that the prewar sovereign could not be. It is this and the possibilities and political space that it has created that triggered debates in the 1980s about bureaucrats versus politicians and the locus of power. Bureaucratic activism (which we have said to be one element in administrative transcendence) underpinned by a reinvigorated sense of the threat of chaos and of the responsibility of officialdom to counter it, was renewed and this greatly facilitated the economic reconstruction and export-oriented industrial policy exercise over a couple of decades to 1975 or so.

However this was secured at a high price. The activism of the bureaucracy was no longer sanctioned by imperial authority. The very weaknesses of the new paramount organ meant that the Diet could not substitute for imperial authority and insure the bureaucracy against failure. From the end of the Pacific War the only guarantee was policy success. High growth and the Japanese miracle secured the legitimacy of the bureaucracy and reinforced the activism principle. The Hanshin Earthquake, a decade of economic recession, and the scandals of the 1990s have left the bureaucracy exposed and vulnerable.

Notes

1 We refer the reader to the introduction to this volume.
2 P. Veyne, 'Le Pain et le Cirque' (Bread and the circus), cited by J. D. Faubion (ed.), *Michael Foucault, Power, Essential Works of Foucault 1954-84*, vol. 3, London: Penguin Books, 1994, p. xxiv.
3 Contrast, for example, the accounts of the strength of the Japanese state in Linda Weiss, *The Myth of the Powerless State*, Ithaca and London: Cornell University Press, 1998; and J. O. Haley, 'The paradox of weak power and strong authority in the Japanese state', in R. Boyd and T. W. Ngo (eds), *Asian States: Beyond the Developmental Perspective*, London: RoutledgeCurzon, 2005, pp. 67–82.
4 This is all but the converse of the case regarding the writings of Arnason, Bellah,

and Eisenstadt which draw upon literatures that include a rich body of scholarship by historians of twentieth-century Japanese administrative institutions. Both Bellah and Eisenstadt argue that Japan is a fully distinct civilization that incorporates techniques of government borrowed from Europe (hence the appearance of similarity) but not the underlying assumptions that constitute society as a separate moral and authoritative site (hence the fundamental difference). However, their writings appeared long after the heyday of the developmental state debates in the 1980s the critical moment at which images and understandings of the Japanese state and bureaucracy were popularized and so did not inform these. As is often the case in the social sciences, what is painfully obvious in one subfield (so, for example, the particularity of the Japanese state to and administration to historians of twentieth-century Japan) is all but unknown in another. It is to be hoped that as the works cited here feed into the theoretical mainstream the particularity of Japanese state making and of the institutions it produced will become more apparent and the trend to over generalize conceptions of state and bureaucracy modeled on exclusively Western experiences will be offset. See J. P. Arnason, *Social Theory and Japanese Experience: The Dual Civilization*, London and New York: Kegan Paul International, 1997; R. N. Bellah, *Imagining Japan, The Japanese Tradition and Its Modern Interpretation*, Berkeley and Los Angeles: University of California Press, 2003; S. N. Eisenstadt, *Japanese Civilization, A Comparative View*, Chicago and London: University of Chicago Press, 1996.

5 R. Grew, 'Comparing modern Japan: are there more comparisons to be made?', *New Global History*, July 2002, pp. 1–41, <http://web.mit.edu/newglobalhistory/articles.html> (accessed 30 May 2004).

6 B. S. Silberman, 'The structure of bureaucratic rationality and economic development in Japan', in H. K. Kim, M. Muramatsu, T. J. Pempel, and K. Yamamura (eds), *The Japanese Civil Service and Economic Development: Catalysts of Change*, Oxford: Clarendon Press, 1995, pp. 135–73; B. S. Silberman, 'Bureaucratic development and the structure of decision-making in the Meiji period: the case of the genrō', *Journal of Asian Studies*, 1968, vol. 27, 81–94; B. S. Silberman, 'Bureaucratization of the Meiji state: the problem of succession in the Meiji Restoration, 1868–1900', *Journal of Asian Studies*, 1976, vol. 35, 421–30; B. S. Silberman, 'The bureaucratic state in Japan: the problem of authority and legitimacy', in T. Najita and J. V. Koschman (eds), *Dimensions of Conflict in Modern Japan*, Princeton: Princeton University Press, 1982, pp. 226–57. Silberman's major statement of the local unfolding of universal processes of rationalization is, *Cages of Reason: The Rise of the Rational State in France, Japan, the United States, and Great Britain*, Chicago: University of Chicago Press, 1993.

7 H. H. Gerth and C. Wright Mills (eds), *From Max Weber, Essays in Sociology*, London: Routledge and Kegan Paul, Oxford: Oxford University Press, 1970, pp. 77–9.

8 S. E. Finer, *The History of Government from the Earliest Times 1: Ancient Monarchies and Empires*, Oxford: Oxford University Press, 1997, pp. 2–3.

9 L. Whitehead in this volume.

10 K. Dyson, *The State Tradition in Western Europe*, New York: Oxford University Press, 1980.

11 Gerth and Wright Mills (eds), *From Max Weber*, p. 197.

12 See, for example, T. W. Ngo, 'The political bases of episodic agency in the Taiwan state', in R. Boyd and T. W. Ngo (eds), *Asian States: Beyond the Developmental Perspective*, London: RoutledgeCurzon, 2005, pp. 83–109; Y. P. Wu, *A Political Explanation of Economic Growth: State Survival, Bureaucratic Politics, and Private Enterprises in the Making of Taiwan's Economy 1950-85*, Harvard East Asian Monographs, Cambridge, Mass.: Harvard University Press, 2005.

13 T. Ikuta, *Kanryō, Japan's Hidden Government*, translated by H. Yanai, New York, Tokyo, Osaka, and London: ICG Muse Inc., 1995, pp. 40–1.

14 Ibid., pp. 98–104.

15 Ibid., pp. 23–33.

16 J. I. Kyōgoku, *The Political Dynamics of Japan*, translated by N. Ike, Tokyo: University of Tokyo Press, 1987, pp. 217–18.

17 Ibid., p. 218.

18 M. Maruyama, 'The structure of Matsurigoto: The basso ostinato of Japanese political life', in S. Henny and J. P. Lehmann (eds), *Themes and Theories in Modern Japanese History*, London: Athlone, 1988, pp. 27–43.

19 K. van Wolferen, *The Enigma of Japanese Power*, London and Basingstoke: Macmillan, 1989, p. 40.

20 Ibid., p. 38.

21 B. A. Shillony, *Politics and Culture in Wartime Japan*, Oxford: Clarendon Press, 1981, p. 29.

22 C. Johnson, 'Japan: who governs? An essay on official bureaucracy', *Journal of Japanese Studies*, 1975–76, vol. 2, 1–28.

23 R. Boyd and S. Nagamori, 'Industrial policy making in practice: electoral, diplomatic and other adjustments to crisis in the Japanese shipbuilding industry', in S. Wilks and M. Wright (eds), *The Promotion and Regulation of Industry in Japan and Her Competitors*, London: Macmillan, 1992, pp. 167–206.

24 C. Johnson, *Japan: Who Governs? The Rise of the Developmental State*, New York and London: W. W. Norton & Co., 1995, p. 207.

25 R. Boyd, 'Rents and economic outcomes in Japan and Taiwan', in L. Tomba (ed.), *On the Roots of Growth and Crisis: Capitalism, State and Society in East Asia*, Annale Feltrinelli No. 36, Milan: Giangiacomo Feltrinelli Editore, 2002, pp. 151–91.

26 Ikuta, *Japan's Hidden Government*, p. 31.

27 S. Sahashi, 'Kanryō shokun ni chokugen suru' (Straight talk to the gentlemen of the bureaucracy), *Bungei shunjuu*, July 1971, p. 108, cited by Johnson, *Japan: Who Governs? The Rise of the Developmental State*, p. 339.

28 Van Wolferen would go further, so entrenched is sectionalism in his view that it is misleading to speak of a 'state' at all, see *The Enigma of Japanese Power*, p. 43.

29 Kyōgoku, *The Political Dynamics of Japan*, p. 218.

30 L. E. Carlile, 'Administrative Reform in Japan: Twilight of the Developmental State?' Paper presented at the Annual Meeting of the Association for Asian Studies, San Diego, California, 9–12 March 2000. Before the report even emerged its proposals had been significantly diluted by the bureaucracy. See K. Mizuno, 'Gyokaku Kaigi: Kanryō to no Kobo' (The Administrative Reform Council: fights with bureaucrats), *Bungei shunjuu*, October 1997, pp. 105–7.

31 See, for example, an interesting piece by R. L. Jepperson, 'Institutional Logics: On the Constitutive Dimensions of the Modern Nation-State Polities', Working Paper 2000/36, Florence: Robert Schuman Centre for Advanced Studies, European University Institute, 2000.

32 Y. Nakasone, *The Making of the New Japan: Reclaiming the Political Mainstream*, translated and annotated by L. Connors, Richmond: Curzon, 1999, p. 140.

33 R. Bendix *et al.* (eds), *State and Society: A Reader*, Berkeley and Los Angeles: University of California Press, 1968, p. 296.

34 For a different view, see P. F. Drucker, 'In defense of Japanese Bureaucracy', *Foreign Affairs*, September/October 1998, vol. 77, no. 5, 68–80. Drucker is a recent addition to a long line of commentators interested to assess the utility or otherwise of aspects of Japanese bureaucratic behavior.

35 H. Belz, *A Living Constitution or Fundamental Law? Constitutionalism in Historical Perspective*, Lanham, Boulder, New York, and Oxford: Rowman and Littlefield, 1998.

36 S. Garon, *Molding Japanese Minds: The State in Everyday Life*, Princeton: Princeton University Press, 1997, p. 18.

37 C. Johnson, *MITI and the Japanese Miracle: The Growth of Industrial Policy, 1925- 1975*, Stanford: Stanford University Press, 1982, pp. 35–82.

38 B. McVeigh, *The Nature of the Japanese State: Rationality and Rituality*, Japanese Studies Series, London and New York: Nissan Institute/Routledge, 1998, p. 81.

39 J. O. Haley, 'Japan's postwar civil service: the legal framework', in Kim *et al.* (eds), *The Japanese Civil Service*, p. 82.

40 From our perspective not only is the debate problematic in respect of its 'zero-sum' power predicate but also in that it cannot in this form address the critical question of how the senior bureaucrat in Japan understands his role. It is quite conceivable that politicians are powerful and simultaneously that bureaucrats are 'activist' – see below.

41 Ikuta, *Kanryō*, p. 12. The *amakudari* phenomenon is much studied. See M. Muramatsu, *Sengo Nihon no Kanryōsei* (The bureaucratic system in postwar Japan), Tokyo: Tōyō Keizai, 1981.

42 T. Inoki, 'Japanese bureaucrats at retirement: the mobility of human resources from central government to public corporations', in Kim *et al.* (eds), *The Japanese Civil Service*, p. 217.

43 T. Okada, 'The unchanging bureaucracy', *Japan Quarterly*, 1965, vol. 12, 175.

44 John Dower, *Empire and Aftermath, Yoshida Shigeru and the Japanese Experience, 1878- 1954*, Cambridge, MA, and London: Harvard University Press, 1988, p. 308.

45 Carlile, 'Administrative Reform in Japan'.

46 Ibid., p. 5.

47 Ibid., pp. 5–6.

48 Ibid., pp. 5–6.

49 Compare B. S. Silberman, 'The bureaucratic role in Japan, 1900–1945: the bureaucrat as politician', in B. S. Silberman and H. D. Harootunian (eds), *Japan in Crisis: Essays in Taisho Democracy*, Princeton: Princeton University Press, 1974, pp. 183–216.

50 Johnson, *MITI and the Japanese Miracle*.

51 Ibid., p. 89.

52 Ibid., p. 67.

53 Ibid., p. 129.

54 For a succinct statement of the 'political economy of war and security', see M. Woo-Cumings, 'Introduction: Chalmers Johnson and the politics of nationalism and development', in M. Woo-Cumings (ed.), *The Developmental State*, Ithaca and London: Cornell University Press, 1999, p. 23.

55 Johnson, *MITI and the Japanese Miracle*, p. 149.

56 Ibid., p. 243.

57 There are two sets of issues here: one is that of institutional borrowing, 'learning from Japan' and so on. This is already difficult terrain, the possibilities, the limits, and so. The borrower needs as clear and sharp a sense as possible of what it is he is seeking to emulate and so how the object of the modeling and borrowing is packaged and presented is critical. See R. Rose, 'What is Lesson-Drawing?', *Journal of Public Policy*, 1991, vol. 11, no. 1, 3–30. This touches in turn upon how what is researched and learnt by students of the periphery (where institutions bearing apparently familiar labels can have different functions and meanings that derive from radically unfamiliar contexts) is fed back to the centre for communication to other points on the periphery by international organizations such as the World Bank. Plainly something of the detail and the particularity must be lost if we are to retain a communicable core so we cannot be too purist. If that core does not contain the essentials then there are problems. The brute essentials of Japan's elite administrative corps – and these are precisely what makes it interesting are

better captured in terms of activism, intervention, leadership, and guidance than they are in the notion of 'civil service'.

58 Garon, *Molding Japanese Minds*, p. 15.
59 K. Inoue, *Tennōsei* (Emperor system), Tokyo: Tokyo Daigaku Shuppankai, 1958.
60 Garon, *Molding Japanese Minds*, p. 58.
61 Ibid., p. 151.
62 J. C. Campbell, *How Policies Change: The Japanese Government and the Aging Society*, Princeton: Princeton University Press, 1992.
63 Garon, *Molding Japanese Minds*, p. 229.
64 There is an enormous literature on the prewar and postwar Japanese bureaucracy. An excellent starting place is the collection of articles (and the extensive references they contain) in Kim *et al.* (eds), *The Japanese Civil Service*; B. C. Koh, *Japan's Administrative Elite*, Berkeley: University of California Press, 1989, is an earlier but valuable study.
65 See J. O. Haley, *Authority without Power: Law and the Japanese Paradox*, New York: Oxford University Press, 1991; E. Isomura and M. Kuronuma, *Gendai Nihon no gyōsei* (Contemporary Japanese administration), Tokyo: Teikoku Chihō Gyōsei Gakkai, 1974.
66 Johnson, *MITI and the Japanese Miracle*, p. 75.
67 M. Wright, *Japan's Fiscal Crisis, the Ministry of Finance and the Politics of Public Spending, 1975- 2000*, Oxford: Oxford University Press, 2002, p. 366.
68 The Council of Economic and Fiscal Policy met for the first time in January 2001.
69 Ikuta, *Kanryō*, p. 152.
70 To enhance the ability to defend the section the bureaucrats draw close to those interests within their jurisdiction so as to present a united front to other sections. The rewards for adopting a united front are various but can include control over market entry. To open a liquor store a license must be purchased. The Ministry of Finance stopped issuing liquor store licenses decades ago. Would-be entrants can only gain entry by buying the license of someone willing to exit the market.
71 Wright, *Japan's Fiscal Crisis*, p. 96.
72 Ikuta, *Kanryō*, p. 152. On the role of the Prime Minister in regard to policy making, see K. Hayao, *The Japanese Prime Minister and Public Policy*, Pittsburgh and London: University of Pittsburgh Press, 1993.
73 A. Miyachi, *Bringing Accountability to Japan's Bureaucracy*, National Institute for Research Advancement, Spring 1999, <http://www.nira.jp/pub/review/99spring/miyachi.html> (accessed 30 June 2004).
74 G. Curtis, 'Japanese Political Parties: Ideas and Reality', Research Institute of Economy, Trade and Industry (RIETI), Discussion Paper Series 04-E-005. Curtis notes in the abstract of his paper that 'Political reformers would be better advised to focus on how to strengthen the Prime Minister vis-à-vis his own cabinet and own party than and on how to restructure the relationship between bureaucrats and politicians.'
75 K. Tsuji, *Gendai Nihon no Seiji Katei* (Political processes in contemporary Japan), Tokyo: Iwanami Shoten, 1958.
76 Bendix *et al.* (eds), *State and Society*, p. 302.
77 Ibid., pp. 303–4.
78 T. Najita, *Japan, The Intellectual Foundations of Modern Japanese Politics*, Chicago and London: University of Chicago Press, 1974, p. 84.
79 Ibid., p. 83.
80 B. B. Schaffer, 'Deadlock in development administration', in C. Leys (ed.), *Politics and Change in Developing Countries*, Cambridge: Cambridge University Press, 1969, pp. 177–212.
81 E. Barker, *The Development of Public Services in Western Europe 1660- 1930*, London: Oxford University Press, 1944, pp. 1–2.

82 As Peter Duus has shown 'the imperial symbol lost its legitimizing function, and the emperor was placed at an even further remove from politics than he had been in the prewar period. On the other hand, no new legitimizing symbol replaced the imperial institution. Consequently, Japan may be the only contemporary democratic polity lacking a widely accepted myth of legitimacy. The notion of *kokutai* has disappeared but the notion of "popular sovereignty" has not quite superseded it.' (P. Duus, 'Bounded Democracy: Tradition and Politics in Modern Japan', unpublished article cited by Eisenstadt, *Japanese Civilization*, p. 96.)

83 Dower, *Empire and Aftermath.*

84 M. Maruyama, *Thought and Behavior in Modern Japanese Politics*, Oxford: Oxford University Press, 1963.

85 S. Araki, 'The spirit of soldiers in the emperor's land', cited by Maruyama, 'The structure of Matsurigoto', p. 8.

86 Ibid., p. 15.

87 T. Inoguchi, 'The pragmatic evolution of Japanese democratic politics', in M. Schmiegelow (ed.), *Democracy in Asia*, New York: St Martins Press, 1997, pp. 217–32.

88 H. Ooms, *Tokugawa Ideology: Early Constructs, 1570-1680*, Princeton: Princeton University Press, 1985, p. 297.

89 Kyōgoku, *The Political Dynamics of Japan*, pp. 202–13. Interestingly enough, Garon opens his study of the Japanese state and social management with the sentence, 'The specter of impending crisis is never far from the minds of those who govern Japan', see Garon, *Molding Japanese Minds*, p. ix.

90 Kyōgoku, *The Political Dynamics of Japan*, p. 210.

91 Ibid., p. 212.

92 This is a synoptic account of Ooms, *Tokugawa Ideology*, p. 297; and Kyōgoku, *The Political Dynamics of Japan*, pp. 205–8.

93 M. A. Centeno and F. Lopez-Alves (eds), *The Other Mirror, Grand Theory through the Lens of Latin America*, Princeton: Princeton University Press, 2001.

4 Citizen, state, and nation in China

R. Bin Wong

The development of states since the nineteenth century has involved governments engaging their subjects as citizens defined in one of two basic ways or some mix of the two. From the French Revolution came the emergence of European 'citizens' as individuals negotiating rights and responsibilities with their governments. In contrast to citizens whose rights and responsibilities were based explicitly on their interests and those of their governments, citizens under another kind of state responded to government appeals of a shared national identity usually anchored in a set of beliefs about a common history and destiny. While governments in some places could seek to reach their citizens with beliefs in a shared past and destiny as a nation, groups in other situations challenged their rulers by labeling themselves nations demanding a state separate and independent from that ruling them.

For Asian states subject to the pressures of Western colonialism and imperialism, a common sense of nation could also be forged in resistance to external threats. Whether this appeal to nation was led by the state or groups in society varied depending on how closely tied the state was to external powers. Politically independent Asian states in the early twentieth century appealed to their citizens through some set of beliefs far more often than they negotiated with them over interests. By the end of the twentieth century, all Asian states were independent of Western colonial rule and most recognized, at least on paper, citizen rights and responsibilities. In one way or another all states in Asia that succeeded in consolidating their power and control over a set of subjects during the course of the twentieth century grappled to define the nation that they ruled and to engage their citizens through appeals to popular interests and beliefs.

Looking at Asian states in terms of the relationships among citizen, state, and nation allows us to apply a set of categories used to examine states more generally without assuming that political transformations necessarily all follow some set of simple patterns. Usually studies applying the concepts of 'citizen', 'state', and 'nation' to non-Western parts of the world focus on quite recent times. As a consequence they rarely account for the historical factors that can shape the ways in which these terms take on meaning in the twentieth century outside Europe and the Americas. This chapter addresses twentieth-century Chinese meanings of citizen, state, and nation in historical perspective. A distinctive arc of political transformation in China explains the persistence of a state that rules much of the territory of an earlier agrarian empire, the only such case in world history, and suggests possible scenarios for the future character of relations between the Chinese state and its citizens that turn on the ways in which the Chinese nation is conceived and affirmed.

The first problem to consider is how the twentieth-century Chinese state ends up after 1949, and nearly a half-century of fragmented political units, to claim sovereignty over roughly the same territories claimed by the Qing empire. The next section suggests that twentieth-century possibilities for a Chinese nation depended on competing definitions of nation, each of which could span much of the territory of the former empire. As the issues of defining 'nation' have been worked through in post-1949 China, the third section of this chapter examines how the government-inspired alternative to interest-based citizenship that was spreading in other parts of Asia after World War II drew upon earlier ways of linking subject and ruler under the Qing dynasty. The fourth and final section of the chapter considers the political pressures on the Chinese state to reconfigure its relations with its citizens and how possible future changes in citizen–state relations will define the character of the Chinese nation in the coming decades.

Ancient and modern nations

The flood of writing on 'nations' in the past quarter century has a number of major streams, some of which crosscut each other while others flow quite independently of each other. One approach stresses the antiquity of 'nations' and 'peoples' with histories of a common fate often beginning many centuries ago.[1] An alternative approach stresses the modern nature of 'nations', arguing for the emergence of conditions such as printing and newspapers, industry, or governments seeking to mobilize their subjects against governments of other countries before the term 'nation' can take on meaning.[2] In those cases where modern 'nations' are formed in part by leaders asserting the antiquity of a common destiny of the people they rule there may be little difference in practice among these two views of 'nation', at least for the modern period. Only if the veracity of the assertions of common past are by some standards dubious and yet still credible to others would there be a serious discrepancy. The 'nation' can be invented in the nineteenth century but if it often uses certain materials of an older pedigree to be persuasive, then the gap between the two approaches to studying the 'nation' need not be large.

In the Chinese case there were clearly cultural resources fashioned in late imperial times that contributed to modern national identity. Across most of the urban and rural areas of the Qing empire, one can find multiple markers of distinctive social identities associated with cultural variations, including dialect differences, culinary preferences, and religious practices. Indeed, linguistics teaches us that the language differences between Mandarin and Cantonese are as pronounced as those between English and Dutch. The various regional cuisines of the northern and southern extremes of the empire differ greatly in their starch staple, sources of protein, and spices. Some deities popular in one part of the empire are unknown in another part, while other deities common to more than one region need not perform the same functions in all cases. Specialists have long recognized some of this diversity. Other features have been discovered more recently. Even in the recent past it was important to bring these differences to broader audiences because many people previously assumed that Chinese were all the same culturally, an assumption borne of ignorance and nurtured by further assumptions about national stereotypes.

But now we realize that most societies are themselves diverse; moreover, with greater numbers of Chinese migrating overseas, recognition of differences among them is becoming more common. Within these changed conditions of our world, it becomes more important to ask how multiple social identities of the Qing empire became joined to form a common cultural identity. At first glance we should not expect this to happen since we have considerable evidence of this not happening in other agrarian empires. In contrast to other empires like the Ottoman or Austro-Hungarian states which allowed groups under their rule to maintain varying degrees of local autonomy and the expression of distinct social identities, the Qing empire imposed a set of Confucian cultural expectations on the vast majority of its subjects whether they were Han Chinese or non-Han minority peoples such as Miao, Yao, Dai, or Yi.[3] While the Confucian ideas of family forms, kinship rituals, and respect for authority and hard work were hardly new in the eighteenth century, the Qing state aggressively implemented an agenda of social control and administrative integration that included the promotion of Confucian cultural practices. Wherever sedentary non-Han peoples lived, the eighteenth-century government recognized that they could be brought more firmly under imperial rule when Chinese language and customs were adopted. This Confucian-inspired project of creating a set of cultural practices deemed the foundation of proper personal behavior and social order spanned a society within which popular beliefs ranged far beyond the dimensions of a Confucian template. Yet, whatever its limitations, the state's drive to control Chinese cultural practices contributed to the definition of a Chinese identity. A late imperial fusion of culture and politics was part of the basic construction of state-society relations. The state played an explicit role in promoting this identity, especially in periods of official activism (both local and central) and in frontier areas where Han Chinese sometimes came into contact with people whose customs differed dramatically from their own.

Confucianism's capacity to culturally create social identity was basic to its status as the hegemonic discourse in late imperial China. Not only did Confucianism create and manipulate the conceptual categories within which human experience was constructed, but also the state played an active role in shaping this process, both for elites and for common people. The process began no later than the tenth century when the Song state began to shape elite thought through the civil service examination system; almost all educated men studied a curriculum heavily influenced by what was necessary to know on the exams. For common people, the Song state began to specify the pantheon of deities deemed worthy to receive the people's offerings and prayers. To these practices the Qing state added in the eighteenth century a system of monthly moral lectures through which a Confucian discourse permeated society. Beyond culture as ideas and practices, the state relied upon elites outside formal government service to help create the institutions of public order considered appropriate for a Confucian society, including schools, granaries, orphanages, and charitable halls. These institutions in turn suffused society with a Confucian culture.

The Chinese case illustrates the relevance to the twentieth-century nation of elements both ancient and modern. An important component of the older beliefs contributing to a Chinese national identity confounds the expectations of analysts following Ernest Gellner who argued that the concept of 'nation' was modern in part because not until the nineteenth century did states take an active and effective role in defining culture within political boundaries.[4] In this view, the formation of nations requires a close correspondence between politics and culture; previously, Gellner argues, elite cultures spanned political borders while popular cultures were far more local in scale. In late imperial China, however, the state took an active role in promoting what it deemed orthodox beliefs at both elite and popular levels. Official success at promoting certain cultural practices, including marriage and funeral rituals, as well as the worship of state-sanctioned deities, created shared customs that gave people some basis for a social identity that became 'national' in the new international context in the decades on either side of 1900 when the survival of China as a country was very uncertain and people feared that foreign powers might carve the country like a melon.

At the same time as the foreign challenges of the late nineteenth and early twentieth centuries encouraged people to draw upon a culturally based social identity promoted by the state to fashion a sense of a national identity, the perceived gap between Western countries and China in terms of wealth and power led many leaders to identify past cultural practices as fundamental problems obstructing the development of a modern China. Confucian ideas about family relationships and social conventions more generally were considered outmoded. Those who modeled their social and political practices on older Confucian norms, consciously affirming their relevance to the early twentieth century were seen by those who rejected such moves as conservative and backward-looking. Radical and iconoclastic intellectuals of the 1920s rejected their cultural past which made the project of crafting a national identity very difficult to build out of native resources. Instead, focusing on common external enemies gave definition to the Chinese nation. The tension between affirming a cultural identity rooted in past practices and confronting old traditions that were believed to be blocking modern developments made a shift to a focus on the nation's external enemies a convenient focus for identity definition.

This Chinese situation contrasts with conditions in Japan where cultural elites reached into the country's past to select activities and attributes intended to symbolize the national character and distinguish Japanese socially and culturally from the Westerners with whom they were competing politically and economically. Both judo and sumo wrestling, for instance, took on distinctive forms in the early twentieth century. Judo was portrayed internationally as a particularly Japanese sport drawing on centuries of martial arts and used within the country to promote the modern concerns for physical health and effective police training. Sumo wrestling became a spectator sport through new systems of competitions and rankings combined with rituals and dress drawn from earlier practices.[5] These recreational activities were independent of the social and economic demands of urban industrial life that were making the lives of many Japanese increasingly similar to those of people in Western Europe and North America.

The Japanese success at developing industry and cities also gave conceptual space to idealizing the countryside. For certain thinkers, the countryside became the locus of the true or authentic Japanese people, untainted by the new customs emerging in cities.[6] The ability of the village to be conceived as an escape from urban changes depended upon the success of cities as sites of modern activity. When the countryside's growing economic poverty became increasingly troubling in the late 1920s and 1930s, political leaders thought to resolve the difficulties through overseas colonization, especially to Manchuria.[7] Japanese success at becoming politically and economically competitive with Western powers and hence 'modern' in an important, perhaps the most important, way afforded its leaders and peoples opportunities to craft a national identity that affirmed selected traits and habits of the past even, as in the case of certain rural traits, when these were held up as an alternative to urban and industrial lifestyles. The Chinese could hardly celebrate the rural scene as an alternative to cities and industries when the latter had not transformed society to the extent that they had in Japan. Nor could Chinese have the cultural confidence to affirm recreational activities as a marker of national identity when so many other more basic cultural practices seemed closely linked to the country's backward condition.

The early twentieth-century Chinese 'nation' was an almost schizophrenic creature due to its two quite distinct sources of identity, a late imperial social identity strongly shaped by state-guided cultural activities and a separate social identity forged in opposition to twentieth-century foreign political and economic threats. The tensions between the two, in particular the tendency of a nationalism born of opposition to foreigners to be critical of earlier cultural practices made it difficult for the state to develop an easy relationship to the Chinese 'nation'.[8]

Republican-era governments wanted to find persuasive means of appealing to their subjects' shared needs and aspirations as a nation. This could mean appeal to either a culturally defined nation as a historically distinct people or to a politically defined nation besieged by foreign threats. The Nationalist government's New Life Movement of the mid-1930s appealed to Confucian sensibilities regarding manners and respect for hierarchy, but the exhortation to people had limited attraction amidst economic difficulty and political uncertainty. The alternative focus on foreign challenges was far more important to people, but also difficult for the government to address successfully. The ability of governments to call upon the common concerns of their subjects to resist foreigners was never easily achieved because they usually lacked the capacities to thwart foreign demands placed upon them. Instead it was social movements of students, workers, and businessmen that called upon governments to resist foreign pressures and demands. The Japanese became the main threat after the establishment of the Republic in 1912. Its Twenty-One Demands of 1915 that formed the proposed conditions for a large bank loan that the Chinese government needed to stay afloat included a call for Japanese control or influence over Manchuria, Inner Mongolia, Shandong, China's southeast coast, and the Lower Yangzi Valley which housed the country's economic center of Shanghai. The Japanese government proposed that the Chinese government hire Japanese advisors for political, financial, and military affairs and establish a joint Sino-Japanese police administration. When the Chinese government agreed to a reduced set of conditions, public opinion mobilized against it. A boycott of Japanese goods began in major cities. Opposition to the Chinese government's acceptance of an expanded political and economic presence by the Japanese reached a far greater degree of intensity in 1919 when students were joined by workers, businessmen, and other urban residents in demonstrations in several Chinese cities to protest the agreement of the Allies to transfer German leaseholds to the Japanese. This May 4th Movement pressured government representatives to refuse to sign the peace treaty and forced officials in China to agree to some of the popular demands for limiting Japanese political influence in order to avoid further social unrest. The 'nation' figured centrally in the statements made by protestors. Here is how the initial May 4th call to protest concluded:

> We now approach a crisis in which our country is threatened with subjugation and her territory is going to be ceded. If her people still cannot unite in indignation in a twelfth-hour effort to save her, they are indeed the worthless race of the twentieth century. They should not be regarded as human beings. Are there not some of our brethren who cannot bear the torture of being slaves and beasts of burden and steadfastly desire to save their country? Then the urgent things we should do right now are to hold citizens' meetings, to make public speeches, and to send telegrams to the government in support of our stand. As for those who willingly and traitorously sell out our country to the enemy, as a last resort we shall have to rely on pistols and bombs to deal with them. Our

country is in imminent peril – its fate hangs on a thread! We appeal to you to join our struggle.[9]

The definition of the nation as the object of foreign threats persisted amidst parcelized sovereignty, first among competing warlords and then between the Nationalist government and the warlords nominally under its authority. With the Japanese invasion of 1937, political authority was divided among Japanese, Nationalists, and Communists. Though recent scholarship has demonstrated that Communist appeal to peasants during the anti-Japanese War included, in at least some places, a response to their dissatisfactions toward Nationalist officials, it remains crucial that the Communists were able to demonstrate effective opposition and thus to portray themselves as defenders of the nation. The Communist movement that defeated the Nationalists and established a new government in 1949 could make the claim more than any previous twentieth-century Chinese government to represent the nation, a nation conceived as one with a long and glorious history marred by a century of humiliation at the hands of foreigners. The Communists built on a patriotic pride in China standing up and taking its rightful place in the family of nations.

The Chinese nation of the 1950s was a nation with centuries of history and culture, but its identity was no longer consciously conceived in the Confucian terms bequeathed from late imperial times because these were generally labeled feudal and traditional categories inappropriate to socialist China. The Qing conquests had provided the opportunity to define the twentieth-century nation as a multiethnic nation of Han, Manchu, Mongol, Muslim Hui, and Tibetan peoples. This early Republican formulation became the foundation for elaboration by the Communists who have made the Chinese nation multiethnic and multicultural by adding to the main ethnic groups another fifty some peoples, many of whom in Qing times had been the objects of a civilizing project intended to transform at least some of their social practices to conform with those of the Han majority. With a multiethnic and multicultural nation the PRC state appealed in the 1950s to what it expected to be a shared sense of patriotic pride in China's strengthened position *vis-à-vis* foreigners. This continued a sense of nation derived from earlier twentieth-century experiences. To this dimension of national identity, the government added a new definition of the people as Communists. Communist categories of analysis and interpretation framed Chinese experiences in the 1950s and 1960s to the virtual exclusion of other ways of seeing the world. Just as an earlier Confucian cultural hegemony contributed to a broadly shared social identity that could serve to define 'nation', so too was a Communist identity a component of a more recent Chinese national identity after 1949. The most intense moments of identity formation within a Communist framework came during the Cultural Revolution when Mao Zedong Thought was considered the basic guide to living life as Chinese revolutionaries.

With the disavowal of the Cultural Revolution and the attendant collapse of the cultural hegemony of Chinese Communist ideology, Party government leaders have faced a crisis regarding their claims to lead and represent the Chinese nation that are most often made in narrow terms of patriotic pride. The country's bureaucrats based in the northern capital of Beijing have faced an ideological challenge to their self-representation as the heart and soul of the Chinese nation. In the 1980s and 1990s, a southern alternative to the government's brand of nationalism celebrated China's maritime commercial connections to foreign countries over the internal integration under an agrarian political authority. This southern view of Chinese social identity did not make the intellectual and political move typical of a region within a far larger country, namely, to claim a regional distinctiveness supporting a claim to recognition as a separate 'nation'. Rather, the claim of a southern-centered Chinese nation as a maritime and entrepreneurial people was intended to cover the entire country as an alternative to and replacement for the state's 'nation'.[10] What this conceptual move made possible was a resolution between the country's past and its relations to outsiders. While previous notions of nation had either focused on a shared history or alternatively on antagonistic relations with foreigners as alternatives, the southern-centered Chinese nation summoned a different past of peaceful and profitable foreign relations in order to affirm positive connections to the outside world in the late twentieth century.

The competition to claim the 'nation' helps to explain how China can continue to survive as the only state ruling a nation that roughly corresponds to the territory and peoples of a former agrarian empire. Other empires were broken into smaller national states. The Chinese state has managed its survival, despite the collapse of its cultural hegemony and its recognition of a multiethnic and multicultural nation. In many ways the Communist Chinese state was able for some three decades to stress relationships of shared beliefs to form a nation of people whose relationship to the state differed from the norms of interest-based negotiation of rights and duties typical of citizens in more democratic settings.

Citizenship and nation in China

Since the French Revolution, one of the basic ways in which the nation has been constituted is through the relationships that the state forges with its individual subjects through principles of citizenship grounded in a recognition of interests. Citizens also respond to government appeals that are based on shared beliefs, but in democratic settings especially, much of the relationship between state and nation is defined by interest-based principles of citizenship. Citizenship accords to individuals a bundle of rights and responsibilities. The composition of the bundle can change over time according to a give and take between officials and subjects. Some decisions are the products of negotiations and changes in law. Others result from protests that demand certain rights or make particular claims. In these kinds of situations, citizens are individuals able to negotiate with officials to pursue their interests. There is, not surprisingly, a range of possible scenarios. At one extreme is the ideal of autonomous individuals protected by a series of legal safeguards who have numerous freedoms and many entitlements that derive from their member-ship in the nation. At the other extreme are cases in which individuals struggle to assert more limited claims on their governments with few guaran-tees of protection against state exactions, demands, and punishments. What unites all these cases is a definition of citizenship based on some set of legally defined rights and responsibilities comprising the relationship between the state and individuals. These citizens in turn define the nation.

This kind of 'nation' initially marked a changed relationship between several European governments and their subject populations. What did this 'nation' replace? Most eighteenth-century European rulers faced corporately organized elites who had enjoyed in earlier centuries their own autonomous bases of power and authority. Nobles had their aristocratic pedigrees and an earlier political authority over some set of lands now qualified by integration into kingdoms. Clergy were parts of organized church hierarchies, the Catholic structures being most developed and formidable. Urban elites had ruled within their town walls; over time their autonomy was qualified by subordin-ation to royal rule. It was out of the varied ways in which rulers engaged with their elites that principles of representation, concepts of 'liberties,' and prac-tices of negotiation were all developed.[11] Nineteenth-century governments extended their negotiations from those centered on elites to include broader strata of the population, culminating in democratic political logics stressing the free and equal status of citizens.

The United States, of course, belongs on the list of nineteenth-century countries in which the relations between the government and its citizens are based on legally defined rights and responsibilities that create separate spaces of individual autonomy and government intervention. The boundar-ies have shifted over time, but much of American domestic political history can be embraced within a framework focused on changing citizenship claims as a key diagnostic for explaining the relationships between the American nation and the state. Citizenship is legally defined and open to immigrants under specified conditions. Becoming an American is in important measure a transformation that is at the heart of what makes up the American nation.

Little of the ideological and institutional nexus that created European and American citizenship amidst processes of state formation existed in late imperial China.[12] China lacked a tradition of municipal autonomy and a tradition of corporately organized elites. In addition, European conceptions of sovereignty and the shift from locating the right to rule in kings to people were absent from China's domestic scene.[13] European elites forged a 'public sphere', a realm of public opinion and political activity that accompanied the state-making process and attempted to influence its direction toward democratic ends.[14] They constructed new kinds of civil society in which autonomous spaces, before the nineteenth century especially those for elites, became demarcated from the spaces in which state power was expanding.

Sharp divisions between state and society depended upon the institutional resources of elites to create their own organizations and social practices and to safeguard them from government interference. These ideological and institutional conditions which supported European constructions of citizenship did not exist in China in the eighteenth century – indeed, they could not even be imagined at that time. In the late nineteenth century, when Western ideas about citizenship were introduced to China, they could not easily replace older political sensibilities and social practices. Instead, they were introduced as components of larger visions of political reform, the agreed upon purpose of which was to strengthen China to withstand the pressures of international competition that threatened to dismember the empire.

Consider how ideas of Western citizenship fit within broader late nineteenth-century Chinese agendas of political reform and how these were in turn still linked to older strategies of rule within which there was no obvious space for European notions of citizenship. The key institutional innovation supporting the late nineteenth-century Chinese development of citizenship was representative assemblies which sought to create a political role for themselves and advocated constitutional monarchy. Inspired by Western examples, these assemblies created China's first 'citizens,' in the sense of individuals with a claim on a form of political participation, from those propertied and educated men who were eligible to vote for representatives drawn from a yet smaller pool of men. Representative assemblies were flanked by other institutions, like newspapers and study societies, which aimed to forge a set of political reforms, the basic purpose of which was to promote the state's capacity to resist foreign threats. The freedom that officials and elites were both seeking in this period was the freedom of the Chinese nation from foreign domination.

Chinese citizenship in the first half of the twentieth century can be conceived more broadly than so far presented. Henrietta Harrison, for example, has argued that Republican-era governments created Chinese citizens through new rituals of statehood and symbols of national day and the flag; these Chinese citizens participated in major ritual events such as Sun Yat-sen's funeral and subsequent burial, and from them gained a social identity as modern Chinese. Harrison identifies 'citizenry' with membership in government-sponsored associations which were usually occupational in nature.[15] Members of such associations are not defined by their rights and duties to the state. Nor are such associations or others successful at establishing representative government. If one thinks of citizen-based nations in a manner more closely connected to the principles of the French Revolution, then Republican-era China does not seem to be much of a citizen-based nation. The identity-generating processes of citizenship in Harrison's analysis lead to a nation in cultural terms different from those of the late imperial era without clearly fostering greater autonomy and agency for the state's subjects.

Prospects for a nation of interest-negotiating citizens did not improve under the Communists. Citizens existed in the post-1949 constitutions with changing sets of rights which the government was authorized to grant and revoke as it deemed circumstances demanded. But citizens included enemies of 'the people' such as former landlords and capitalists. Thus, being a citizen was not as desirable as being a member of the people.[16] To engage the people, Communist leaders repeatedly relied on mass movements to mobilize great efforts on the basis of shared beliefs in a struggle to create a better future. The logic of mass movements in Mao's day offered an alternative to the political engagement created by voting citizens who form voluntary associations and interest groups in a public sphere or civil society.[17] The logic of mass movements in key ways extended an earlier political logic of campaigns used in more limited ways in late imperial times.[18] European people secured rights and freedoms that came to include material ones in the twentieth century. These material rights followed other quite firmly secured political and individual rights that were basic to defining a citizen-based nation and the individual's relationship to the state. A strongly developed citizen-based nation promotes the recognition of distinct interests of citizens and of their governments. In contrast, an ethnically or culturally defined nation, like that in China, tends to obscure competing interests and to highlight in their stead shared beliefs.

Citizenship and nation: the state, interests, and beliefs

Interest-based citizenship and culturally or ethnically defined nations stress two different logics. The former work on the basis of people negotiating their 'interests' with the state; officials and people negotiate claims they understand to represent their respective interests. The latter exist on foundations of shared beliefs; officials and people share with each other and consciously affirm habits, customs, stories, and myths that bond them to each other and distinguish them from others. The late imperial political project of creating common cultural practices which became a basis for belief in a 'national' identity was supplemented by people pursuing their interests through social institutions like guilds and native-place associations that also came, in the twentieth century, to mobilize urban elites against foreign threats. The 'interests' of association members sometimes mattered politically in a city like Shanghai, but lacked the means to make very effective demands on the city's rulers.[19]

After 1949, the government dismantled many of the social organizations that were intermediaries between individuals and the state, including many guilds and some native-place associations. The intent of these actions was in part to undermine social bases of identification and platforms from which to express interests that were independent of the state. Ironically, as people lost associations through which they expressed various kinds of interests, it became more important to pursue their interests by engaging bureaucracies. Political participation in Communist China has therefore often meant manipulating the political system in order to realize personal interests.[20]

Beginning in the 1980s the formation of voluntary associations for professional, cultural, and social purposes has at times included those expressing opinions that broaden the dimensions of political discourse. These kinds of organizations might come to include vehicles for articulating the interests of citizens, though how and when this would happen is by no means clear. While officials have favored or at least allowed the formation of groups pushing the envelope of acceptable political debate, they have in general been unwilling to include groups that explicitly represent particular interests seeking to negotiate with the government – farmers with their increased tax burdens, for example, stage protests, they threaten to become a social movement, but they do not currently have much organizational structure or means by which they can routinize negotiations with the state.

Voluntary associations largely based in urban areas have yet to involve large numbers of people who act as citizens with the capacity as individuals and in groups to negotiate their interests with the government. In contrast, rural areas have been the site for village members to elect their local leaders according to assessments of who will best serve their interests. This is a kind of democratic activity that contributes to making people into citizens and defines their membership in the nation in terms of their rights. But there are limits to how far a citizen-based 'nation' can develop given the state's persistent reluctance to negotiate other kinds of rights and freedoms on larger spatial scales. Village-level elections conform to political constraints similar to those faced by local self-government efforts earlier in the twentieth century. In both cases top-down bureaucratic systems place limits on local capacities to pursue broader and larger interests. For voluntary associations, a parallel exists with earlier twentieth-century practices as well, since governments of both eras were far more comfortable allowing organizations with nonpolitical purposes to function and occasionally even flourish. Both the urban and rural situations emerge out of late imperial situations in which the ideological and institutional bases for a citizen-based nation were lacking. Despite the development of a discourse using the categories of 'citizens', 'rights', and 'nation', the institutional practices of twentieth-century China did not create a citizen-based nation along the lines of an English or French model.

The logic of an ethnically or culturally defined nation worked in more than one way in twentieth-century China. The late imperial state's cultural construction of Chinese identity continued to promote a 'national' identity over lower-level regional or provincial identities. Within this broader nation, the Confucian civilizing project came to be replaced by a Communist socializing project which embraced ethnic diversity and sought to create a common understanding of what were politically very different kinds of ethnic groups – those within China proper and those who live in territories brought into the agrarian empire by the Qing dynasty. Most groups within China proper had long histories mixing movements of assimilation and separation, cooperation and conflict. Their membership in the Chinese nation under the People's Republic no longer depended upon cultural practices promoted by the state;

instead, certain cultural particularities could be combined with social and political commonalities with the country more generally that made them members of socialist China. For the Inner Asian minority peoples who never had been part of the Confucian project of cultural transformation, the Communists have recognized them politically by making them autonomous regions with systems of rule institutionally separate in some ways from those present in most of the country. But the social differences, a vestige of the Qing empire, are not officially sanctioned to be the bases of separatist national identities; the People's Republic has persistently defended its inheritance via the Republic of the Qing empire's dominions and reaffirmed the Nationalist government's claim of Chinese society being composed of many peoples (or ethnic nations).

For the vast majority of its subjects, the state continues to invoke the 'nation' as the object of defense and salvation against internal and external threats more frequently than it engages the nation in terms of citizens seeking to negotiate claims with the government. Unwilling to develop interest-based claim making for any of its citizens and recognizing the inadequacy of 'nationalist' calls to minorities within and without China proper, the state has offered more material benefits and opportunities. These appeals to material interests do not include much in the way of greater abilities among minority peoples to bargain with the government. When moral suasion and material advantages have proved inadequate, coercion and repression have become the preferred instruments of control.

The Communists have long refrained as much as they can from engaging their subjects as citizens in the sense of individuals with a bundle of rights and responsibilities defined by their relationship to the state. Through the mid-1970s they pursued the alternative of mobilizing people through mass movements for both economic and political purposes. These movements were in part an extension of late imperial movements in the same way that nineteenth-century European mass politics built on ideas and institutions of elite-state relations under the *ancien regime*. The Chinese Communist movements depended upon the ability of leaders to persuade people about the value of their proposed beliefs and practices, though the threat of coercion discouraged those more skeptical of a movement's principles to openly oppose them. Mass movements did not give people the means to negotiate their interests with the government. To the contrary they had to mask any interests that threatened to contradict the political beliefs of the particular moment.

Now that the era of Maoist mass mobilization campaigns has been over for a quarter of a century, we realize that their reduced appeal and efficacy have not led naturally to the adoption of ideas and institutions which make the articulation and negotiation of interests the basis of relations between the government and its subjects. As interests become more explicitly the basis for economic activities and the persuasiveness of Communist ideology wanes as political belief, there is a possibility for economically inspired principles of interest to make their way more explicitly into politics. Whether or not the

Chinese state comes to understand the advantages it can gain by negotiating with its citizens over their interests may well tell us about the kind of state and nation China becomes in the future. Whatever the twenty-first century brings, the main outlines of the Chinese state's twentieth-century transformations are becoming clear. These include understanding that the Communist success in achieving authority over the entire country after decades of division depended in part upon its appeals to subjects as members of a common nation, some cultural components of which had been formulated by earlier dynastic regimes. Like governments before it, the Communist state has preferred to stress what its subjects share in terms of beliefs and interests rather than negotiate with individuals and groups over the distinct interests that citizens in an industrial society often compete. In Western cases, the capacities of citizens to negotiate with their states developed out of ideas and institutions, the antecedents to which were at the foundation of relationships that rulers and elites had previously formed. Only after we better attend to differences in historical experiences can we appreciate more fully the future possibilities that emerge out of past principles and practices.

Notes

1 A. Smith, *The Ethnic Origin of Nations*, Oxford: Blackwell, 1986.
2 E. Gellner, *Nations and Nationalism*, Ithaca, NY: Cornell University Press, 1983; B. Anderson, *Imagined Communities*, 2nd edn, London: Verso, 1991.
3 R. B. Wong, 'Two kinds of nation, what kind of state', in T. Brook and A. Schmid (eds), *Nation Work*, Ann Arbor: University of Michigan Press, 2000, pp. 109–23.
4 E. Gellner, *Nations and Nationalism*; R. B. Wong, *China Transformed: Historical Change and the Limits of European Experience*, Ithaca, NY: Cornell University Press, 1997, pp. 170–1, 174.
5 S. Inoue, 'The invention of the martial arts: kanō jigorō and kōdōkan judo', in S. Vlastos (ed.), *Mirror of Modernity: Invented Traditions in Modern Japan*, Berkeley and Los Angeles: University of California Press, 1998, pp. 163–73; L. A. Thompson, 'The invention of the *yokozuna* and the championship system, or, futahaguro's revenge', in S. Vlastos (ed.), *Mirror of Modernity: Invented Traditions in Modern Japan*, Berkeley and Los Angeles: University of California Press, 1998, pp. 174–87.
6 M. Hashimoto, '*Chihō*: Yanagita Kunio's "Japan"', in Vlastos (ed.), *Mirror of Modernity*, pp. 133–43; S. Vlastos, 'Agrarianism without tradition: the radical critique of prewar Japanese modernity', in Vlastos (ed.), *Mirror of Modernity*, pp. 79–94.
7 L. Young, 'Colonizing manchuria: the making of an imperial myth', in Vlastos (ed.), *Mirror of Modernity*, pp. 95–109.
8 Wong, 'Two kinds of nation'.
9 Young, 'Colonizing Manchuria', pp. 107–8.
10 E. Friedman, 'Reconstructing China's national identity: a southern alternative to Mao-era anti-imperialist nationalism', *Journal of Asian Studies*, 1994, vol. 53, no. 1, 67–91.
11 R. Bates, A. Greif, M. Levi, J. L. Rosenthal, and B. Weingast, *Analytic Narratives*, Princeton, NJ: Princeton University Press, 1998; P. T. Hoffman, and K. Norbert, *Fiscal Crises, Liberty, and Representative Government, 1450- 1789*, Stanford, Calif.: Stanford University Press, 1994; Wong, *China Transformed*, pp. 129–35.

12 Some of the following discussion of Chinese citizenship is based on R. B. Wong, 'Citizenship in Chinese history', in M. P. Hanagan and C. Tilly (eds), *Extending Citizenship, Reconfiguring States*, Lanham, Md.: Rowman and Littlefield, 1999, pp. 97–122.

13 The Chinese emperor's mandate to rule was conditioned by the possibility of peasants rising up in righteous opposition, but this did not become a basis for sovereignty being vested in the people.

14 The term 'public sphere' has been made famous, of course, by J. Habermas. For an evaluation of its relevance for China, see R. B. Wong, 'Great expectations: the "public sphere" and the search for modern times in Chinese history', *Chūgoku shi gaku*, 1993, vol. 3, 7–50, as well as the articles cited therein.

15 H. Harrison, *The Making of the Republican Citizen: Political Ceremonies and Symbols in China 1911- 1929*, New York and Oxford: Oxford University Press, 2000, p. 119.

16 X. Yu, 'Citizenship, ideology and the PRC constitution', in M. Goldman and E. J. Perry (eds), *Changing Meanings of Citizenship in Modern China*, Cambridge, Mass.: Harvard University Press, 2002, pp. 288–307.

17 Wong, 'Citizenship in Chinese history', p. 111.

18 R. B. Wong, 'Formal and informal mechanisms of rule and economic develop-ment: the Qing empire in comparative perspective', *Journal of Early Modern History*, 1991, vol. 5, no. 4, 387–408; 402–6.

19 B. Goodman, 'Democratic calisthenics: the culture of urban associations in the new republic', in Goldman and Perry (eds), *Changing Meanings of Citizenship*, pp. 70–109.

20 T. Shi, *Political Participation in Beijing*, Cambridge, Mass.: Harvard University Press, 1997.

5 Sovereignty, survival, and the transformation of the Taiwan state

Jenn-hwan Wang

This chapter discusses the formation and transformation of the Taiwanese state, with the intention of deciphering the idiosyncratic characteristics of its governance structure and its restructuring at the current stage. The Taiwanese state has since 1949 had many characteristics that are distinctive in world politics. First of all, in terms of the state's status and its name (the Republic of China), before 1970 Taiwan was recognized in the international political arena as the only 'China', even though its sovereign power had never out-reached that of 'China' and its rule only encompassed Taiwan and its adjacent isles. This created a discrepancy between the state's claims regarding its sovereignty and the reality of its actually ruled territory. Secondly, as the Kuomintang regime's state status was derecognized in 1970 when the US and other major international political powers began to recognize the People's Republic of China (the PRC) as the only 'China', which consequently forced Taiwan to withdraw from the United Nations as a sovereign state, the Taiwanese state henceforth became an *orphan state* in the international polit-ical arena, in spite of the Kuomintang regime in Taiwan having in every respect the features and apparatus of a state. This created another discrep-ancy between the state *reality* and the state-less *status* in the international arena. Now Taiwan is often merely regarded as a 'province of the PRC' or an economic entity in the international arena.

Thirdly, as Taiwan has gone through a political democratization process since the late 1980s in which Taiwanization has been an essential ingredient, a new nation-building project that has intended to expel the 'Chinese fea-tures' of the old regime so as to enable Taiwan to establish its own national identity[1] has emerged from the political scenery. This new nation-building project has not only been intended to promote Taiwan as a sovereign state in the international political arena, but has also caused the state to seek to restructure itself so as to be consistent with its political sovereignty. However, this effort has resulted in Taiwan's being unable to gain recognition from major world powers, and has also evoked strong reactions from the PRC that has never given up on its project of national reunification. This has as a consequence generated yet another discrepancy between building the nation as a 'Taiwan state' and the international political reality. Naming the name has become a hotly contested issue in both the local and international political arenas.

The Taiwanese state was born out of a civil war, and the above-mentioned features of the state have shaped the development of Taiwan's political economy in distinctive ways. In particular, the issue of survival when faced with the Chinese military threat has always been the priority concern among state policies. Indeed, as Woo-Cumings correctly argues, '[East Asian] states were born of civil wars that have not ended, and that this fact continues to shape state actions. Specifically, social and economic policies are much affected by the issues of national survival.'[2] This survival issue has changed little and has even been strengthened during the current stage when the democratization process that has taken place since the late 1980s has finally brought about a new nation-building impulse which has heightened the tensions across the Taiwan Strait even further.

This chapter is divided into six sections. Following this introduction, I will discuss in the second section the formation of the Taiwanese state in the 1950s and argue that the Taiwanese state was then largely backed by the US government in the Cold War atmosphere through which a security and authoritarian state was established. In the third and fourth sections, I will examine the process of democratization and the internal power struggle of the state that finally gave impetus to the building of a new nation-state. In the fifth section, I will review the hotly contested issues regarding the formation of a new Taiwanese state both internally and externally. I will argue that the Taiwanese state's legitimacy at the current stage is mainly derived from its internal democratic process. It should be noted, however, that this nation-building impulse has not only met with resistance internally, but has also encountered external opposition from major international players in addition to the military threat from the PRC. The complexity of the politics of nation building has been further exacerbated as Taiwan's economy has at the same time become increasingly integrated with the Chinese market. Finally, in the concluding section I will argue that the survival issue continues to preoccupy the state, but that this time it takes the form of both military and economic threats from the PRC.

The formation of the Taiwanese security state in the 1950s

In 1949, the Kuomintang regime was defeated by the Communists on the Chinese mainland and retreated to Taiwan, which marked the beginning of an era of authoritarian rule on the island. The Korean War that broke out in 1950 saved the Kuomintang regime, for the US perceived that the Communists were a threat to both Asia and the capitalist world. A huge amount of financial and military aid was subsequently channeled into Taiwan while the US encompassed Taiwan as part of its Cold-War military protection region. Under these circumstances, the US helped the Kuomintang regime to consolidate its rule in Taiwan while the emigrated Kuomintang regime focused on the survival issue rather than development as its number one priority. During these years, the state-building process was predominated by this principle.

The US government and the Kuomintang regime's rule in Taiwan

The development of Taiwan's political economy during this period was overwhelmingly influenced and backed up by the hegemonic US power. Initially, the US government thought that Taiwan might fall to the Communists, and therefore a hands-off policy was implemented. The outbreak of the Korean War changed the US's assessment regarding Taiwan's geopolitical position in the global containment strategy against communist expansion.[3] Military and economic aid to Taiwan poured into the island.

There were two types of US aid to Taiwan: direct military assistance and economic aid, which was handled by the Agency of International Development of the US government in Taiwan (AID). The former mainly consisted of the supply of heavy military equipment. The total amount of this assistance over the fifteen-year aid period, 1951–65, was approximately $2.5 billion, or an average of $167 million each year.[4] Indeed, in order to survive militarily in Taiwan and later return to China, the Kuomintang regime constantly maintained a military force of 600,000 men, which was equal to 7.6 per cent of Taiwan's civilian population at the end of 1951, and ranked among the world's largest in terms of the ratio of military to civilian of the country's population.[5] To sustain such a military force, the military spending constantly drained 85 to 90 per cent of the central government's expenditure, or over 50 per cent of the expenditures at all levels of government, or about 9 to 12 per cent of GNP. However, this amount of military spending merely 'consisted of pay and allowance for personnel and their dependents, and for operation and maintenance of equipment'.[6] Heavy military equipment, comprising airplanes, ships, and vehicles, was mainly supplied by the US as a gift to the Kuomintang regime.

The other type of assistance was economic aid, the main objective of which, in the early 1950s, was to stabilize Taiwan's economic and social order. During the fifteen fiscal years of aid, a total of $1,465 million in economic aid was sent to Taiwan. Of that total, military support amounted to $792 million, or 54 per cent of all assistance, and was intended to maintain the Kuomintang regime's military strength. Second, direct military support amounted to $124 million or 8.5 per cent of the total, which was designed to enable Taiwan to maintain the military forces necessary to carry out mutual Chinese–US objectives. These two categories occupied more than 62 per cent of the total economic aid, or approximately $915.78 million, or an average of $61 million annually.

Jacoby estimated that the total annual budget of the military establishment of the Kuomintang regime, including the US military assistance program, ranged from $325 to $375 million in the late 1950s.[7] This meant that the US assistance was responsible for 60.8 per cent to 70.15 per cent of the total military spending each year in Taiwan during the aid period. In other words, the Kuomintang regime's military was largely maintained by the US.[8] Moreover, during this period, the Kuomintang regime also suffered from serious state budget deficits and economic inflation, which in turn were also largely financed by the US in order to reduce the damage.[9] The US aid on average accounted for 34 per cent of Taiwan's gross domestic capital formation and supported 74 per cent of its infrastructural investment during the 1950s.[10] Indeed, as Jacoby argued, 'certainly, US economic assistance helped to preserve the cohesion of the mainlander minority to consolidate its political power. Had no external assistance come to douse the fires of inflation and improve the material conditions of the Taiwanese during the early 1950s, it is doubtful whether the R.O.C. would have endured in its present form.'[11]

In addition, it was the US that supported the Kuomintang regime's status in the international political arena. Therefore, although the Kuomintang regime only ruled Taiwan and its adjacent isles, in terms of its status and its name (the Republic of China), Taiwan was recognized in the international political arena up until 1970 as the only 'China'. The almost unlimited support from the US that was extended to the Kuomintang regime therefore not only enabled the Taiwanese state to gain legitimacy in international politics, but also validated its internal political rule.

The Kuomintang regime's state building and governance structure

For the Kuomintang regime, to survive on the island and to retake China constituted a sacred mission. Under the banner of recovering the mainland, a series of state-restructuring projects were undertaken. The state building of the Kuomintang regime had the following features. First, the Kuomintang regime was led by a party that had quasi-Leninist characteristics. Its party structure and party–state relationship was very similar to its socialist counterpart.[12] Party organizations controlled administrative units at various levels of government as well as the military via a commissar system. Party cells penetrated the existing social organizations, including production organizations. The internal decision-making rules of the party were very centralized and managed by narrow elites.[13] Opposition parties were not allowed, and the regime prohibited alternative ideologies as well as organized opposition. Moreover, the party–state used mass organizational techniques to mobilize popular support for national purposes, particularly in order to 'take back the mainland'.[14]

Second, by claiming a state of emergency, the state enacted martial law which prohibited civil rights from being realized in order to prohibit possible anti-governmental activities and also prevent communist infiltration. This inevitably led to a system in which the surveillance force was so powerful that it suppressed civil freedoms and any potential political activity other than support for the state in the name of national security.

Third, the Kuomintang regime claimed to be the only government of China and therefore the national-level elections were frozen, although elections at the sub-national levels were allowed to be contested in order to present Taiwan as the 'free China'.[15] The regime for many years kept the original congressional incumbency intact, merely adding a minority of elected seats until 1991. Major governmental leaders were elected indirectly by one of the three congresses (the National Assembly, the Legislative Yuan, and the Control Yuan) or appointed by the President. Fourth, a comprehensive land reform program was installed, with support from the US, which consequently eliminated the landlord class and built up social support among the peasantry.[16] This historical contingency gave the emigrated regime a chance to abolish the most powerful social class that might have affected its stern rule on the island.

All these features consequently centralized political power in the hands of the mainlander minority (who migrated from mainland China mostly after 1949) and in the leader of the Kuomintang party that marginalized the majority native Taiwanese and kept them outside the power circle.[17] These developments inevitably created an ethnic cleavage between mainlanders and the native Taiwanese and became the institutional origin of the ethnic tensions on the island.

However, the Kuomintang regime also built social support in Taiwan through two preemptive channels. The first was through clientelist mechanisms.[18] This included, first of all, the regime's building of a patron–client network with major Taiwanese families and loyal native Taiwanese during the initial stage of its stay in Taiwan by awarding them the monopoly of finance, trade, and land development privileges in exchange for political loyalty. Second, as the regime lacked local connections, it needed local political elites to mobilize votes in local elections so as to create mass support. In doing so, the Kuomintang leadership built a clientelist relationship with local political factions by awarding them economic privileges and benefits at the local level. These included a hold on regional oligopolistic economic activities through institutions such as banks, farmers' associations, and so forth; access to special loans offered by provincial banks; special treatment regarding contracts for public construction; and a large degree of freedom in conducting economic activities that might have appeared illegal.[19]

The other channel through which the regime built up its social support was the state corporatist mechanism, through which the regime manipulated the organizations by representing the interests of various social groups.[20] This included setting up national capitalists', workers', and farmers' organizations, subsidizing them with financial support, and rewarding those who were in the highest positions. In addition, only one organization in each category was allowed at each level of government and it had to be set up under the umbrella of the national organization. Like the communist regime, the Kuomintang's party cells penetrated all of these organizations and carefully observed their operations. As regards the trade unions, the Kuomintang regime on the one hand built a labor regime that attempted to mobilize workers for political support by giving them some material benefits such as labor insurance and medical treatment. On the other hand, the state used political and legal strategies to prevent the workers from escaping its control.[21]

The security objective of the state was to make the regime authoritarianist, which resulted in the militarization of the society. Social organizations were under the control of the regime, whereas those who might have had the potential political power to challenge the state were incorporated into the clientelist or corporatist mechanisms.

The shift from militarism to developmentalism

When it retreated to Taiwan, the primary objectives of the Kuomintang regime were to both stabilize the socioeconomic order in order to survive and to retake China. The mainland recovery philosophy was a sacred goal beyond dispute; development as such was not a goal but had to serve the function of militarism.[22] As Jacoby observed, 'the dominant aim of President Chiang Kai-shek and his government was to build a socially and politically, and an economically capable base for the recovery of all of China ... The purpose of developing Taiwan into a viable independent economy did not exist.'[23] If this was the case, how does one explain Taiwan's later policy of pursuing economic development?

Amsden[24] suggests that there were two contradictory trends – militarism and developmentalism – within the Kuomintang regime in the 1950s, with militarism as the dominant one championed by President Chiang Kai-shek, who 'more than any other person ... was responsible for asserting and perpetuating the concept of mainland recovery ... He insisted on tighter authoritarian control and a greater diversion of resources to military and security purposes.'[25] However, the shift in US policy in the late 1950s greatly affected the tendency to slide toward developmentalism.

From 1956 on, US economic aid began to refine and improve programs designed to enable Taiwan to achieve its goal of becoming a self-supporting economy. In 1958, the Development Loan Fund and an Office of Private Enterprises were approved by the US Congress, and were directly targeted at Taiwan's economic infrastructure and industrial projects. In 1958, a 19-point program of economic and financial reform was raised by the AID in order to speed up Taiwan's economic development. The AID made it clear that US aid would be phased out in the mid-1960s. This shift in the AID's objectives from pure military assistance to economic development immediately influenced Taiwan's economic policies. In essence, the 19-point economic reform program was intended to liberalize the state's control over trade and industry, to promote exports and create a sound investment environment in order to stimulate private investment. Although there was resistance from the military, this reform was eventually implemented in 1960.[26]

Under pressure from the US government, Chiang Kai-shek, among other Kuomintang leaders, supported this reform, 'because it would enable Taiwan to get off the dole and become self-reliant'.[27] Amsden suggested that the military's eventual acceptance of the export-led industrialization policy was mainly due to the following factors. First, economic development not only would not affect the military's interest in warfare but on the contrary would support it. Second, focusing on economic development was the only way to get support from the US and this was particularly important for the regime. Third, successful economic development had the potential to become a new propaganda tool for the military in the geopolitical struggle against the Communists.[28] As Amsden contested, 'the reality of economic development itself both seduced the military away from its initial orientation and changed its position within the state apparatus, which then freed up the process of capital accumulation still further'.[29]

The above authoritarian features of the political regime, supported by the US, ultimately led the state to have a high degree of autonomy in making development policy. As the new export-led industrialization policy was implemented in 1960, the state liberalized its economic controls over various important sectors and encouraged foreign investment, which as a consequence greatly changed Taiwan's politico-economic landscape.[30]

To sum up, it was the US that in the 1950s supported the Kuomintang regime and protected it from a military invasion by the PRC, thereby enabling it to survive on the island and gain legitimacy in the international arena. Guided by the principle of survival, the Kuomintang regime built a security state to rule over the society. Moreover, it was also due to the US's influence that the security state changed its priority to economic development. The militarized society plus the export-led industrialization finally linked the Taiwan economy in a significant way with the world market.

Democratization and the rise of civil society

The Kuomintang regime's suppression of civil society consequently created a weak society. However, there were three factors that created opportunities for the civil society to surface. The first was the US's derecognition of Taiwan as the 'China' in 1971 that delegitimized the Kuomintang regime both externally and internally. The second was the periodic local elections under the authoritarian rule that opened a channel that enabled the opposition to survive. The third was the export-led industrialization that nurtured a nascent middle class, which in turn supported the opposition movement that challenged the Kuomintang's rule. All of these factors pushed the Kuomintang regime to implement reforms and dismantle the existing governance structure.

The challenges to the Kuomintang's authoritarian rule

In 1971, the US government changed its geopolitical strategy when President Richard Nixon decided to improve relations with the PRC, a move that ended the American effort to sustain the Kuomintang regime as the sole legitimate government in the United Nations. In February 1972, the Shanghai Communiqué was signed by the US and the PRC, in which the US 'acknowledged' that Chinese on both sides of the Strait 'maintain' that there is only one China, including Taiwan. Over the course of the 1970s, almost every country in the world recognized the PRC as the legitimate 'China', breaking off diplomatic relations with Taiwan in the process. The Kuomintang regime has faced a serious legitimacy crisis ever since.[31]

One of the most influential strategies that the Kuomintang regime adopted to meet the legitimation crisis was a partial political reform – a limited degree of Taiwanization – that opened more channels for Taiwanese to participate at the national level.[32] In the 1950s and 1960s, Taiwanese were only allowed to participate in political elections at the local level. Now, more positions were opened at the national level, including membership of the Legislative Yuan and the National Assembly. Moreover, the Kuomintang, led by Chiang Ching-Kuo (Chiang Kai-shek's son), recruited more Taiwanese into the main decision organs of the party and into the state bureaucracy from the early 1970s onwards in order to strengthen the social support base. Winckler referred to this process of transforming the Kuomintang regime as a shift from hard to soft authoritarianism.[33] The recruitment of more Taiwanese into the power circle itself finally created a political faction within the regime that was more sympathetic to the opposition movement during the regime's transitional period in the late 1980s.

The limited reforms of the Kuomintang regime created more space for the opposition. The periodic local elections that began in the 1950s had already enabled the opposition to survive the suppression of the authoritarian regime, and now the more open attitude of the Kuomintang regime to gain internal legitimacy during this period gave the opposition more opportunities to publicize its ideas during the electoral period and to recruit supporters. The opposition demanded civil freedoms, the formation of opposition parties, the inclusion of more Taiwanese in the power circle, an end to martial law, and so on. This eventually gave rise to an election culture that disseminated alternative ideas in a legitimate way. However, the growing challenges to the regime mounted by the opposition were largely due to the changes in the social structure.

The opposition was mainly supported by the urban middle class that was nurtured by the long-term process of economic development. Taiwan had changed from an agricultural society to an industrial one by the 1970s. In the early 1950s, the primary sector accounted for 50 per cent of all employment. By 1970, however, this share had fallen to 36.7 per cent, and by 1980 to 19.5 per cent. The share accounted for by the industrial sector rose from 16.9 per cent to 28.0 per cent and to 42.4 per cent at these same points in time, whereas the share attributed to the tertiary sector rose from 27 per cent to 35.3 per cent and to 38.1 per cent, respectively. The transformation of the social structure had given rise to an urban middle class that demanded more political participation. Indeed, the opposition movement was led by the urban professional strata, particularly lawyers and professors, and followed by workers and urban masses that challenged the rule of the Kuomintang regime.[34]

The limited opening up of the Kuomintang regime in the 1970s effectively speeded up the process by which the opposition mobilized and challenged the authoritarian governance structure, which consequently created cleavages in the governance structure. The regime was no longer able to control local politicians through its clientelist structure as the opposition became more organized. Although the opposition movement was suppressed by the regime in the late 1970s,[35] it still enjoyed about 30 per cent of the electoral support in every election. In the early 1980s, it had become a semi-organized party that challenged the Kuomintang's rule.[36] The challenge posed by the opposition to the Kuomintang forced the regime to depend more on local political factions to win in every local election. This electoral challenge created leverage to enable those Kuomintang-affiliated local political factions to have more bargaining power in relation to the national elites. The party no longer enjoyed the absolute control over the local elites that it had previously exercised.

In addition, various types of collective movements emerged, along with the opposition political movement, that were beyond the control of the state corporatist structure.[37] Included among them were movements composed of environmentalists, women, veterans, farmers, workers, and students. These movements and their collective actions challenged the existing regime's governance structure and pushed it to meet their demands in relation to their respective rights and interests. According to one study, the incidence of street demonstrations rose sharply during the 1983–1988 period, with the annual number of demonstrations increasing from 107 in 1983 to 204, 272, 337, 734, and 1,172, respectively, in each consecutive year until 1988.[38] The social movements in this period, however, had become very politicized, for two structural reasons. The first one was the state's suppression of autonomous social organizations. Under martial law, no social collectivities were allowed outside of the state corporatist structure. The organizations and collective actions of the social movements inevitably encountered the state's repressive power. The second was the affinity between the opposition movement and the social movements. This was due to the necessity for mutual support. The opposition could provide social movements with political skills and resources, whereas the latter could offer electoral support in exchange.

These above cleavages within the governance structure, plus some serious contingent crises in the early 1980s,[39] led the Kuomintang regime to institute a reform program that was intended to further co-opt those challenging forces into a new framework in the mid-1980s. These included the abolition of martial law, allowing new political parties to be formed, the reelection of national representative bodies, and the protection of civil rights under the constitution. However, this 'passive revolution' – to use Gramsci's[40] term – was abolished when the then President Chiang Ching-Kuo died in early 1988 and there began a new era of political struggle within the regime, that led to a new era of democratization.

Political struggle and the role of civil society[41]

The death of President Chiang Ching-Kuo led to an internal power struggle within the party state. The reformers were led by Lee Teng-Hui, then the president and chairman of the Kuomintang and one of the earliest Taiwanese to be recruited by the Kuomintang into the power circle, and his followers. The hard-liners were those mainlanders who had remained in the power circle for a long time.[42] The internal struggle within the regime provided civil society with more opportunities to mobilize as the reformers sought to find social support outside of the power bloc. The internal power struggle within the regime took place during the 1988–1993 period, in the course of which the reformers ousted the hard-liners from the power circle of the regime.

As Przeworski describes, 'the first critical threshold in the transition to democracy is precisely the move by some groups within the ruling bloc to obtain support from forces external to it'.[43] At the initial stage of the transition, President Lee, the reformers' leader, was not as powerful as other hard-liners who had been established in the circles of power for a long time. He did not have his own power base within the state bureaucracy and the party, nor did he have commanding power with respect to the military. He therefore needed to build up his own social base in the struggle. As a nominal party chairman and the president, he had the institutional capacity to do this. The cleavage within the former governance structure provided him with the very opportunity to do so. President Lee's weakness in the ruling bloc became his strength in finding social support in the political struggle. The local political elites, the rising capitalists, the opposition, and social movements all directly and indirectly helped him to consolidate this power base.

As discussed above, the local political elites were confined to local politics. However, as the Kuomintang needed them to win in local elections against the opposition, those local elites were inspired to enter politics at the national level. The existing governance structure, which was designed by the former regime (therefore by the hard-liners), prevented this from being realized. By contrast, President Lee not only had the ethnic affinity (Taiwanese) with local politicians, but he also promoted reform programs that were intended to transform the rules for reelection to national representative bodies. This would provide local politicians with an opportunity to enter national politics. This factor was favored by the reformers rather than by the hard-liners in terms of building a social basis of support.

The rising capitalist class also supported the reformers. The state capitalist mode of development that had been in place since the 1950s had prohibited private enterprises from entering the strategic upstream industries.[44] However, as these private enterprises became bigger, they wanted to step into these areas. As a liberal economist, President Lee promoted economic liberalization and deregulation encompassed not only the privatization of state firms but also the opening up of every kind of market to private investment. This idea was welcomed by the capitalists. Therefore, the reformers also gained more support from the capitalists than did the hard-liners. This consequently enabled the capitalists to have a greater influence in the decision-making process.[45]

The opposition groups in this power struggle process within the Kuomintang regime also preferred to ally with the reformers as opposed to the hard-liners. The opposition movement had both democratic and ethnic/national characteristics. In 1986, it formed the first opposition party, the Democratic Progressive Party (the DPP), and forced the regime to recognize it. Since then, the DPP has become an organized opposition party that has countered the Kuomintang in politics. As for the opposition groups, the hardliners (and the mainlanders) were the power-holders within the authoritarian regime deemed responsible for the suppression of the Taiwanese. The DPP's political objective was mainly to transform the state and thereby resist the rule of the hard-liners. Compared to the hard-liners, the opposition groups preferred to ally themselves with President Lee (who was the first Taiwanese president) and reformers within the regime.

The last factor was the role played by the social movements. As Przeworski argued, the split within the regime and the popular mobilizations fed each other during the transitional period. These popular movements signaled to the reformers 'the possibility of an alliance that could change the relations of forces within the power bloc to their advantage'.[46] The power struggles and internal splits within the regime provided the social movements with more opportunities to mobilize themselves.[47] Furthermore, the popular mobilization in turn forced the regime to decide whether to repress, co-opt, or devolve power. This in turn exacerbated the internal division within the regime. In March 1990, the largest student demonstration ever to occur in Taiwan took place in Taipei, and demanded the reform of the regime and the reelection of national representative bodies. This mobilization indirectly helped the reformers to win over the hard-liners. On the one hand, the mobilization of social movements created serious problems for social order, which were harmful to economic development. The capitalists demanded that the regime maintain order. On the other hand, the reformers used this pressure to force the hard-liners to face the demands that arose from the civil society. The social movements thus indirectly helped the reformers to win the power struggle.

All the social and political forces favored the reformers over the hardliners in the power struggle. The initially weak reformers gradually gained the dominant position within the regime and finally forced the hard-liners to step down from the power circle in early 1993. From then on, a much more pro-capitalist, Taiwanized, and liberally oriented regime was in the making.

The transformation of the state in the 1990s

From 1993 onward, the Taiwanese state entered a new era. A new regime was established, and the old governance structure of the state was gradually transformed to one characterized by a process of 'de-China-lization' and Taiwanization.

First, whereas the old regime structure was designed to represent sovereignty over China, now the new regime claimed that its sovereignty held sway only over Taiwan and its adjacent isles. Therefore, the Constitution had been reformed year by year through which various types of national representative bodies were reconstructed and the related elections were held. In addition, for the first time in history the Taiwanese were able to choose their leader beginning in 1996, the year in which President Lee was popularly elected. This reform of the state structure largely reduced the representative characteristics of China and created a greater correspondence to the territorial reality of Taiwan.

Second, the democratization of the regime also led to a Taiwanese nation-building movement propagated by the regime itself. In the old regime's rhetoric, Taiwan was a local government that was attached to the 'Chinese' state. The central state in Taiwan was an emergent one that would finally return to China. Therefore, to have a Taiwanese consciousness was regarded as treason and open discussion in relation to it was not allowed before the 1980s. Now the new regime not only promoted Taiwanese consciousness but also treated it as a legitimate national identity. Various mechanisms were set up by the state with the intention of constructing an 'imagined community' – to use Anderson's term.[48] For one, the rewriting of Taiwan's history through state-sponsored projects and turning them into school curriculums were aimed at building up a new collective memory. In a way that differed from the old regime that treated Taiwan's history as a local one that was part of the long Chinese history, the new regime rewrote it as a national history. Together with Taiwan's economic success, the new regime intentionally wanted to differentiate the new Taiwanese regime from the old 'Chinese' regime. Indeed, the state's discourses called for a new Taiwanese identity and assigned to it a new form of nationalism. The most aggressive action taken by the regime in terms of calling for a new Taiwanese national identity was that in July 1999 when President Lee announced through the German media that the cross-Taiwan Strait relationship was a 'special state-to-state relationship'. This act officially declared that Taiwan had a 'two-nation states' policy and proclaimed its nation-state status in the international political arena.

Third, the new regime made efforts to reenter the international political arena to be recognized as a sovereign state. Diplomatic efforts were made in particular with a view to entering the United Nations. As compared with the old Kuomintang regime, which treated this as a two-China policy that was prohibited, now the new regime wanted to be recognized as a Taiwanese state. Other efforts were also made to enter other international organizations under the UN structure.

Furthermore, the governance structure of the old regime was transformed under the new regime so as to build up and maintain its social support. The clientelist structure was reinforced as the opposition groups became more organized, so that the Kuomintang depended more on local factions to compete with the DPP in each election. Furthermore, as more local politicians entered the arena of national politics, they gained more power in the decision-making process. The reformation of the clientelist structure produced a dual effect. On the one hand, national politics became 'pork barrel' politics that replaced the centralized decision-making model that had existed in the old regime. On the other hand, because the locals gained more resources from the central state, this gave rise to severe competition among local social and political groups.

As regards the corporatist structure, the existing framework lost its controlling power. While there was still a national organization in each category and it played the role of interest representation, there were many self-organized groups that were not under the national framework. For example, with respect to the unions, a new labor law was drafted that aimed to give up the 'one union, one shop' policy and attempted to allow workers to organize their own unions and compete among themselves within the firm. The capitalists also gained more power in regard to the state-business relationship during this period. They had representatives in all major decision-making organs that influenced social and political policies. When compared with the former stage where the state took the lead in initiating industrial policies, the capitalists now became a junior partner in making decisions.[49] All of these tendencies indicated that the state corporatist structure had undergone transformation into a pluralist model.[50]

Social movement organizations at this stage were either incorporated by the opposition parties or became interest groups. As Schmitter argued, the democratizing social movements and actors would inevitably decline in the consolidation stage of democratization, whereas political parties and interest groups would take center stage.[51] Most of the movement organizations had now become affiliates of the DPP. Still, there were other newly formed, national or local, organizations that were more politically neutral and sought to influence public policy. These recruited and trained movement activists that contributed to the activation of the civil society. They tended, however, to become interest groups that directed pressure toward politicians of all parties and allied themselves with those who could help push their respective policy agendas.

In sum, as the new regime instigated its nation-building and state-restructuring projects, it also reconstructed the old governance structure into

Table 1 The state–civil society relationship and governance structure

State- civil society relationship	Old KMT regime	New KMT regime
State form	Authoritarian party–state: based on suppressive apparatuses and a Chinese identity	Democratic state: based on elections and a Taiwanese identity
State–social groups	State corporatism	Pluralism
State–local politicians	Clientelism	Interest politics
State–business	State-led capitalism	Partnership
State–social movements	Suppressive	Interest groups
Identity	A 'Chinese' state discourse prevailed	A 'Taiwanese' state discourse prevailed

a new one that also left space for more freedom within civil society. The governance structure and state–civil society relationships discussed above are depicted in Table 1.

The contested issues in building a new nation

As discussed above, the undermining of the legitimacy of the Kuomintang regime due to the withdrawal of the US support in the 1970s, together with other social and political structural factors, finally forced the Kuomintang regime to implement limited reform programs. These internal legitimation processes as a consequence created a democratization process that inherited with it a new nation-building impulse in the 1990s. The restructuring of the Kuomintang regime, however, did not have hegemonic power over the society internally, and did not gain international support externally. Even worse, the nationalist project tended to contradict its tendency to become economically integrated with the Chinese market.

Internally, the new nation-building process created ethnic conflicts in national politics, in that many politicians within the Kuomintang became detached from the party and formed a new party to resist this inclination towards independence. Because these politicians mainly consisted of mainlanders, this triggered serious ethnic tensions that revolved around the national identity as being Taiwanese versus Chinese, or involving a 'Taiwanese nation' versus a 'Chinese nation'. The new party members accused the new regime of retreating from the legacy of the Republic of China and possibly putting Taiwan in danger of being invaded militarily by the PRC. By contrast, the DPP not only hailed the efforts of the new Kuomintang regime, but also charged the new party with betraying the 'Taiwanese' nation. Naming the name of the nation became hotly contested as ethnic tensions entered the political arena.

Externally, all the moves taken by the new regime were regarded by the PRC as actions to become independent. Verbal threats as well as military exercises that were continuously held by the PRC in the southeastern parts of China posed a major challenge to Taiwan. Military tensions again heightened across the Taiwan Strait, to an extent unheard of since before the 1970s. Moreover, since the nation-building effort had not been hailed by the major powers within the international political arena due to their 'one-China policy', the new regime had to depend on its own efforts to maneuver the cross-Strait relationship and engage in international politics.

Moreover, this difficult issue became even harder for the regime to deal with as its economy became increasingly integrated with the Chinese market. As compared with the economy before 1990, when Taiwan's major trading partner was the US, the economy now came to depend more and more on the China side. There are two indicators that illustrate this tendency.

First, Taiwan's major export market gradually shifted from the US to China (via Hong Kong). As discussed above, Taiwan's industrialization was mainly based on the expansion of the US market. This market in 1985 comprised over 48 per cent of the value of all export commodities.[52] However, its importance subsequently declined. By contrast, the Chinese market gained importance during the same period. This also meant that, as an export-oriented economy, Taiwan depended on China much more than before for its economic prosperity (Figure 1). Second, China became the main destination of Taiwan's capital outflow (Table 2). As many have noted, because of the hostility surrounding the cross-Strait relationship, many investments went through second and third channels. Therefore, the actual percentage ought to be much higher than the official figures.

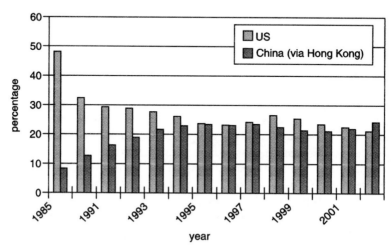

Figure 1 US and China as Taiwan's export market.

Source: CEPD 2002.

Table 2 Taiwan's investment in China (amount and number of cases)

Year	Amount ($ million)	Cases	Average/case ($ million)
1991	174.2	237	0.73
1992	247.0	264	0.94
1993	3,168.4	9,329	0.90
1994	962.2	934	1.03
1995	1,092.7	490	2.23
1996	1,229.2	383	3.21
1997	1,614.5	728	2.22
1998	2,034.6	1,284	1.58
1999	1,252.7	488	2.57
2000	2,607.1	840	3.10
2001	2,784.1	1,186	2.35
Total	**20,092.9**	**24,270**	

Source: CEPD 2002.

All of these figures indicate that the Taiwan economy has become deeply integrated with that of China. Politically, the Taiwanese state perceived that the deepening economic integration would eventually be in China's favor in that the PRC could use the strategy of businesses interests to circumscribe the Taiwanese state to comply with its 'one-state, two-systems' policy. Economically, the deepening economic integration would not only bring about a massive inflow of capital into China that would eventually hurt the Taiwanese economy, but it would also upgrade the Chinese economy, thereby enabling it to compete in the world market. In order to avoid the threat to the Taiwan economy posed by the PRC through its business interests, the new regime adopted new methods to hold back this tendency.[53] However, the regime's strategies did not have the required deterrence effect as the Taiwanese capitalists continued to invest on a huge scale in the Chinese market. These conflicting issues continued to trouble the DPP regime as it came to power in 2000.

In 2000, the Kuomintang stepped down from its ruling position for the first time in the post-Second World War era as a result of the presidential election. A democratic system was consolidated, and the DPP took over the power of the state. However, the divergence in political development in terms of building a new nation-state and the Taiwanese economy's tendency to become integrated with China became even clearer. It was mainly the DPP's in-built ideology regarding Taiwan independence that largely amplified the new nation-building process, which as a consequence increased the tension across the Taiwan Strait. For example, in August 2002, the president insisted that Taiwan and China were 'one country on each side' of the Taiwan Strait and said that Taiwan should consider passing a referendum law to protect its sovereignty. In November and December 2003, following the passage of a law allowing for a limited referendum, the president said that he would call for a vote demanding that China remove its 496 missiles aimed at Taiwan, and that he would push for the rewriting of Taiwan's Constitution in 2006 in order to make 'Taiwan a normal, complete, great country'.[54] These acts triggered strong reactions from both the PRC and the US as they perceived that Taiwan might want to change the status quo, which might have destabilized the geo-political environment. The US rebuked Taiwan for the first time, but also warned China that it would intervene if it were to attack Taiwan. All of these actions indicated that it was the DPP's determination to pursue independent sovereignty that exacerbated the political tension across the Taiwan Strait.

The DPP regime, as it continued to pursue its goal of independent sover-eignty, faced an even harder economic integration issue in that the Taiwan economy was becoming even more integrated with that of China. At the end of 2001, China was absorbing over 42 per cent of Taiwan's approved outward investments, while the Chinese market had already replaced the US as the major export destination for Taiwanese exports.[55] For the DPP regime, the goal of building a new nation-state took priority over economic develop-ment, and therefore it prevented the 'Three Links' policy (direct trade, mail, and transportation) from being realized in order to counter the tendency for the two economies to become more integrated. The economic integration with China was regarded as a national security issue and was handled by political means. The inexperience of the DPP regime and its political stance at the current stage has been in serious conflict with developments that have taken place in Taiwan's economy. Indeed, Taiwan experienced for the first time in 2001 the most serious economic downfall (a −2.18 per cent growth rate) after over 50 years of rapid growth. This contradiction between the political and economic aspects gave rise to some serious problems that the DPP regime's leadership had to face as it assumed state power. The survival issue continues to be the major concern of the DPP regime, but this time careful attention needs to be paid to both the military and economic threats from the PRC.

Discussion and conclusion

This chapter discusses the specificities of the formation of the Taiwanese state and its transformation both during and after the democratization pro-cess. It is argued that the survival issue led the Kuomintang regime to build up a security and militarized state that consequently constituted a polity with an authoritarian governance structure. It was also due to the support from the US in the 1950s that the Kuomintang regime was able to consolidate its rule on the island and to gain legitimacy in the international political arena. However, Taiwan's indeterminate status as a sovereign state after 1970 in international politics and the inconsistency of the 'one China' acclamation against the actual sovereign power finally from the late 1980s onwards gave impetus to building a new nation as part of the process of democratization.

The regime has since 1993 experienced both state-restructuring and new nation-building processes which have diverged from its economic trend. This decoupling of the polity and the economy at the current stage has led to a new legitimacy problem for the DPP regime as the economy continues to be in trouble.

The national survival issue thus remains the essential element that the current state has to deal with, as was the case in the 1950s. However, there are major differences between these two stages. First, the Kuomintang regime in the 1950s was fully supported by the US as it sought to establish its rule on the island. The state's legitimacy in this sense mainly came from external forces. However, the state's legitimacy at the current stage arises from a democratic electoral system. Nevertheless, this internal legitimacy of the state's power still cannot gain recognition in the international political arena as a sovereign state when most of the major states in the world still consider the PRC as the only 'China' of which Taiwan is but a province.

Second, while the issue of the state's survival in the 1950s was mainly concerned with a military invasion by the PRC, today both the military and economic threats need to be considered. In the Cold War era, under the protection of the US, the Taiwanese economy was deeply integrated with the US market. Now, in the post-Cold War era, the Taiwanese economy has become integrated with the Chinese market while the political regimes on either side of the Taiwan Strait remain hostile toward each other. The PRC's 'one-China policy' and the pro-independence position of the DPP regime has become an unsolvable issue even though the two economies have become integrated within the 'Greater China region'. The survival issue of the Taiwanese state becomes even more serious when the economy goes against the politics.

Indeed, while the Cold War atmosphere has become more relaxed, the cross-Strait relationship by contrast has intensified. The national survival issue continues to be the state's main concern. For the Kuomintang regime before democratization, the national survival issue was concerned with preventing a military takeover by the PRC in the name of 'China'. For the state both during and after the process of democratization, the issue becomes one of survival from the same military threat in the name of 'Taiwan'. The new DPP regime is now caught in between nation building and delinking its economy with China. The issue of survival has become like a double-edged sword. If it follows the economy and integrates with China, the state may disappear and become a local state in the style of Hong Kong. However, if it does not want to follow this trend and instead makes claims to be an independent and sovereign state, further economic development may be fraught with difficulties. The future of Taiwan appears to be in a kind of stalemate that requires Solomon's wisdom. All of these features show that the formation and transformation of the Taiwanese state have typically idiosyncratic characteristics that have rarely been seen in the history of international politics.

Notes

1 T. Gold, 'Taiwan's quest for identity in the shadow of China', in S. Tsang (ed.), *In the Shadow of China: Political Development in Taiwan since 1949*, London: Hurst and Company, 1993, pp. 169–92.
2 M. Woo-Cumings, 'National security and the rise of the developmental state in South Korea and Taiwan', in H. Rowen (ed.), *Behind East Asian Growth: The Political and Social Foundation of Prosperity*, London: Routledge, 1998, pp. 319–37.
3 J. Ballentine, *Formosa: A Problem for U.S. Foreign Policy*, Washington, DC: The Brookings Institution, 1952.
4 N. Jacoby, *U.S. Aid to Taiwan: A Study of Foreign Aid, Self-Help, and Development*, New York: Frederic A. Preager, 1966, p. 118.
5 Ibid.
6 Ibid.
7 Ibid., p. 119.
8 J. H. Wang, 'Taiwan de zhengzhi zhuanxing yu fandui yundong' (Political transformation and the opposition movement in Taiwan), *Taiwan: A Radical Quarterly in Social Studies*, 1989, vol. 2, no. 1, 71–116.
9 During the aid period, the regime suffered from budgetary deficits that averaged about 26 per cent of central and provincial expenditures, and were a result of the heavy military burden. More than 90 per cent of these deficits were financed by US aid that was not part of the regular budget – Jacoby, *U.S. Aid*, pp. 92–3. Moreover, because of the sudden inflow of over one million refugees from the mainland and the financial difficulties experienced by the state, an easy money supply policy was adopted. Bank credit expanded rapidly and the money supply doubled in 1950. The result was serious inflation. The arrival of aid in late 1950 largely brought the inflation under control and helped rehabilitate the economy, see S. Ho, *Economic Development in Taiwan, 1860- 1970*, New Haven: Yale University Press, 1978, p. 113.
10 Jacoby, *U.S. Aid*, p. 152.
11 Ibid., p. 165.
12 J. Bruce, 'Paradox in the politics of Taiwan', *Politics*, 1978, vol. 13, no. 2, 239–47; T. J. Cheng, 'Democratization of a quasi-Leninist regime in Taiwan', *World Politics*, 1989, vol. 41, 477–99; T. J. Cheng and S. Haggard (eds), *Political Change in Taiwan*, Boulder, Colorado: Lynne Rienner, 1992, pp. 6–7.
13 A. J. Lerman, 'National elites and local politicians in Taiwan', *American Political Science Review*, 1977, vol. 71, no. 4, 1406–22; E. Winckler, 'National, regional, and local politics', in E. Ahern and H. Gates (eds), *The Anthropology of Taiwanese Society*, Palo Alto, Calif.: Stanford University Press, 1981, pp. 13–37.
14 J. K. Kallegren, 'Nationalist China: the continuing dilemma of the mainland philosophy', *Asian Survey*, 1963, vol. 3, 11–16; G. Kerr, *Formosa Betrayed*, Boston: The Riverside Press, 1965; R. N. Clough, *Island China*, Cambridge: Harvard University Press, 1978.
15 Lerman, 'National elites'; Winckler, 'National, regional, and local politics'.
16 Ho, *Economic Development*; F. C. Deyo (ed.), *The Political Economy of the New Asian Industrialism*, New York: Cornell University Press, 1987; T. Gold, *State and Society in the Taiwan Miracle*, Ithaca, NY: M. E. Sharpe, 1986.
17 Clough, *Island China*; Gold, *State and Society*.
18 cf. S. N. Eisenstadt and L. Roniger, 'Patron-client relations as a model of structuring social exchange', *Comparative Studies in Society and History*, 1980, vol. 22, 42–75; L. Roniger and G. Ayes, *Democracy, Clientelism, and Civil Society*, Boulder, Colorado: Lynne Rienner, 1994.
19 Y. H. Chu, 'Guazhan jingji yu weiquan zhengzhi tizhi' (The oligopolistic economy

and authoritarian political system), in M. H. H. Hsiao (ed.), *Monopoly and Exploitation: The Political Economy of Authoritarianism*, Taipei: Taiwan Research Foundation, 1989, pp. 136–60 (in Chinese); M. T. Chen and Y. H. Chu, 'Quyu xinglian he duzhan jingji, difang paixi, yu shengyiyuan xuanju: yixiang shengyi-yuan houxuanren beijing ziliao fenxi, 1950–1986' (Regional oligopoly, local factions, and provincial assembly elections: an analysis of the socio-economic background of candidates, 1950–1986), *National Science Council Proceedings - Social Sciences and Humanities*, 1992, vol. 3, 77–97 (in Chinese); M. T. Chen, *Paixi zhengzhi yu Taiwan de zhengzhi bianqian* (Factional politics and Taiwan's political change), Taipei: Yue-dan Press, 1995; C. L. Lin, 'Weiquan shicong zhengti xia de Taiwan fandui yundong' (Opposition movement under an authori-tarian clientelist regime), *Taiwan: A Radical Quarterly in Social Studies*, 1989, vol. 2, no. 1, 117–43.

20 cf. P. Schmitter, 'Still the century of corporatism?', *Review of Politics*, 1974, vol. 36, 85–131.

21 J. H. Wang, 'Labour regimes in transition: changing faces of labour control in Taiwan: 1950s–1990s', in A. Y. Hing, C. T. Chang, and R. Lansbury (eds), *Work, Organization, and Industry: The Asian Experience*, Singapore: Armour, 1998, pp. 250–74; F. C. Deyo, *Beneath the Miracle: Labor Subordination in the New Asian Industrialism*, Berkeley and Los Angeles: University of California Press, 1989: Y. J. Lee, *Taiwan gonghui zhengce de zhengzhi jingji fenxi* (The political economy of Taiwan's union policy), Taipei: Ju-liu Books, 1992 (in Chinese).

22 Kallegren, 'Nationalist China'.

23 Jacoby, *U.S. Aid*, p. 36.

24 A. Amsden, 'The state and Taiwan's economic development', in P. Evans, D. Rueschemeyer, and T. Skocpol (eds), *Bringing the State Back In*, Cambridge: Cambridge University Press, 1985, pp. 78–106.

25 Ibid., p. 84.

26 Amsden, 'The state'; Gold, *State and Society*. The resistance mainly came from the military. The import-substitution industrialization in the 1950s was consistent with the interests of the military, especially since the manufacturing industry produced goods for the military without being affected by the world market. The export-led industrialization would eventually expose Taiwan to the world economy and make Taiwan vulnerable to external forces.

27 Gold, *State and Society*, p. 77.

28 Amsden, 'The state', pp. 99–100.

29 Ibid., p. 78.

30 Amsden, 'The state'; Deyo, *The Political Economy*; Wade, *Governing the Market: Economic Theory and the Role of Government in East Asia*, Princeton, NJ: Princeton University Press, 1990; S. Haggard, *Pathways from the Periphery*, New York: Cornell University Press, 1990; Gold, *State and Society*; Weiss and Hobson, *States and Economic Development*, Cambridge: Polity Press, 1995.

31 S. Tsang (ed.), *In the Shadow of China: Political Development in Taiwan since 1949*, London: Hurst and Company, 1993.

32 Wang, 'Political transformation'.

33 E. Winckler, 'Institutionalization and participation on Taiwan: from hard to soft authoritarianism', *The China Quarterly*, 1984, no. 99, 481–99.

34 M. H. H. Hsiao (ed.), *Bianqian zhong de Taiwan shehui de zhongchan jieji* (Taiwan's middle class and social change), Taipei: Ju-liu Press, 1989; Wang, 'Political transformation'.

35 The conflict between the regime and the opposition resulted in the arrests of the leaders of the opposition in late 1979 when a rally held in the city of Kaohsiung turned into a violent confrontation between the police and the movement's supporters.

36 Y. H. Chu, *Crafting Democracy in Taiwan*, Taipei: Institute for National Policy Research, 1992; Wang, 'Political transformation'.

37 C. K. Hsu and W. L. Shong (eds), *Taiwan xinxing shehui yundong* (New social movements in Taiwan), Taipei: Ju-liu Press, 1989 (in Chinese); M. K. Chang, *Shehui yundong yu zhengzhi zhuanhua* (Social movements and political transition), Taipei: Taiwan National Policy Center Press, 1990.

38 J. M. Wu, 'Zhengzhi zhuanxing qi de shehui kangyi: Taiwan 1980 niandai' (Social protests in political transition: Taiwan in the 1980s), M.A. thesis, National Taiwan University, 1990 (in Chinese), p. 45.

39 cf. J. H. Wang, *Shui tongzhi Taiwan: zhuanxing zhong de guojia jiqi yu quanli jiegou* (Who rules Taiwan: the transformation of the state and power structure), Taipei: Ju-Liu Books, 1996 (in Chinese).

40 A. Gramsci, *Selections from the Prison Notebooks*, London: Lawrence and Wishart, 1971.

41 This section and the subsequent ones are based on my former works (see Wang, *Who Rules Taiwan*; J. H. Wang, 'Civil society, democratization, and governance in Taiwan', in National Science Council, Taipei, Bonn Office (ed.), *Conference Prague 1999: Transitional Societies in Comparison: Central East Europe vs. Taiwan*, Frankfurt am Main: Peter Lange, 2000, pp. 17–34.

42 T. J. Cheng and S. Haggard (eds), *Political Change in Taiwan*, Boulder, Colorado: Lynne Rienner, 1992; Wang, *Who Rules Taiwan*.

43 A. Przeworski, 'Some problems in the study of transition to democracy', in G. O'Donnell, P. C. Schmitter, and L. Whitehead (eds), *Transitions from Authoritarian Rule*, Baltimore, Md.: The Johns Hopkins University Press, 1986, p. 56.

44 Amsden, 'The state'; Gold, *State and Society*.

45 Chu, *Crafting Democracy*; J. H. Wang, 'Guojia jiqi, ziben han Taiwan de zhengzhi zhuanxing' (The state, capital and Taiwan's political transition), *Taiwan: A Radical Quarterly in Social Studies*, 1993, vol. 4, 123–64 (in Chinese); M. H. H. Hsiao, 'Formation and transformation of Taiwan's state-business relations: a critical analysis', *Journal of Ethnology*, 1993, vol. 74, 1–32.

46 A. Przeworski, *Democracy and the Market: Political and Economic Reforms in Eastern Europe and Latin America*, Cambridge: Cambridge University Press, 1991, p. 57.

47 Chang, *Social Movements*.

48 B. Anderson, *Imagined Communities*, London: Verso, 1983.

49 Wang, 'The state'.

50 Wang, 'Labour regimes'.

51 P. Schmitter, 'Civil society: East and West', in L. Diamond, M. Plattner, H. M. Tien, and Y. H. Chu (eds), *Consolidating the Third Wave Democracies*, vol. 1, Baltimore: Johns Hopkins University Press, 1997, pp. 239–62.

52 Mainland Affairs Council (MAC), *Cross-Strait Economic Statistics*, Taipei: MAC, 2002.

53 The first method that the new regime adopted was to propagate a new 'Southward Investment Policy' in 1994 that encouraged firms to invest in the ASEAN countries rather than China. The second was to deter big firms from investing in China. On 14 September 1996, President Lee announced a new policy that upheld the strategies of 'patience over haste' and 'steady for the long haul' in the areas of trade and investment in China. This policy subjected investment projects on the mainland involving high-level technology and infrastructure construction amounting to more than $50 million to appropriate regulations and restrictions.

54 S. Lawrence and J. Dean, 'A whole new conflict', *Far Eastern Economic Review*, 18 December 2003, pp. 16–21.

55 MOEA (Ministry of Economic Affairs), *Investment Commission Statistics*, Taipei: MOEA, 2002.

6 Constructing the state in the Tibetan diaspora

Ann Frechette

State building involves the organization of a central government apparatus, the expansion of its administrative reach throughout a territory, and the institutionalization of its control over that territory and its population.[1] In this chapter, I analyze the activities of the Tibetan exiles in India and Nepal as a case of state building. I make two arguments. The first is that the activities of the Tibetan exiles do, indeed, constitute a case of state building, albeit an atypical case. Typically, state building takes place either prior to, or simultaneous with, the establishment of exclusive sovereignty over territory. The Tibetan exiles lack exclusive sovereignty over any territory, yet they have been able to construct most of the elements of statehood due to the considerable autonomy they have been able to exercise within their resettlement camps. I propose the concept of a latent state to characterize the political organization of the Tibetan resettlement camps. I define a latent state as a state-in-the-making, an organization that is in the process of assembling the elements of statehood (a people, a territory, a government, and the capacity to enter foreign relations) yet that presently lacks exclusive sovereignty.[2]

The second argument I make is that there is much to learn by analyzing state building from the perspective of atypical cases. I discuss the case of the Tibetan exiles below in order to highlight four major themes in the state-building literature. They are the increasing importance of external relations to the state-building process, the cultural limitations of externally imposed models of the state, the multivalence of the concept of sovereignty in the contemporary global political order, and the influence of historical contingency in how state building proceeds. I discuss these themes both to illustrate the value of analyzing atypical cases and to advance what I propose as a constructivist view of the state. A constructivist view contrasts both with the realist view, which emphasizes the importance of legitimate coercion (such as an army, navy, police force, prison system) to the definition of a state, and the legalist view, which emphasizes mutual recognition (such as membership in the United Nations). A constructivist view takes a processual, rather than absolutist, approach to what constitutes a state and focuses on what Rosenau describes as a state's underlying relational dynamics.[3] It asks not 'Is element x present or not?', but rather 'What are the underlying relational dynamics that enable element x to emerge or not?' A constructivist view thus takes into account the entire state-building process, from inception to collapse, as well as a broad range of states and state-like entities from what we may consider to be full fledged states (that is, members of the United Nations that exercise considerable governing capabilities) to a variety of latent states, nascent states, quasi-states, and collapsed states. I compare the case of the Tibetan exiles with these other atypical cases to highlight the variety of political arrangements that constitute the contemporary global political order and to argue for an expansion of the concept of the state to include them.

Constructing a state: a view from the Tibetan resettlement camps

I first began to consider the activities of the Tibetan exiles under the general rubric of state building while conducting a survey project in a Tibetan resettlement camp in Jawalakhel, Nepal in 1995. My purpose in conducting the survey was to map changes in camp residence from the time the camp was initially settled in 1961 until the time of my fieldwork. To conduct the survey, I spent my afternoons at the camp drawing the layout and interviewing members of each household. One day, as I was drawing, an old woman, a Tibetan who lived in the camp, led me to the boundary of the camp land. She pointed along a line in the land that divided hard-packed earth, on our side, from overgrown weeds on the other. 'That land over there', she said, as she pointed at the weeds, 'is Nepali land. This land here', where the earth was more compact, 'is Tibetan land'. I asked her what made the land Tibetan land. She replied that Tibetans owned it. I asked her who was the owner (*dag-po*) of the Tibetan land. She replied '*shung*', the government. I asked her which *shung*, which government, and she replied '*pö shung*', the Tibetan government. Having interviewed the administrators of the camp land, I knew that it was legally registered as the property of the Nepal Red Cross Society. The woman's answer, therefore, made me pause. I asked her, then, had she heard of a particular Nepali organization who were the owners of the land, and she responded, 'Oh, maybe the *marpo tsogpa*', the Red Cross Society, 'it is possible they are the owners of the land'.

As I continued my survey, I found that most camp residents talked about the camp land in the same manner, as if it were Tibetan land. They acknowledged the existence of Nepal's Red Cross only when prompted, and even then, many insisted on Tibetan ownership. They had many reasons to think that way. Tibetan exile officials perform most of the administrative functions within the camp, from settling disputes to organizing public construction to registering, taxing, and providing for the camp inhabitants. Even Nepal's police prefer to work through Tibetan officials in their interactions with the camp and its inhabitants. Tibetan exile officials are the only government administrators camp residents interact with on a regular basis. To the residents, the land is Tibetan territory and they, as inhabitants of the land, are 'citizens' (*mi-ser*) of a Tibetan community.

Based on the perspective within the camps, it seems as if the Tibetan exiles have already assembled a number of the elements of statehood. They have achieved considerable autonomy in the management of their camps. They have recruited and trained specialized personnel to govern the camps. They have developed a concept of citizenship within the camps that is further reinforced through the issuance of Tibetan identity booklets.[4] They have developed a taxation system, a social welfare system, an electoral system, and a system of laws and regulations, including the constitution-like 1990 Charter for the Tibetan Exiles. For most purposes, the camp residents interact with each other based on the idea that they constitute a type of Tibetan state.

The view from the Dalai Lama's exile administration further supports the idea that state building is, indeed, what the Tibetan exiles are doing. The exile administration, first established as a small private office in 1960 in Dharamsala, India, where the Dalai Lama had resettled upon fleeing Tibet, has since expanded into a highly structured bureaucracy with an estimated 3,500 full-time staff members working in departments of finance, security, international relations, education, religion and culture, health, home affairs, planning, and public service.[5] It has written a constitution, a charter, and internal rules and regulations for recruiting, training, and promoting staff members. It has instituted the idea of the five-year plan to develop the Tibetan exile communities, and it had since expanded its administrative reach throughout all of the Tibetan communities in exile. The presence of the Dalai Lama's exile administration in Nepal, for example, is broad, deep, and highly diversified. It consists of a 'Tibet Office' (a centralized office in Kathmandu that oversees the governance of the camps and liaisons with foreign governments); Tibetan welfare offices, schools, local assemblies, tax offices, and a district election commission in each of the camps; and at least thirteen for-profit businesses. The Tibetan exiles, in other words, have organized a central government apparatus, expanded its administrative reach throughout a territory (albeit a non-contiguous patchwork of camps), and institutionalized its control over that territory and its population. They have constructed a type of state.

There are arguments to be made even to the legalists and the realists that the Tibetan case constitutes a type of state building. Take the capacity to enter foreign relations, for example, the *sine qua non* of statehood from a legalist perspective. Although the Dalai Lama's exile administration lacks formal, official relations with any state, it engages in considerable unofficial diplomatic activity. The Dalai Lama, for example, regularly meets with state leaders and speaks at government meetings.[6] The exile administration has 'Tibet Offices' in London, Paris, Moscow, Tokyo, Geneva, Pretoria, New York, Zurich, Toronto, Budapest, Canberra, New Delhi, and Kathmandu.[7] The US State Department has appointed a 'Special Coordinator for Tibetan Issues' to liaise with the Dalai Lama's exile administration, an appointment similar to the unofficial diplomatic arrangements the US has made for Taiwan.[8] When unofficial diplomatic relations are taken into account, it seems that the Tibetan exiles have made considerable progress toward mutual recognition and have achieved a form of unofficial diplomacy, similar to that of Taiwan today, or to the People's Republic of China prior to the 1970s.[9]

The Tibetan exiles have assembled the elements of an unofficial coercive apparatus as well. The Dalai Lama's exile administration has its own judicial commission, for example, that is in the process of developing both constitutional and procedural law. Tibetan resettlement camp leaders settle disputes and even expel people whom they determine to have broken the law from the resettlement camps. Tibetan exile leaders exercised the use of coercive force, in the form of CIA-supported guerrilla fighters, until the 1970s, and they continue to develop their military capabilities through the enlistment of Tibetan troops in the Indian army's all-Tibetan twenty-second battalion.[10] Viewed in processual rather than absolutist terms, therefore, the Tibetan exiles may be said to be on the way toward the development of a legitimate coercive apparatus. From even a realist perspective, therefore, it can be argued that they are engaged in state building.

The Tibetan exiles, to be sure, have not (yet) achieved full fledged statehood. They do not exercise exclusive sovereignty over any territory, whether their resettlement camps in exile or their homelands in Tibet. They do not have a seat in the United Nations General Assembly. I therefore propose the concept of the latent state to describe their political organization. I consider the Tibetan exiles' case to be a latent state, and not just an exile government, based on the extent to which the Dalai Lama's exile administration has institutionalized its control over the Tibetan resettlement camps. Its institutional control far exceeds that of most other exile governments worldwide[11] and most closely resembles that of the Palestinians' state-building efforts, particularly in Lebanon from 1969 to 1982.[12] Latent states are most likely to develop, I suggest, within an exile community. They thereby require external supporters (host states and other political patrons) to help maintain their state-building efforts.

The importance of external relations to the Tibetans' state-building efforts

External support is fundamental to the Tibetan exiles' state-building efforts. Their host states, primarily India and Nepal, are the most important of their supporters, as they have allowed the Tibetan exiles considerable autonomy in the governance of their resettlement camps. The Tibetans' other patrons, primarily the United States and Switzerland, play important roles as well. External support is important not only for the Tibetan exiles, and other latent states, however. It is an increasingly important part of the state-building process more generally.

The first theme that I use the Tibetan case to highlight, therefore, is the importance of external relations to the state-building process. Much of the early literature on state building emphasized the importance of internal relations. The debates focused on the respective roles of coercive force, economic control, and ideological control in enabling a political elite to organize and institutionalize its domination over a territory and its population.[13] Equally important, and increasingly more important, are the external relations that enable state building. Tilly and Carneiro argued early on for the role that war plays in the state-building process, but in the present political era, after the organization and institutionalization of a worldwide system of nation-states, a variety of other types of external influences have come into play. One of the most important is the rise in intergovernmental organizations, membership in which conveys mutual recognition of statehood. States exist, on one level, in other words, because other states recognize that they exist. Hence, it is necessary for states-in-the-making to seek this type of recognition (Taiwan is a notable example in this regard).[14] Another external influence involves the dissemination and accommodation of foreign models of the state. Foreign models may be imposed in a direct manner, as in the colonial context,[15] or disseminated in an indirect manner, when they are portrayed as the natural or self-evidentially necessary way in which to organize political life.[16] This process of dissemination and accommodation can be traced back to the mid-nineteenth century (Meiji Japan is a notable example), yet it has become increasingly common as worldwide institutional norms have developed[17] and as governments have begun to interact at deeper organizational levels.[18] A third way in which external relations influence state building is through the use of foreign economic assistance as a tool to encourage or compel states to develop in particular directions.[19] Strong states, acting either unilaterally or multilaterally through institutions such as the World Bank and the International Monetary Fund, are making increasing use of foreign economic assistance to influence others' state-building efforts (contingencies on loans to Indonesia in the late 1990s are a notable example).[20] The use of foreign aid in this regard has become increasingly widespread with the increasing expansion of the global capitalist system.[21]

External relations have come to play such an important part in the state-building process that some scholars argue that they are now more important than internal relations. There are states, in other words, that are supported largely from above with little support from below; the fact that they remain in existence in this manner demonstrates that they follow a fundamentally different set of rules. Jackson proposes the idea of 'negative sovereignty' to characterize these new rules, in which outside intervention is not just permissible but is necessary to enable states (his examples are postcolonial African states) to exist. Jackson defines negative sovereignty as a formal legal condition of freedom from outside interference that lacks practical substance due to the lack of an internal capacity to govern.[22] He describes the role that diplomatic and economic support from international organizations plays in enabling such states to exist. He coined the term 'quasi-states' to describe their condition of being formally, legally recognized as states but requiring foreign assistance to remain in existence.

Like Jackson's quasi-states, latent states, like the Tibetan case, require foreign assistance to remain in existence. They require host states to enable their state-building efforts as well as foreign economic assistance to finance them. With the Tibetan case, India and Nepal serve as host states. Foreign assistance from Switzerland and the United States helps to finance the Tibetans' state-building efforts. Based on this support, the Dalai Lama's exile administration has expanded its administrative reach throughout the Tibetan exile communities and institutionalized its control over them. The Tibetan resettlement camps in Nepal serve here as an example of the role that external support plays in the Tibetan exiles' state-building efforts.

Nepal is host to twelve formal Tibetan resettlement camps that house about a third of its 20,000 Tibetan exiles.[23] The camps were initially established in the 1960s through a series of negotiations between Swiss intergovernmental officials and the Nepal government.[24] Swiss support was, and continues to be, extensive, particularly on behalf of the four initial resettlement camps in Chialsa, Dhorpatan, Pokhara, and Jawalakhel. Swiss intergovernmental organizations provided the funds to purchase the camp lands; negotiated a 1964 agreement to entrust the lands to the Nepal Red Cross Society (with the Swiss government itself as guarantor); negotiated two further agreements, in 1966 and 1971, to bring two additional camps under the same ownership arrangements; and negotiated a 1972 frame agreement to institutionalize Swiss intergovernmental involvement with the camps indefinitely.[25]

Swiss intergovernmental involvement went beyond the ownership of camp lands to include ownership of the camp businesses as well. Under Nepali law, non-citizens cannot hold shares in small-scale village and cottage industries, yet in accordance with the 1964 and 1972 Swiss-Nepal agreements, Swiss officials were allowed to hold shares in the camp businesses on behalf of the Tibetans.[26] The Swiss were very active shareholders. They helped the Tibetans build factories within each of the resettlement camps and to register an export company, based in Kathmandu, to sell their goods internationally; they located the first international buyers for the Tibetans' goods; they provided the Tibetans with loans from Swiss banks; and they trained the first generation of Tibetan factory managers. Swiss involvement helped the Tibetans to establish a dominant position in the export market for hand-woven woolen carpets. Carpet manufacture is now one of Nepal's largest industries and a major source of economic support for its Tibetan resettlement camps.

Swiss intergovernmental involvement was, and continues to be, so extensive that it raises the question of why Nepal's government was, and is, willing to cede such control to a foreign organization. In the early years of the Tibetan exile, according to Toni Hagen, the first Swiss official to become involved in the Tibetan project, the sole concern of the Nepal government was that the Nepali population benefit from whatever programs the Swiss designed for the Tibetan exiles.[27] Over time, Swiss intergovernmental organizations began to play an increasingly important role in funding other development projects in Nepal as well – from the construction of hydroelectric dams to forestry projects to projects to promote women's and children's health. Overall, inter-governmental aid finances some 70 per cent of Nepal's development-related expenditures as well as much of its regular budget.[28] The extent of the aid relationship gives Swiss intergovernmental organizations a certain amount of leverage in Nepal.

The extent of Swiss involvement raises the question of why the Tibetans, and particularly the Dalai Lama's exile administration, would cede such control as well. The basic fact of the matter is that the Dalai Lama's exile administration initially exercised very little control over the Tibetan exiles in Nepal, as it lacked the institutional presence to do so. It initially expanded into Nepal only through the institutions that the Swiss initially helped to create. The Dalai Lama's exile administration established its first presence in Nepal only in 1970, for example, by granting an official title, 'Representative of His Holiness the Dalai Lama to Nepal', to a Tibetan who was already serving as general manager of the Jawalakhel Handicraft Center, the first of the Swiss-Tibetan resettlement camp businesses. In the mid-1970s, when the Dalai Lama's exile administration began to build institutional strength, Swiss and Tibetan officials came into conflict over a number of issues as they negotiated the Tibetans' relative autonomy.[29] The Tibetans, as a result of these negotiations, gained considerable autonomy even from the Swiss officials who still serve on the boards of directors of the Tibetan businesses.

Swiss support thereby enabled the establishment of the camps, the establishment of an economic base for the camps, and the expansion of the administrative reach of the Dalai Lama's exile administration within them. Swiss support continues to remain important to the camps, as the Swiss continue to serve as guarantors to the camps and their businesses. Other forms of external support, in the meantime, have emerged and have served to support the Tibetan exiles' continuing state-building efforts. The exile administration's tax collection system is a good example of the role that US support has come to play in that regard.

The Dalai Lama's exile administration collects a number of taxes from the inhabitants of the Tibetan exile communities. All Tibetan exiles in Nepal, for example, are required to pay a standard two rupee per month tax.[30] Employees of the Dalai Lama's exile administration are required to pay 2 per cent of their salaries as tax, and business owners are required to pay 10 per cent of their annual business income as tax. Tax payments are recorded in what are called 'freedom booklets' (*rangzen lagteb*) in Tibetan or, based on the color of their covers, 'green books' in English. The same size and shape as a passport, green books contain a personal information page and then a number of additional pages for tax payment stamps. Tibetan exile officials describe tax payments as voluntary, as they claim that they have no means through which to enforce payment, yet the simultaneous use of green books to determine eligibility for foreign assistance programs provides adequate means of enforcement. For most assistance programs, Tibetan exiles must pay their taxes up-to-date to become eligible. For some particularly desirable programs, such as US-sponsored Fulbright scholarships or resettlement opportunities in the US, Tibetan exiles must pay all of their own taxes, as well as all of their parents' taxes, to become eligible. The exile administration's middleman position in the provision of foreign assistance thus facilitates its tax collection efforts. It is but one example of continued importance of external support to the Tibetan exiles' state-building efforts.

External support to the Tibetan exiles played a fundamental role in the establishment and maintenance of the Tibetan resettlement camps; it continues to play a role in financing the activities of the Dalai Lama's exile administration within them. The role that the Tibetan exiles' external supporters play enables them, at times, to influence the Tibetans' internal activities, as with the disbandment of the Tibetan guerrilla movement in northern Nepal[31] and the introduction of democratic reforms into the exile administration's governance system.[32] For the most part, however, the Tibetan exiles exercise considerable autonomy in their own governance, even more so than what Jackson describes as typical for quasi-states, and considerably more so than what Woodward describes for Bosnia.[33] External support is important to the Tibetan exiles not just because they are in exile, therefore; it is an increasingly important part of the state-building process more generally. Worldwide norms as to what a state is supposed to look like have developed. Both full fledged states and other state-like organizations are taking steps to accommodate them.

The limits of external models: Tibetans' debate over the concept of the citizen

The emergence of worldwide norms as to what constitutes a state has its origins in the colonial era, when Western governments imposed new institutional norms on their colonies.[34] Colonized peoples at times resisted the imposition of norms and developed alternative institutional forms, yet the colonial era is marked by the overall dissemination of Western ideas about states and state formation throughout the world. This dissemination of institutional norms has continued, even accelerated, in what has been called the postcolonial era. There are many reasons why, including the continued role of Western governments, and Western-financed intergovernmental organizations, in supporting development projects throughout the world;[35] the portrayal of Western institutional norms as natural and necessary;[36] and the expansion in transgovernmental working relationships among increasingly specialized parts of the state (courts, regulatory agencies, executives), a process that Slaughter[37] describes as transgovernmentalism. The imposition and accommodation of Western models of the state is an old process that has continued in the present political era and has developed new variations.

The Tibetan exiles in India and Nepal, like many other peoples worldwide, draw on Western institutional norms in their state-building efforts. Their 1963 constitution for the future of Tibet, for example, was based on the US model.[38] The 1990 Charter for the Tibetan Exiles, similarly, draws on the US model in its balance of powers among three branches of government and on the United Nations Charter in its guarantee of basic human rights and social welfare. The Tibetan exiles' electoral rules and regulations draw on emergent worldwide norms as to what constitutes a free and fair election. The formation of their Planning Council, and its use of the five-year plan, similarly reflects emergent worldwide norms outlining the state's role in economic development.

The role that external models of the state play in the Tibetan exiles' state-building efforts should not be overstated, however. The Tibetans arrived in exile with their own model of the state in mind, that of Tibet as it was governed under the Dalai Lamas (1642–1959). Even as they draw upon external models, the Tibetan exiles interpret those models through their own political and historical legacy. Even when they appear to imitate external models of the state on a structural level, therefore, they often read different meanings and operational values into them.

The second theme in the state-building literature that I use the Tibetan case to highlight, therefore, is that there are cultural limitations on external models of the state as they are disseminated throughout the world. Theorists writing about state-building in China have been particularly influential in highlighting these cultural limitations and in proposing alternative models of the modern state that emerge out of fundamentally different values.[39] One basic argument that emerges out of their work is that the European experience with state building proceeded with reference to particular ideas about liberty, equality, private property, and legal due process that do not have the same salience throughout the rest of the world. They propose that modern states can exist based on different value systems such as communitarian duty-consciousness, filial piety, and the moral transformation of ritual.[40] They point to the economic successes of Hong Kong, Singapore, and Taiwan as evidence that modern states can succeed, even prosper, based on these fundamentally different values.

The Tibetan exiles have similarly encountered cultural limitations in their efforts to accommodate modern Western models of the state. I explore here their efforts to translate and interpret the concept of the citizen as an example of the cultural dissonance they must negotiate. The concept of the citizen is critical to the organization of the modern Western state. Scott describes it as fundamental to the development of centralized political control.[41] Writing about the French case, in particular, he argues that all of the other administrative projects that the central government initiated (for example, the standardization of weights and measures, inheritance laws, taxation systems, and market regulations) depended upon the concept of a uniform, homogenous citizenship. With the concept of national citizenship, he writes, one can imagine 'a national French citizen perambulating the kingdom and encountering exactly the same fair, equal conditions as the rest of his compatriots. In place of a welter of incommensurable small communities, familiar to their inhabitants but mystifying to outsiders, there would rise a single national society perfectly legible from the center.'

The Tibetan exiles have worked toward the development of the concept of the citizen in their own state-building efforts, yet in the process, they have struggled with the concept in their attempts to justify their own ideas about political membership with the ideas about liberty, equality, private property, and legal due process that the concept of the citizen entails. Their struggle derives not just from the heightened importance that political exiles place on preserving traditional values;[42] the very language that the Tibetan exiles use to discuss political membership derives from a fundamentally different political ideology. The Tibetan exiles struggle with the concept of the citizen, therefore, not necessarily out of deliberate defiance or conscious resistance to an externally imposed model, but because they are engaging with new concepts from within a different cultural context.

Tibet, as it was governed under the Dalai Lamas, did not have a single homogenous category of the citizen. The relationship between Tibet's inhabitants and the Tibetan state depended upon whether or not they held land, and if so, what type of land they held. Toward the end of the Dalai Lama regime (roughly 1930–1950), approximately 250–300 families held land as government-service aristocrats (*kudrak*); they paid taxes to the Dalai Lama's government and held broad authority over the estate lands they held.[43] The remainder of the population consisted of serfs (*mi-ser*) of two types – tax-paying serfs, who hereditarily held land on their lords' estates, and nontaxpayers, who did not have any hereditary claims to land.[44] Tibetan serfs, whether taxpayers or not, were not without rights *vis-à-vis* the Tibetan state – they could, for example, initiate legal action against their lords – yet there was no uniform legal code outlining what those rights were.[45] If we understand the concept of the citizen to imply uniform homogenous rights, then it is fair to say that the Tibetans, as they were governed under the Dalai Lamas, lacked that concept.

The Tibetan exiles, as part of their state-building efforts, have begun to use the concept of the citizen and to formulate a code of uniform homogenous rights that all citizens are supposed to hold in common. Their 1963 constitution, for example, outlines the rights of Tibet's citizens, as does the 1990 Charter for the Tibetan Exiles. These rights include, among others, free speech; free assembly; rights to life, liberty, and property; and the right to vote. As they have formulated these rights, however, they have struggled with how even to express them in Tibetan. The very language that the Tibetans use is laden with rules and meanings inimical to the idea of uniform homogenous rights. Its distinct lexicons for common people, aristocrats, and lamas (enlightened teachers) provide but one example of the hierarchical legacies embedded in the language itself.[46] As a result, there are at least three translations of the concept of the citizen in use in the Tibetan exile communities.

The first term that the Tibetan exiles used to translate the concept of the citizen, in their 1963 constitution, is *nga-wang*, which connotes the idea of a 'subject' (someone who is subject to, or subordinate to a territory and its lord).[47] The authors of the constitution used the term *nga-wang*, a fundamentally hierarchical concept, even though it is clear from the context that at least one of the meanings they intended to convey is equal citizenship. In both its English and Tibetan versions, the 1963 constitution states clearly that all Tibetans are equal before the law (article 8) and that all Tibetan 'citizens' (*nga-wang*) have equal rights to speech, assembly, movement, residence, property, and professional occupation (article 18). Elsewhere in the 1963 constitution, however, there is evidence that the latent hierarchical connotations of *nga-wang* are still present. Article 25, for example, stipulates that all land in Tibet belongs to the state; combined with article 29, which invests the Dalai Lama with absolute powers of state, it seems as if all Tibetans are actually subjects of the Dalai Lama rather than equal citizens.

The 1990 Charter for the Tibetan Exiles uses a different term for the concept of the citizen. It uses *yul-mi*, which translates as 'local inhabitant' or 'native' (someone from a particular place). The use of *yul-mi*, instead of *nga-wang*, represents a significant movement away from a sovereign-subject or ruler-ruled conceptualization of political membership. It connotes greater equality. The 1990 Charter, like the 1963 constitution, outlines the rights that *yul-mi* are entitled to hold, such as to life, liberty, property, equality, free speech, free assembly, and the right to vote (articles 10–12). Significantly, however, the Charter continues to invest the Dalai Lama with supreme authority (articles 19, 20, 36). Although the use of *yul-mi* implies greater equality, therefore, the Charter clearly distinguishes the Dalai Lama, at least, as more equal than others.

Tibetan exiles in Nepal, in their everyday discussions, use a different term for the concept of the citizen. That is *mi-ser*, which translates as 'agricultural tenant' or 'serf', and which was used for all non-aristocrats in Tibet under the Dalai Lamas. In Tibet, the term *mi-ser* was used most often as part of a possessive phrase, naming the estates from which particular serfs derived.[48] In that context, it clearly connoted patrimonial belonging. In exile, inhabitants of the Tibetan resettlement camps use the term *mi-ser* both to translate the English word 'citizen' and to refer to their relationship with the Dalai Lama's exile administration. What they intend is unclear. Does the term now connote equality under the law, as with the concept of the citizen? Or does it continue to refer to a relationship of patrimonial belonging? The Tibetan woman who pointed me to the boundary of the Jawalakhel resettlement camp land used the term *mi-ser* to connote her status as a subject of *pö shung*, the Tibetan (exile) government. She was clearly positioning herself as a subject of the Dalai Lama and his administration.

The many terms that the Tibetan exiles use to translate the concept of the citizen demonstrate their ongoing struggle to develop a political ideology that reflects both their achievements in constructing a modern state and their own culture and tradition. The process is by no means simple, as it involves the fundamental reconsideration of the very language that the Tibetan exiles use to discuss political relationships. The efforts of the Tibetan exiles, in this regard, are best viewed as a struggle, rather than as active resistance, as it often proceeds in a context of genuine efforts at reform. Translation is thus a fundamental challenge to the imitation of foreign models of the state that at best involves an ongoing process of negotiation, interpretation, and accommodation of foreign ideas.

The multivalence of the concept of sovereignty

Another idea that is critical to the concept of the modern state that is being reconsidered and renegotiated in the present political era is the concept of sovereignty. Sovereignty is under reconsideration not just as a result of local-ization, as with the concept of citizenship among the Tibetans, but as a result of intransigent international issues that challenge the principle of exclusive sovereignty as the basis for the international political order.

Sovereignty is a concept that derives from Rome's civil law tradition, and in particular, its ideas about property and patrimonial ownership; it signifies supreme authority within a territory.[49] It developed into the basis for the international political order through such events as the Peace of Westphalia; the realignment of Europe's states after the world wars; the decolonization of Asia, Africa, Latin America, and the Middle East throughout the 1960s and 1970s; and the establishment of international organizations such as the League of Nations and the United Nations.[50]

Recent debates raise the issue of whether the world is in the midst of another transformation in the concept of sovereignty. Jackson, writing about newly independent African states, proposes the idea of negative sover-eignty.[51] Hashmi, in examining newly independent post-communist states, makes a distinction between procedural sovereignty (that is, minting curren-cies, exchanging ambassadors, sending a representative to the UN General Assembly) and substantive sovereignty (that is, providing adequate external defense, maintaining internal order, engaging in effective economic plan-ning).[52] Philpott discusses recent NATO and UN actions in Bosnia, Kosovo, Somalia, and other places, and suggests a decoupling of the concepts of sovereignty and nonintervention in a state's internal affairs.[53] He suggests that state sovereignty is undergoing a process of circumscription with refer-ence to standards of international justice, such as peace, order, and basic human rights.[54] What is clear from all of their arguments is that the basic concept of sovereignty is being reconsidered in a context of post-Cold War political uncertainty and that new political arrangements are being negotiated.

The most interesting development for my purposes here is the re-emergence of the idea of multiple sovereignties. The organization of the worldwide system of nation-states is predicated upon a principle of exclusive sovereignty, that is, the state is the single supreme authority within a territory. Scholars who analyze the development and expansion of nation-states worldwide describe the difficulties that the concept of exclusive sovereignty posed for areas of the world in which multiple sovereignties (embedded relationships of authority, as with tributary states) had more often been the rule. Winichakul, for example, describes how the process of 'mapping Siam', in response to British colonial incursion, forced the Thai kingdom to transform its relationships with its various dependents.[55] Oksenberg describes how China's engagement with the international system of states forced it to transform, particularly in its relationships to Hong Kong, Taiwan, and Tibet.[56] A number of recent events suggest that new forms of multiple sovereignty are emerging. Writing about international intervention in the former Yugoslavia, Gow suggests that it may be time to entertain the concept of shared sovereignty.[57] About Bosnia, in particular, Woodward forwards the idea of compromised sovereignty.[58] Writing about the establishment of the European Union, Philpott proposes the idea of 'pooled' sovereignty to characterize the EU's decision-making authority in relationship to its member states.[59]

Krasner, in response to these events, contends that the basic concept of sovereignty has always been subject to negotiation so that what is happening now in the international political arena is not altogether new.[60] He describes how international political actors have always used such strategies as conventions, contracts, coercion, and imposition to challenge what is possible internationally.[61] As such, he asserts that exclusive sovereignty is, and has never been, applied as rigidly as one might expect. In place of the idea of a single concept of exclusive sovereignty, he suggests a disaggregation of the concept into four types, any of which may be transacted to another political actor: domestic sovereignty (the organization of authority within a given state); interdependence sovereignty (the ability of states to control transborder flows); international legal sovereignty (formal recognition as a state); and Westphalian sovereignty (the ability to exclude external authority structures). His typology allows for the analysis of a variety of forms of multiple sovereignty in the contemporary global political arena without predicting its immanent collapse. He portrays these various arrangements as exceptions to the general rule of exclusive sovereignty as the basis for the global political order.

It is with his typology in mind that I approach the analysis of the Tibetan resettlement camps in India and Nepal, which I suggest, can be viewed as another example of multiple sovereignty in the contemporary global political arena. The Tibetan exiles' host states maintain international legal sovereignty, in Krasner's terms,[62] over the territory within their borders, including the camps, yet the Dalai Lama's exile administration exercises domestic sovereignty within the camps. Sovereignty over the camp territory is shared between them. This arrangement of multiple sovereignty provides a territorial base on which the exile administration's state-building efforts may proceed. The arrangement is maintained, however, only through the discursive association between the Tibetan resettlement camps and the Tibetan homelands. The Dalai Lama's exile administration portrays its state-building efforts in the resettlement camps as intended for the governance of the Tibetan homelands (as a dress rehearsal, so to speak, for a future independent Tibet) rather than for governance in exile. In that manner, the exile administration avoids the portrayal of its state-building efforts as a challenge to the international legal sovereignty of its host states.

The Dalai Lama's exile administration has developed a number of strategies to enable the discursive association of the Tibetan resettlement camps with the Tibetan homelands. It uses these strategies not only to avoid a challenge to its host states but also to recruit support for its state-building efforts from within the Tibetan exile communities. Part of the legitimacy of the exile administration rests on its ability to return Tibet to Tibetan control, thereby maintaining continuity in Tibet's history as a nation. The Dalai Lama's exile administration thereby narrates a story of Tibet's continuous history as a nation that starts in the Tibetan homelands (as they were governed under the Dalai Lamas), continues within the Tibetan resettlement camps (under the control of the Dalai Lama's exile administration), and ends back in the Tibetan homelands (imagined again as an independent political entity under Tibetan control).

One such strategy that the Dalai Lama's exile administration uses is the myth of return to Tibet.[63] It is unlikely in the present political context that the Tibetan exiles will return to Tibet. Tibetan exile officials, nevertheless, maintain the myth of their impending return. A speech the Director of the Tibet Office made at a 1995 meeting of the Kathmandu branch of the Tibetan Youth Congress, for example, illustrates one way in which he imagined that a return could occur:

> The United Nations intervenes in many conflicts around the world. They helped free Kuwait after Iraq occupied their country, and they sent peacekeeping forces to prevent Iraq from invading again . . . It has happened everywhere. In Bosnia-Herzegovina, in Afghanistan, in Somalia, in Beirut . . . The UN Security Council, which includes America, England, France, China, and Russia, has veto power over all UN decisions, and in the past, China has blocked the UN from helping Tibet. These days, however, many countries are splitting apart, like Russia, Czechoslovakia, Yugoslavia, and as they do, they form new countries that become members of the UN . . . Maybe in the future, they will become as strong as the Security Council . . . Then, the United Nations would have to implement its resolutions on Tibet . . . We need to try ways tried in the past as well as new ways to make Tibet independent.

Another example of this myth of return involves a referendum the exile administration conducted within the Tibetan exile communities from 1995 to 1997. The referendum asked the Tibetan exiles to vote on which path they considered to be most effective in returning Tibet to Tibetan control: (1) the 'middle path' (*lam u-ma*), meaning negotiation with China for some type of political control short of complete independence; (2) 'independence' (*rangzen*), meaning violent struggle, if necessary, to return Tibet to the Tibetans; (3) 'self-determination' (*rang-thag rang-chö*), meaning use of the United Nations to achieve some type of international agreement; and (4) 'peaceful resistance' (*den-pay u-tsug*), meaning a Gandhi-inspired resistance movement to force China to withdraw from Tibet. Although in the end, the referendum was quietly deemed to have failed on procedural grounds, for two years it served to remind Tibetan exiles of the idea of an impending return. Through this myth of return, Tibetan exile officials create a sense of continuity between Tibet in the past (governed by Tibetans), the resettlement camps in the present (governed by the exile administration), and Tibet in the future (under Tibetan control).

Another more subtle way in which the exile administration discursively associates the Tibetan resettlement camps with the Tibetan homelands is through the structure of the Assembly of Tibetan People's Deputies (ATPD), a legislative organization elected from within the Tibetan exile communities. The ATPD is structured to represent the interests not of the various resettlement communities in India and Nepal (such as Jawalakhel, Chialsa, Mussorie, Dharamsala) but rather the various regional and sectarian communities that existed in Tibet as it was governed under the Dalai Lamas. Of the forty-six members of the ATPD, ten represent Tibetans from Central Tibet (*U-tsang*); ten from eastern Tibet (*Kham*); ten from northeastern Tibet (*Amdo*); and two from each of five major sectarian groups (Gelugpa Buddhists, Kagyupa Buddhists, Nyingma Buddhists, Sakya Buddhists, and Bonpos). Of the remaining six members, two represent Tibetans in Europe; one represents Tibetans in North America; and three are subject to appointment by the Dalai Lama. The ATPD is thereby structured with reference largely to the Tibetan homeland rather than to the Tibetan exile communities (with the notable exception of the European and North American representatives). The implication is that the ATPD, although in exile, represents homeland constituencies over which it exercises (or will someday soon exercise) some control. The Tibetan exiles, through this discursive strategy, bridge the spatial disjuncture between the resettlement camps and the Tibetan homelands, avoid the implication that the ATPD poses a challenge to the law-making organizations of the Tibetans' host states, and create a sense of continuity in Tibet's national history.

The discursive association between the Tibetan resettlement camps and the Tibetan homelands has been useful to the Dalai Lama's exile administration, as it has enabled it to engage in its state-building efforts without a challenge to its host states, while simultaneously serving to recruit support for its state-building efforts from within the Tibetan exile community. It thereby helps the Tibetan exiles to maintain domestic sovereignty over the camps without challenging the international legal sovereignty of their host states. It also helps maintain the resettlement camps' multiple-sovereign arrangement without a challenge to the general rule of exclusive sovereignty as the basis of the global political order.

The historical contingencies of the state-building process

Whether or not the Tibetan exiles will ever be able to return to Tibet and construct a Tibetan state in their homelands is a question that no one can, at present, answer definitively. Just as no one could have predicted the rise of the nation-state system,[64] its expansion worldwide,[65] or the transformation of China into a national state,[66] no one can predict what will happen to China and its various territories in the future. Historical contingency is a fundamental part of the state-building process both for the Tibetan exiles and for China's leaders in Tibet.

The fourth theme in the state-building literature that I use the Tibetan case to explore, therefore, is the considerable historical contingency that influences how state-building proceeds. Historical contingency is a long-standing theme in the state-building literature. For Tilly and others, conflict among states is the source of contingency.[67] War, and all of the uncertainties that it unleashes, plays a determining role in which states, and which of many models of the state (feudal, theocratic, mercantile, national), prevail. For Migdal and others, it is conflict within states that creates contingencies in the state-building process. Migdal, for example, explains:

> As the state organization comes into contact with various societal groups, it clashes with and accommodates to different moral orders. These engagements, which occur at numerous junctures, change the social bases and the aims of the state. The state is not a fixed ideological entity. Rather, it embodies an ongoing dynamic, a changing set of goals, as it engages other social groups . . . Resistance offered by other social forces . . . as well as the incorporation of groups into the organization of the state, change its social and ideological underpinnings.[68]

Societal forces, in other words, play as much of a role in the state-building process as the activities of state builders themselves.

Both types of contingency come into play in the state-building efforts of the Tibetan exiles. The Tibetan exile communities came into existence, and are continuously sustained, for example, due to a conflict among states.[69] Conflicts within states, including the People's Republic of China and the Tibetan exiles' host states, continue to influence how state building among the Tibetan exiles proceeds. Historical contingency is a factor in how all states, not just the atypical cases, develop. The plethora of predictions about what the new world order will bring – from the end of the nation-state[70] to the rise of transgovernmentalism[71] to the clash of civilizations[72] – is testimony to the fundamental contingencies of the state-building process.

There are distinct differences between China and the Tibetan exiles in their ability to manage the contingencies of history, however. China has far greater economic resources, military capabilities, institutional capabilities, and the benefits of full diplomatic status, including a permanent seat on the UN Security Council. The Tibetan exiles, quite simply, lack China's capabilities. International events that favored the Tibetan exiles are, in addition, on the wane. US support for the Tibetan exiles, for example, was strongest from 1950 to 1970, when China's foreign and domestic policies led to its diplomatic isolation. Swiss support for the Tibetan exiles was strongest in the 1960s, and even then, it arose more out of the personal involvement of Swiss officials than a coherent China policy. Toni Hagen, the Swiss geologist and development official who initiated Swiss intervention on behalf of the Tibetan exiles, writes of his personal interest in their situation:

> I was deeply impressed by the Tibetan culture in which religion based on a philosophy of tolerance, non-violence, and respect for all living creatures is woven into the fabric of daily life . . . [and] I recalled, knowing it for the outrage it was, the infamous slogan 'the boat is full,' with which Switzerland justified sending back thousands of Jews to certain death in Hitler's Germany during the last war.[73]

Hagen's involvement went against the spirit of Switzerland's 1950 recognition of the People's Republic of China. Swiss involvement began and remains strictly defined as a humanitarian issue.

Since the 1970s, the Tibetan exiles have positioned themselves well within what Madsen describes as an alternative sovereignty regime,[74] meaning unofficial diplomatic relations, the support of non-governmental organizations, and the adoption of liberal political and economic policies favorable to Western governments. The Tibetan exiles, as a result, continue to receive support from Western governments, most notably the United States, as well as from such organizations as Human Rights Watch, Amnesty International, and a plethora of Tibet-specific groups such as the Tibet Information Network and the Tibet Justice Center. These relationships have been able to sustain the Tibetan exiles' state-building efforts, but there are limits to what they can enable. They have not been able to force China into negotiations with the Tibetan exiles over the status of the Tibetan homelands, for example. China has claimed the Tibetan homelands as its own territory, and that claim is consistently supported through the actions and non-actions of other states worldwide.

As a result, the ultimate goal of the Tibetan exiles – the construction of a Tibetan state within the Tibetan homelands – is, at present, dependent upon negotiations with China. Only China can grant the Tibetans the degree of autonomy they seek over the Tibetan homelands. Such negotiations depend, most importantly, on the Dalai Lama, whom China sees as the Tibetan exiles' only real asset. Negotiations with China have been stalled for decades over a number of issues including Tibet's historical status, the status of the Dalai Lama in a future Tibet, and the political activities of the Dalai Lama's exile administration.[75] Until some sort of breakthrough over these issues occurs, it is safe to assume that, for the present, the Tibetan exiles' state-building activities will remain confined to the Tibetan resettlement camps.

One hope that the Tibetan exiles continue to maintain for a substantial change in their political situation is for an impending China crisis, precipitated by China's relationships with Hong Kong and Taiwan and compounded by its efforts at internal economic and political reform. Such a crisis is, indeed, possible. What it would entail for the Tibetans, however, is unknown. It could lead to some form of greater autonomy for Tibet, yet it could just as likely lead to the reinforcement of China's nationalist goals throughout the mainland, including Tibet. China's greater economic, political, and institutional resources render the Tibetans in a far less favorable position to weather a China crisis. The Tibetan exiles can only hope that a China crisis renders the Tibetan homelands too expensive for China to maintain, so that China decides, for its own reasons, to devolve authority over them.

Toward a constructivist view of the state

In the meantime, the Tibetan exiles continue in their state-building activities in the Tibetan resettlement camps in the hope of an imminent return to Tibet. These activities involve not just the imagination of a Tibetan state but also the active construction of the constituent elements of a state within the Tibetan exile communities. The Tibetan exile communities are autonomous; they are governed by a centralized administration; they maintain a taxation system, a social welfare system, an electoral system, and a system of laws and regulations; they engage in a type of foreign relations through the Tibet Office system; and they maintain an embryonic coercive apparatus. They have thereby constructed more than just a government-in-exile; they have constructed a latent state, poised to expand one day into the Tibetan homelands.

The Tibetan exiles are not the only peoples worldwide who have constructed a latent state. The Palestinian case is the most obvious comparative example. The Palestinians developed a latent state first in the East Bank; then in Lebanon, where the Palestinian Liberation Organization exercised greater control throughout the 1970s than even the collapsed Lebanese government itself; and now finally in the West Bank and Gaza, where they seek international recognition as a full fledged member of the international system of states. In order to understand what will ultimately occur with the Tibetan and Palestinian cases, among others, it is important to understand how latent states develop, what supports their ongoing existence, and what their various options are, whether or not they achieve full fledged statehood.

It is for that reason that I propose a constructivist view of the state to account not just for latent states but for the broad range of atypical cases – latent states, nascent states, quasi-states, and collapsed states – that exist worldwide. A constructivist view shifts the locus of analysis from the elements that constitute a state to the underlying relational dynamics that enable those elements to emerge. The presence or absence of certain elements of statehood, such as mutual recognition or a legitimate coercive apparatus, tells us little about how such elements come into being, what supports their existence, or why they fall apart. A constructivist view of the state, in contrast, raises our awareness of the considerable unofficial arrangements that are contracted within and between states and expands our understanding of how state-building proceeds. We may then be in a better position to predict what the uncertainty of the post-Cold War new world order will yield, as we gain an understanding of the alternatives to the nation-state system that are already in existence.

Notes

1 The definition I propose here derives from a number of theories of states and state building, including L. Krader, *Formation of the State*, Englewood Cliffs, NJ: Prentice-Hall, 1968, p. 27; C. Tilly, 'Reflections on the history of European state-making', in C. Tilly (ed.), *The Formation of National States in Western Europe*, Princeton: Princeton University Press, 1975, p. 70; H. Claessen and P. Skalník, 'The early state: theories and hypotheses', in H. Claessen and P. Skalník (eds), *The Early State*, The Hague: Mouton, 1978, pp. 533–96; and R. Cohen, 'Evolution, fission, and the early state', in Claessen and Skalník (eds), *The Early State*, pp. 92–5. My concern here is with theories of state building that acknowledge the agency of the people involved rather than the macro-level environmental or economic conditions that also play a role (hence my preference for the term 'state building' rather than 'state development'). For useful commentaries on the literature on state development writ large, see R. Cohen, 'State origins: a reappraisal', in Claessen and Skalník (eds), *The Early State*, pp. 31–75; and G. Poggi, *The Development of the Modern State*, Stanford: Stanford University Press, 1978.

2 I define the state here in terms of four attributes (a people, a territory, a government, and the capacity to enter foreign relations) following R. H. Cox, *The State in International Relations*, San Francisco: Chandler, 1965, p. 11.

3 J. N. Rosenau, 'The state in an era of cascading politics: wavering concept, widening competence, withering colossus, or weathering change?', in J. A. Caporaso (ed.), *The Elusive State: International and Comparative Perspectives*, Newbury Park, Calif.: Sage Publications, 1989, p. 18.

4 Studies of the Tibetan resettlement camps in India further support the state-building thesis I develop here. For an analysis of the use of Tibetan identity documents in the Tibetan settlement camps in India, for example, see D. M. Devoe, 'Keeping refugee status: a Tibetan perspective', in S. Morgan and E. Colson (eds), *People in Upheaval*, New York: Center for Migration Studies, 1987, pp. 54–65.

5 The most comprehensive description of the structure of the Tibetan exile administration I have seen is Planning Council of the Central Tibetan Administration of His Holiness the Dalai Lama, *Tibetan Resettlement Community Integrated Development Plan, 1995- 2000*, Dharamsala: Central Tibetan Administration, 1994. The

information I present here derives also from personal interviews I conducted with the directors of the various departments of the Dalai Lama's exile administration while living in Dharamsala, India, in the summer of 1994. For further information about the development of the Dalai Lama's exile administration, see also J. F. Avedon, *In Exile from the Land of Snows*, London: Michael Joseph, 1984, p. 107; Dalai Lama XIV, *Freedom in Exile: The Autobiography of the Dalai Lama*, New York: HarperCollins, 1990, p. 166; and R. French, 'The new snow lion: the Tibetan government-in-exile in India', in Y. Shain (ed.), *Governments-in-Exile in Contemporary World Politics*, New York: Routledge, 1991. The estimate of the number of employees in the exile administration I provide here derives from L. Sangay, 'Tibet: Exiles' Journey', *Journal of Democracy*, 2003, vol. 14, 119–30.

6 Sangay, 'Tibet: exiles' journey', p. 123 reports that the Dalai Lama made 183 trips to 57 countries from 1954 to 2000.

7 See <http://www.tibet.com>, the Tibetan exile administration's official website, for ongoing changes to the list.

8 For an account of Taiwan's unofficial diplomatic exchanges, see R. Madsen, 'The struggle for sovereignty between China and Taiwan', in S. Krasner (ed.), *Problematic Sovereignty*, pp. 141–93.

9 For an account of the PRC's unofficial diplomatic exchanges prior to the 1970s, see Madsen, ibid.

10 Avedon, *In Exile*, p. 129.

11 Y. Shain, *The Frontier of Loyalty: Political Exiles in the Age of the Nation-State*, Middletown, Conn.: Wesleyan University Press, 1989.

12 For details on the Palestinians' state-building efforts, see L. A. Brand, *Palestinians in the Arab World: Institution Building and the Search for a State*, New York: Columbia University Press, 1988; M. Beker and R. van Oordt, *The Palestinians in Lebanon: Contradictions of State-Formation in Exile*, Amsterdam: Middle East Research Associates, 1991; B. Schiff, *Refugees into the Third Generation: UN Aid to Palestinians*, Syracuse: Syracuse University Press, 1995; D. E. Arzt, *Refugees into Citizens: Palestinians and the End of the Arab-Israeli Conflict*, Washington, DC: Brookings Institution Press, 1997; M. Heller, *Toward a Palestinian State*, Tel Aviv: Jaffee Center for Strategic Studies, 1997; G. Robinson, *Building a Palestinian State: The Incomplete Revolution*, Bloomington: Indiana University Press, 1997; and H. Frisch, *Countdown to Statehood: Palestinian State Formation in the West Bank and Gaza*, Albany: State University of New York Press, 1998.

13 For arguments about the role of coercion in the state-building process, see C. Tilly, 'Reflections on the History of European State-Making'; C. Tilly, *Coercion, Capital, and European States, AD 990- 1990*, Cambridge, Mass.: Basil Blackwell, 1990; and R. L. Carneiro, 'A theory of the origin of the state', *Science*, 1970, vol. 169, 733–8. For various arguments about the role of economic control, see S. F. Nadel, 'The Kede: a riverain state in Northern Nigeria', in M. Fortes and E. E. Evans-Pritchard (eds), *African Political Systems*, London: Oxford University Press, 1940, pp. 164–95; K. Wittfogel, 'The theory of oriental society', in M. Fried (ed.), *Readings in Anthropology*, New York: Crowell, 1968, pp. 179–200; G. Ardant, 'Financial policy and economic infrastructure of modern states and nations', in C. Tilly (ed.), *The Formation of National States*; and C. Tilly, *Coercion, Capital, and European States*, pp. 164–242. For arguments about the role of ideological control in state-building, see C. Geertz, *Negara: The Theatre State in Nineteenth-Century Bali*, Princeton: Princeton University Press, 1980; B. Cohn, *Colonialism and Its Forms of Knowledge: The British in India*, Princeton: Princeton University Press, 1996; and J. C. Scott, *Seeing Like a State: How Certain Schemes to Improve the Human Condition Have Failed*, New Haven: Yale University Press, 1998.

14 For an analysis of Taiwan's efforts to secure mutual recognition, see Madsen, 'The struggle for sovereignty'.

15 Cohn, *Colonialism and Its Forms of Knowledge*.

16 J. Boli, 'Human rights or state expansion? Cross-national definitions of constitutional rights, 1870–1970', in G. M. Thomas *et al.* (eds), *Institutional Structure:
   Constituting State, Society, and the Individual*, London: Sage Publications, 1987,
   pp. 15–49; S. Huntington, *The Third Wave: Democratization in the Late Twentieth
   Century*, Norman: University of Oklahoma Press, 1991; L. Malkki, 'Citizens of
   humanity: internationalism and the imagined community of nations', *Diaspora: A
   Journal of Transnational Studies*, 1994, vol. 3, 41–68.

17 Boli, 'Human rights'.

18 A.-M. Slaughter, 'The real new world order', *Foreign Affairs*, 1997, vol. 76, 183–97.
   For an analysis of Meiji Japan's accommodation of Western institutional forms,
   see D. E. Westney, *Imitation and Innovation: The Transfer of Western Organizational Patterns to Meiji Japan*, Cambridge, Mass.: Harvard University Press, 1987.

19 R. H. Jackson, *Quasi-States: Sovereignty, International Relations, and the Third
   World*, Cambridge: Cambridge University Press, 1990; J. Ferguson, *The Anti-
   Politics Machine: Development, Depoliticization, and Bureaucratic Power in
   Lesotho*, Cambridge: Cambridge University Press, 1990.

20 For accounts of the loan negotiations, see David E. Sanger, 'U.S. Is Set to Lend $3
   Billion to Help Bolster Indonesia', *New York Times*, 31 October 1997; David E.
   Sanger, 'U.S. Warning to Indonesia: Comply on Aid', *New York Times*, 8 January
   1998; Seth Mydans, 'Pressed by I.M.F., Indonesia Accepts Economic Reforms',
   New York Times, 15 January 1998; and Seth Mydans, 'Indonesia Agrees to
   I.M.F.'s Tough Medicine', *New York Times*, 16 January 1998.

21 I. Wallerstein, *The Modern World System: Capitalist Agriculture and the Origins of
   the World Economy in the Sixteenth Century*, New York: Academic Press, 1975;
   Jackson, *Quasi-States*.

22 Jackson, *Quasi-States*, p. 27.

23 Seven of the camps were legally registered as the property of the Nepal Red Cross
   Society. They are the focus for my analysis. The other five camps were negotiated
   under extenuating circumstances, as part of the process of demilitarizing the CIA-
   supported Tibetan guerrilla movement in northern Nepal. Their establishment
   and continuing status are more ambiguous.

24 For accounts of the Tibetan exiles' early years in Nepal, see A. Forbes, *Settlements
   of Hope*, Cambridge, Mass.: Cultural Survival, 1989; H. D. Joshi, *A History of the
   Tibetan Refugees in Nepal*, Kathmandu: Swiss Association for Technical Assistance, 1983; T. Hagen, *Building Bridges to the Third World: Memories of Nepal,
   1950- 1992*, Delhi: Book Faith India, 1994; and A. Frechette, *Tibetans in Nepal:
   The Dynamics of International Assistance among a Community in Exile*, New York:
   Berghahn Books, 2002.

25 Walter Jutzi, Swiss intergovernmental organization official stationed in Nepal
   from 1973 to 1978 and 1990 to 1996, personal communication, 3 May 1995.

26 Walter Jutzi, personal communication, 3 May 1995. It is the 1961 Industrial
   Enterprises Act that restricts ownership of small-scale village and cottage industries to Nepali citizens only.

27 Hagen, *Building Bridges*, p. 206.

28 Nepal defines 'development-related' in such a way as to include much of its regu-
   lar budget. The Nepal Aid Group, which includes Switzerland, provides much of
   the funding. For information on Nepal's development expenditures, see K. Guru-
   Gharana, 'Strategies for Poverty Alleviation in Nepal and the Role of Foreign
   Aid', paper presented at a seminar on the political economy of small states,
   Kathmandu, Nepal, 1995, p. 11.

29 Joshi, *A History*.

30 The rate is higher for Tibetans resettled in Western countries. Tibetan exiles in the
   United States, for example, are required to pay two dollars per month.

31 Avedon, *In Exile*, pp. 126–8.
32 Frechette, *Tibetans in Nepal*, pp. 74–88.
33 Jackson, *Quasi-States*; S. L. Woodward, 'Compromised sovereignty to create sovereignty: is Dayton Bosnia a futile exercise or emerging model?', in S. Krasner (ed.), *Problematic Sovereignty: Contested Rules and Political Possibilities*, New York: Columbia University Press, 2001, pp. 253–300.
34 T. Winichakul, *Siam Mapped: A History of the Geo-Body of a Nation*, Honolulu: University of Hawaii Press, 1994; Cohn, *Colonialism and Its Forms of Knowledge*.
35 Ferguson, *The Anti-Politics Machine*.
36 Boli, 'Human rights'; Malkki, 'Citizens of humanity'.
37 Slaughter, 'The real new world order', p. 184.
38 J. K. Knaus, *Orphans of the Cold War: America and the Tibetan Struggle for Survival*, New York: Public Affairs, 1999, p. 252.
39 P. Duara, *Rescuing History from the Nation: Questioning Narratives of Modern China*, Chicago: University of Chicago Press, 1995; W. Tu, 'Beyond the enlightenment mentality: a Confucian perspective on ethics, migration, and global stewardship', *International Migration Review*, 1996, vol. 30, 58–75; R. Wong, *China Transformed: Historical Change and the Limits of European Experience*, Ithaca, NY: Cornell University Press, 1997.
40 Tu, 'Beyond the enlightenment mentality', p. 70.
41 Scott, *Seeing Like a State*, p. 32.
42 M. Nowak, *Tibetan Refugees: Youth and the New Generation of Meaning*, New Brunswick, NJ: Rutgers University Press, 1984; Y. Shain, *The Frontier of Loyalty: Political Exiles in the Age of the Nation-State*, Middletown, Conn.: Wesleyan University Press, 1989.
43 Goldstein, 'Serfdom and mobility', p. 522.
44 Ibid., pp. 524–5.
45 Ibid., p. 522.
46 My analysis here benefits from T. Shakya, 'Politicisation and the Tibetan language', in R. Barnett and S. Akiner (eds), *Resistance and Reform in Tibet*, Bloomington: Indiana University Press, 1994.
47 All translations that follow derive from M. Goldstein, *Tibetan-English Dictionary of Modern Tibetan*, Kathmandu: Ratna Pustak Bhandar, 1983, with reference also to S. C. Das, *A Tibetan-English Dictionary*, Delhi: Sri Satguru Publications, 1902.
48 M. Goldstein, 'Freedom, servitude, and the servant-serf Nyima: a re-rejoinder to Miller', *The Tibet Journal*, 1989, vol. 14, 56–61, p. 57.
49 D. Philpott, *Revolutions in Sovereignty: How Ideas Shaped Modern International Relations*, Princeton: Princeton University Press, 2001, p. 16.
50 D. Philpott, 'Ideas and the evolution of sovereignty', in S. Hashmi (ed.), *State Sovereignty: Change and Persistence in International Relations*, University Park: The Pennsylvania State University Press, 1997, pp. 15–49; Philpott, *Revolutions in Sovereignty*.
51 Jackson, *Quasi-States*.
52 S. Hashmi, 'Introduction', in S. Hashmi (ed.), *State Sovereignty*.
53 Philpott, *Revolutions in Sovereignty*, p. 31.
54 Ibid., p. 41.
55 Winichakul, *Siam Mapped*.
56 M. Oksenberg, 'The issue of sovereignty in the Asian historical context', in S. Krasner (ed.), *Problematic Sovereignty*, pp. 83–104.
57 J. Gow, 'Shared sovereignty, enhanced security: lessons from the Yugoslav war', in S. Hashmi (ed.), *State Sovereignty*, p. 154.
58 Woodward, 'Compromised sovereignty'.
59 Philpott, *Revolutions in Sovereignty*.
60 S. Krasner, *Sovereignty: Organized Hypocrisy*, Princeton: Princeton University

Press, 1999; S. Krasner, 'Problematic sovereignty', in S. Krasner (ed.), *Problematic Sovereignty*, pp. 1–23.

61 Krasner, *Sovereignty*, pp. 25–42.

62 Krasner, *Sovereignty*; Krasner, 'Problematic sovereignty'.

63 I draw here on the concept of the 'mythico-history' to understand the activities of the Tibetan exiles. See L. Malkki, *Purity and Exile: Violence, Memory, and National Cosmology among Hutu Refugees in Tanzania*, Chicago: University of Chicago Press, 1995, for an account of how refugees use mythico-histories in the construction of their collective national past (she analyzes Hutu in Tanzania). Unlike Malkki, I credit political leadership for the construction of mythico-histories not the structure of the resettlement camps. Although the structure of the camps plays some role in facilitating national consciousness among the Tibetan exiles, political leadership plays a much greater role. Political leadership helps to unite the various resettlement camps throughout India and Nepal, for example, and to propagate the same 'mythico-histories' within them.

64 Tilly, 'Reflections'; H. Spruyt, *The Sovereign State and Its Competitors: An Analysis of Systems Change*, Princeton: Princeton University Press, 1994.

65 Jackson, *Quasi-States*; Philpott, 'Ideas'; Philpott, *Revolutions in Sovereignty*.

66 Duara, *Rescuing History*; Wong, *China Transformed*; Madsen, 'The struggle for sovereignty'.

67 Tilly, 'Reflections'.

68 J. S. Migdal, 'The state in society: an approach to struggles for domination', in J. S. Migdal *et al.* (eds), *State Power and Social Forces: Domination and Transformation in the Third World*, Cambridge: Cambridge University Press, 1994, p. 12.

69 Avedon, *In Exile*; M. Goldstein, *The Snow Lion and the Dragon: China, Tibet, and the Dalai Lama*, Berkeley: University of California Press, 1997; Knaus, *Orphans of the Cold War*.

70 K. Ohmae, *The End of the Nation State: The Rise of Regional Economies*, New York: The Free Press, 1995.

71 Slaughter, 'The real new world order'.

72 S. Huntington, *The Clash of Civilizations and the Remaking of World Order*, New York: Simon and Schuster, 1996.

73 Hagen, *Building Bridges*.

74 Madsen, 'The struggle for sovereignty'.

75 Goldstein, *The Snow Lion*.

7 Nation, ethnicity, and contending discourse in the Malaysian state

Shamsul A. B. and Sity Daud

Discussions on the terms and concepts of 'state' and 'nation-state' in most political science textbooks, rarely take into consideration the variations that exist in contemporary global context of 'state' and 'nation-state' formations. Often, these two terms 'state' and 'nation-state' have been used interchangeably, mostly for pedagogic convenience sacrificing epistemological clarity. This, we believe, has led to the general assumption that when one uses the term 'state' one also means 'nation-state'. At times, some even consider 'state' and 'nation' as two of the same thing.

We wish to avoid this epistemological flaw because the experience of decolonization among independent former colonies tells us a different ontological story compared to that of Europe, the birthplace of the 'modern nation'.[1] We learnt from the postcolonial countries that, first, we cannot assume that the term 'state' could be used interchangeably with the term 'nation-state' because of the wide range of historical trajectories shaping the postcolonial countries. Thus, second, the term 'nation-state' could be used in a number of different fashions. For example, we are aware of the existence of 'state-nation', such as Singapore, in which the 'state', instead of society, not only defines and engineers but also reinvents the 'nation' almost at will to suit the changing demand of the 'state'. In some other cases, there are 'nations-without-state', such as in the case of the Moros of the Southern Philippines who have a 'nation', or a few competing 'nations-of-intent', but who have yet to successfully establish a full-fledged *bona fide* 'state'. Of course, there are also cases of 'states-without-nation'. Malaysia is one such case.

The existence of these variations has conceptual and empirical implications that we intend to address in this chapter. Conceptually, the 'state', defined as 'an entity that has a rule of a law, a territory and citizenship', especially in postcolonial countries, could be separated from the 'nation', defined as 'an imagined community imbued with a notion of a nation-of-intent', because the former has already existed during the colonial period fulfilling colonial needs. Once a country achieved its independence and despite the fact that the natives are at the helm, its main structure of governance remains the same as that of the colonial state.

Depending on how the independence was negotiated, the 'nation' or 'how the nation should be', in most postcolonial countries, remains an unfinished agenda because the struggle for independence during the colonial era rarely takes a homogenous form, especially, in a multiethnic or multicultural societies, such as Fiji, Malaysia, Guyana, Sri Lanka, Congo, India, Pakistan, Nigeria, Sudan, and many more. In these countries, the 'state' exists for many decades after independence without an established nation. Sometimes, bloody civil wars, such as the Biafran War in Nigeria, break out because different ethnic groups within a postcolonial country prefer to pursue their own nation-of-intent.[2] In Asia, as in the case of India, the Muslim anticolonial nationalist movement broke away to form its own state called Pakistan, consisting of West and East Pakistan. A few decades later East Pakistan broke away to form what we know today as Bangladesh.

The Malaysian case is also an interesting one to consider for our conceptual and empirical scrutiny.[3] It is made up of a two-tier federation. In the first tier it is the Federation of Malaya which consists of 11 provinces that became independent in 1957. The second, the Federation of Malaysia, consists of the Federation of Malaya (physically located on the Malay peninsula) plus the provinces of Sabah and Sarawak (both located on the island of Borneo) declared independent in 1963. Not only is the issue of the 'nation' separate from the 'state', even the existence of the state remains a conditional one, in terms of rule of law and citizenship, and this is written into the Malaysian constitution.[4] For instance, Malaysians born in the Federation of Malaya have to have an international passport, or a special document, to enter Sabah and Sarawak. They cannot stay more than three months without a special visa. Should they want to take up employment in Sabah and Sarawak they, like other foreign workers, have to obtain a work permit from the respective provincial government.

We would like to argue, based upon the empirical evidence outlined above, that the 'modern states' and/or 'nation-states' in Asia, and other postcolonial countries, are a distinct lot, for historical and a host of other reasons, when compared to the European ones which have been for so long the main conceptual and empirical source, indeed benchmark, for theorization in the construction of theories about 'the state' and 'nation-state' for the rest of the world.[5] Indeed, in many of the Asian cases, the 'state' and the 'nation' are two quite separate entities. The former is solidly established and usually promotes a version of the latter. The latter, on the other hand, is often being contested by different social groups, hence the proliferation of notions of the nation-of-intent.

A theoretically and empirically informed analysis on the state of modern state making in Asia has to take cognizance of the uniqueness of the patterns of the modern state, nation-state, state-nation, state-without-nation, and nation-without-state. The variety and hybridism of Asian forms of the state and the nation has to be incorporated in the general theorization exercise about modern state making. This chapter on state making in Malaysia is meant as an empirical contribution to support the argument put forward above.

This chapter is therefore a modest attempt to 'reconnect' the 'nation' and the 'state' in the discourse on state formation in Malaysia. It is motivated by a deceptively simple idea put across by Gellner[6] which would describe Malaysian state formation as an attempt by Malaysians, of various ethnic and class backgrounds, to grasp 'the national principle' of seeking to make 'the cultural and the political unit congruent'. And that attempt, ontologically, has been articulated in the contestation of meanings or notions about different forms of what we would call 'nations-of-intent', informed by an epistemological understanding that the Malaysian state is a variant of a developmentalist capitalist state.

The presentation begins with an outline of Malaysia's effort to chart the trajectory of its modernization project, particularly its unfinished political agenda, namely to create 'a united Malaysian nation-state', a *Bangsa Malaysia*, by the year 2020. Then we move on to discuss the ongoing debate amongst various social groups, both *bumiputera* and non-*bumiputera*, regarding the kind of Malaysian nation-state that each is trying to promote. The origin and social roots of these nations-of-intent will be described. Finally, the implications of the Malaysian case on the effort to theorize about the modern state and nation-state will be examined.

Malaysia's modernization project: an unfinished political agenda

At independence, Malaysian society comprised three major ethnic communities, namely, the indigenous community or *bumiputera* (literally sons of the soil), who accounted for 50 per cent of the population, and two sizeable immigrant communities, one Chinese (37 per cent) and the other Indian (11 per cent). Since then, the Censuses of 1970, 1980, and 1990 have shown that, in spite of the general increase in the population, from about 10 to 18 million, the ethnic composition has not changed significantly. However, to most Malaysians, it is the *bumiputera* and non-*bumiputera* ethnic divide that is perceived as significant, used in official government documents as well as in the idiom of everyday interaction, despite the fact that there is heterogeneity within both. Nonetheless, colloquially, the public refers to this ethnic divide simply as '*bumi*' and non-*bumi*, reflecting the delicate demographic balance between the two categories, each constituting about 50 per cent of the population. This has important wider implications in the social life of Malaysians, especially in political terms.[7]

One of these involves the attempt to make 'the cultural principle' (read the different 'notions of nations') and the political unit (read 'the state') congruent. At the level of 'authority-defined social reality', which is *bumiputera*-dominated, the cultural principle question, or in popular idiom referred to as the issue of 'national identity', is perceived by the state as a non-issue because its basis and content has been spelt out in a number of policy documents within the framework of the Malaysian constitution. It is a *bumiputera-*defined cultural principle that has privileged many aspects of *bumiputera* culture as the 'core' of the Malaysian national identity while recognizing, if peripherally, the cultural symbols of other ethnic groups.

On the other hand, at the level of 'everyday social reality', the authority-defined cultural principle has been challenged by three groups, namely, the non-*bumiputera* group, led by the Chinese, and two *bumiputera* ones, the non-Muslim *bumiputera* group and the radical Islamic *bumiputera* group, each offering its own nation-of-intent, that is, its own vision of what the cultural principle should be for the political unit (the state), based on a particular ideological framework. The non-*bumiputera* rejects the *bumiputera*-based and *bumiputera*-defined cultural principle in preference for a more 'pluralized' one, in which the culture of each ethnic group in Malaysia is accorded a position equal to that of the *bumiputera*. For instance, the Chinese suggest that Chinese language and rituals should be considered as an integral part of the cultural principle or national identity.[8] Although both the non-Muslim *bumiputera* and the radical Islamic *bumiputera* accept the authority-defined *bumiputera*-based cultural principle, the former suggest that Christianity and 'native religions' be accorded equal status to that of Islam, as components within it; the latter, on the contrary, rejects what it sees as the secular, modernist Islamic component of the identity in preference for a 'truer and purer' Islam, hence the idea of the Islamic state. The Kadazan of Sabah argue forcefully for the non-Muslim *bumiputera* case and the Parti Islam of Kelantan for the radical Islamic *bumiputera* group.

Those who believe that Malaysia is an authoritarian state, with *bumiputera* hegemony well entrenched, view the opposition to the authority-defined cultural principle as an anomaly, a social aberration, or as minority voices, which the state allows as an act of benevolence or a form of 'social tokenism'. This view is informed, conceptually, by a 'benevolent state' thesis which stresses the fact that *bumiputera* dominance is a foregone conclusion. Hence dissenting voices find space at the behest of the *bumiputera* ruling class, who, in return, use this to demonstrate that 'democracy' is well and alive in Malaysia. We find that this approach, albeit unwittingly, favors a kind of master narrative that downplays and, in an ironic twist, belittles many of the oppositions and differences of human experience that characterize every-day human life in Malaysia. Their 'hegemonic developmentalist' approach ignores most of what is going on behind the public scene.

We find it more instructive to give equal weight to the dominant and the dominated, each representing a different view or approach, and each articulating dissimilar interests. This opens the way for uncertainties, ruptures, and tensions. With such an approach we are in a better position to highlight the alternatives, their attendant differences, however slight, the distances between them, and most significantly the dialogue between them, fruitful or futile, eventful or mundane. As one would have noted from the above, this is the strategy of our presentation. It is an effort to make sense of dissenting voices in the Malaysian present-day social milieu with regard to the question of 'the cultural principle'. In doing so, we are offering a discourse analysis on the origin, social roots, and bureaucratic management of contemporary contestation regarding Malaysia's cultural principle or national identity: a Malaysia which is in a hurry to realize its 'modernization project'.

We have chosen this strategy for two main reasons. First, most analyses of Malaysia's modernization project tend to emphasize the material process. Whereas this, of course, is necessary, we believe that we should also try to grasp the ideological, and in many ways 'abstract' contestation that goes with modernization. There is a need to explore what happens in the political space, beyond politics of parties and numbers, particularly in the realm of ideas, symbols, and perceptions. Second, in so doing we have outlined some of the origins of the present 'abstract' ideological struggle over the definition of the cultural principle that should underpin the functioning of the political unit, both amongst the elites and nonelites. The latter are particularly concerned about the practical consequences of various concepts of community for their everyday lives and the future, such as their children's education, the usefulness of their mother tongue, and other cultural practices. Such concerns, mundane as they seem, are closely linked to the larger issue of Malaysia's future as a nation-state.

Broadly speaking, Malaysia's 'modernization project' has two interconnected main components, the economic and the political. If the economic component is driven by the need to industrialize, the political one is motivated by the need to realize a nation-state. To achieve both has been the central objective of Malaysia's modernization project.

Politicians, policy makers, and most informed observers on Malaysia seem to hold the view that the economic component of Malaysia's modernization effort, as of the last decade, is not as problematic as the political one. Such a view has emerged against the background of Malaysia's spectacular economic growth, particularly from mid-1980s to mid-1990s. But we do know that the Malaysian economy, successful as it is, has a number of weaknesses, as the 1997 economic crises revealed. However, it has been argued that the political difficulties are more serious than the economic ones and they are perceived as obstacles to Malaysia's further economic success. In other words, Malaysia's achievement thus far has been perceived as one-sided, heavily economic, and not matched by a similar achievement in the political sphere (read state/nation formation).

Against such a perceived background as well as a concern for the long-term survival of the society, Malaysia's Prime Minister, Dr Mahathir Mohamed, in 1991, introduced his famous *Wawasan 2020*, or Vision 2020, which simply means that in the year 2020 Mahathir hopes Malaysia to be an advanced industrialized country with an established nation-state, hence a fully modern society.[9] He listed a number of challenges and obstacles that Malaysia has to overcome in order to achieve this vision. It is quite clear that, to him, the political challenge of creating a united Malaysian nation, or a *Bangsa Malaysia*, is the greater and critical one compared to the economic challenge of sustaining the current level of economic growth in Malaysia's effort to become modern.

The fact that Mahathir emphasized the need to create a united Malaysian nation implies that Malaysia is still 'one state with several nations', meaning that in the broad economic sense it is a coherent variant of a capitalist entity but in the political and ideological sense it is still searching for a parallel coherence because there are strong competing nations-of-intent. The political struggle in Malaysia, if put in Gellnerian terms, is over whether or not it is able to make 'the cultural and the political unit' congruent.

Competing nations-of-intent in Malaysia

By nation-of-intent we mean a more or less precisely defined idea of the form of a nation-state, that is its territory, population, language, culture, symbols, and institutions. The idea must be shared by a number of people who perceive themselves as members of that nation, and who feel that it unites them. A nation-of-intent may imply a radical transformation of a given state, and the exclusion or inclusion of certain groups of people. It may also imply the creation of a new state, but it does not necessarily imply an aspiration for political self-rule on the part of the group of people who are advancing their nation-of-intent. It may be an inclusive construct, open to others, and which is employed as the basis for a political platform voicing dissent or a challenge to the established notion of nation. In any case, the concept nation-of-intent depicts an idea of a nation-state that still needs to be constructed or reconstructed. It promises the citizens (or some of them) an opportunity to participate in a 'grand project' which they can claim as theirs. It therefore bridges the authority-defined and the everyday-defined idea of a nation. In the Malaysian case, as admitted by Mahathir, the 'united Malaysian nation-state' is yet to be born. Hence various social groups in Malaysia can still voice their different nations-of-intent.

In some aspects, conceptually, 'nation-of-intent' is not dissimilar to Anderson's concept of 'imagined political community'.[10] By 'imagined', he does not necessarily mean 'invented', but rather the members of the said community 'will never know most of their fellow-members, meet them, or even hear them, yet in the minds of each lives the image of their communion'. However, nation-of-intent is a more open-ended concept. It is more positive, proactive, non-deterministic, and forward-looking. It has a programmatic plan of action articulated in *real politik* which has, in the Malaysian case, emerged not only from a historical context of anticolonialism but also in the postcolonial era. In the latter it serves as an alternative way of formulating political intentions even though, mostly, it remains at the discourse level.

However, in a number of cases, especially in particular localities, the idea of advancing alternative nations-of-intent has found concrete expression, hence political space.

This is what has happened in the local provinces of Kelantan and Sabah. In both provinces, the local ruling party, which opposes the Malaysian National Front Party-dominated government, has made serious attempts not only to continue to articulate its own nation-of-intent but also to implement some aspects of it locally. Even though these attempts have met with limited success, they have demonstrated that it is possible to have and hold on to one's nation-of-intent and implement it within the so-called 'authoritarian' political context in Malaysia. It is in this sense that the Malaysian situation, in some ways, is not unlike the African one. If the latter has been complicated by 'tribal nationalism' thus giving rise to a situation described as 'one state, many nationalisms', the Malaysian case could be described as a situation of 'one state, several nations', or more precisely, nations-of-intent.[11]

The concept of a united Malaysian nation, proposed by Mahathir, could be interpreted in two ways: first, to mean 'the nation as a cultural community', a kind of political innovation which suggests the idea of rural and urban, intra- and interethnic, and interclass solidarity (clearly, here Mahathir is not using the term 'nation' in the traditional 'aspiration for political self-rule' sense); and, second, to mean the construction of a 'national identity', hence 'national integration'. In fact, the latter has been the overriding, but as yet not realized, objective of the New Economic Policy, which was launched in 1971, implemented over two decades, and ended in 1990.

Some observers have said that Mahathir's concept of *Bangsa Malaysia* is not really different from the one proposed by Lee Kuan Yew in 1963, namely a 'Malaysian Malaysia' nation, when he was chief minister of Singapore and Singapore was still in the Federation of Malaysia. However, some Malay bureaucratic intellectuals have contended that Mahathir's concept is qualitatively different. Whereas Lee Kuan Yew argued for a nation-state in which everyone, irrespective of race, color, and creed, would enjoy equal status, Mahathir argues for a nation-state in which the constitutionally recognized special position of the *bumiputera*, hence *bumiputera* political dominance, is retained and accepted by all Malaysians.

Therefore, it could be said that the shaping of the political agenda of Malaysia's modernization project, as outlined by Mahathir, is contextualized within the existing legal-bureaucratic state structures, namely, the Malaysian constitution and the federalist nature of the state. Lee Kuan Yew's 'Malaysian Malaysia' agenda, on the other hand, demands a radical constitutional reform and perhaps the formation of an 'absolutist' unitary state, such as the one in Singapore, which, according to many analysts, has not really been a 'Singaporean Singapore'. In spite of that, the Democratic Action Party (DAP), the Chinese-controlled main opposition political party in Malaysia, has continued, from the late 1960s until the last general election of 2004, to call for a 'Malaysian Malaysia' as its nation-of-intent.

Since it is unlikely that a radical constitutional reform will take place in Malaysia, by implication the formation of a unitary state in the mold of a 'Malaysian Malaysia' is improbable. But, in Mahathir's opinion, there is no reason why Malaysians should not strive to create a 'united Malaysia nation-state' and build their own 'national identity'. Ironically, it is this very suggestion that keeps the debate open, about the kind of *Bangsa Malaysia* the country should have, or at least that is the perception of many social groups in contemporary Malaysia. Hence the dialogue between various nations-of-intent is alive and well in Malaysia at present, arguably, in a redefined political space. Therefore, it is not surprising that elites from various ethnic groups in Malaysia continue to articulate different nations-of-intent. These notions cannot be dismissed as wishful thinking, because some are actively articulated and operationalized in various institutional forms, such as through political parties, NGOs, and cultural organizations.

Conclusion

This chapter has been a modest attempt to reconnect the discourse on 'state' and 'nation' in the context of Malaysian studies motivated by the Gellnerian idea that state making in Malaysia is informed by an attempt to grasp 'the national principle' through making 'the cultural and the political unit congruent'. We have done this by locating this attempt in a wider sociological context, namely, 'the modernization project' of developing countries (read Malaysia), in which, besides the economic program, the political program of nation-state building, hence the national identity issue, is a part.

Many studies have advanced the argument that nationalist ideology often emerges as a reaction to industrialization and the fragmentation of society that it brings. The state realizes that, on the one hand, kinship ideology, feudalism, and religion are no longer capable of organizing people, and yet, on the other, the relatively new industrial system of production urgently requires a kind of sociocultural homogenization of the population to prepare on a large scale, a continuous pool of skillful workers. The success of the process of homogenization is dependent on the success of a mass education system, which is supposed to introduce 'national consciousness', and create cohesion and loyalty amongst individuals involved in a densely populated social system. A 'nationalist ideology' or 'nationalism' is often seen, in this context, as being able to fulfill these cultural and political requirements for what is essentially a materialist objective.

It could be argued that a nationalist ideology is functional for the state for two main reasons; first, it recreates a sentiment of 'nationhood', that is, a feeling of wholeness and continuity with the past, and, second, it may come to terms with the negative consequences of modernity, particularly, the ruptured relationship between individual and society hence alienation resulting from industrialization. 'Nationhood' begets 'national identity', which are both a political ideology and a faith for which previously people have been willing to sacrifice their lives. But, in the context of the newly emerging economies, such as Malaysia, would the state expect its citizens to die for the sake of achieving a statistical target of 'economic growth'? Herein lies the problem which the state faces in introducing a relatively new nationalist ideology in the post-Cold War era in countries such as Malaysia, that are solely motivated by a modernization project intent on transforming the country, through industrialization, into a developed modern nation.

The proclamation by the Malaysian state that there is an urgent need to have created a 'united Malaysian nation-state' with a *Bangsa Malaysia* identity by the year 2020, is a conscious effort on its part to foster a new 'nationalist ideology' to preempt its transformation to an industrialized developed status which, it believes, is now well on its way. Interestingly, the realization of this 'identity' has been put across by the state as the ultimate 'challenge' for all Malaysians; by implication, should this ideology introduced by the urban elites fail, the burden of the blame will fall on the mass of citizens. However, the real challenge is to seek a middle ground or a compromise between an authority-defined nation, framed within the context of *bumiputera* dominance (as articulated by a particular group within the *bumiputera*), and the everyday ideas about nations-of-intent propagated by both the various *bumiputera* and non-*bumiputera* groups. Some of the latter have their social roots deep in the past and others in the recent postcolonial circumstances.

The intervention by the 'new' middle class, in the form of perpetuating ethnicized social scientific knowledge framed in the nation-of-intent perspective, does not help this attempt to find a middle ground. The fact remains that irrespective of ethnic groups, what is being proposed and actively promoted has been a variety of nations-of-intent that could form Malaysia's future 'nationalist ideology' and 'national identity'. The concept of nation-of-intent is analytically useful to understand the contradictions within the general discourse on 'nationalism', 'nationalist ideology', and 'nationhood' in the societies of emerging industrial economies such as in the Asian region, as evident from the Malaysian case. It may also assist us to understand that particular discourse in a more positive light, separating analytically the authority-defined nation-of-intent from the everyday-defined forms, and how these two sets of nations-of-intent are articulated interests and how the state and people come to terms with that of the other. It would also lead to a more interesting exercise in the theorizing process of state making in Asia.

For instance, in Malaysia today the main problem in the *bumiputera*-defined nation-of-intent called *Bangsa Malaysia* is that it has been perceived by non-*bumiputera* as being imbued with strong 'acculturationist', even 'assimilationist', tendencies and the latter prefer the state to adopt a more accommodative position, thus proposing a 'pluralized' nation, where no one single ethnic community predominates. Political, economic, and demographic factors have allowed such a debate to proceed within Malaysia without creating open tension or enmity. Some could argue that perhaps such a debate is not possible in other countries with different historical and structural circumstances and could lead to conflict and bloodshed. However, we wish to argue that such a view, though partially valid, is too 'alarmist' and, in fact, echoes the position of the status quo within the state.

In a postcolonial society, such as the one in Malaysia, when modern institutions and practices have already become 'traditions', 'pillars of authority', and 'measurement of social authenticity', when time and space have been transformed by globalization, creating macro large-scale systems and unleashing a host of contradictions at the micro level, and when everyday 'transnationalist' existence continues to question and challenge the functionality of the state, it is impossible for the state and its authority-defined social reality to impose totally its presence on the more diffused and fragmented everyday social reality of the masses except in a draconian and authoritarian way. Within such a context, the contest may not be in the arena of *realpolitik* but at the discourse level, where concepts like nation-of-intent may become extremely useful not only to express dissent but also resistance in a subtle way.

In conclusion, we find that the Malaysian case presented in this chapter has provided us significant pointers if we were to theorize about modern state making in Asia and beyond, in at least three different ways. First, it is always helpful to treat the 'state' and the 'nation' as two separate analytical constructs and social entities which are actively engaged with each other in the process of state making. This is the result of the historical difficulties confronted by the various social groups as well as the ruling regime to grasp 'the national principle' of seeking to make 'the cultural and the political unit congruent' as a consequence of being in a country and society which is an ex-colony. Second, in order to resolve the said historical difficulties, a variety and hybridism of Asian forms of the state and the nation came to be created in due process. As such, the existence of a variety and hybridism of modern states in Asia has to be taken into consideration and to be incorporated in the effort to theorize about the modern state, in general, and in Asia, in particular. Third, the transplanting of the European institutions, such as the modern state during the colonial period, in Asian societies involved a complex process of embedding, namely, into the local socio-political and cultural mold.[12] Therefore, it should not come as a surprise at all that the imported 'modern state' and 'nation-state' idea and practice that reached Asia came to be transformed as they began to get embedded and rooted in a variety of local contexts.

Notes

1 For a recent interesting discussion on decolonization and state making in Southeast Asia, see M. Frey, R. W. Pruessen, and T. Y. Tan (eds), *The Transformation of Southeast Asia: International Perspectives on Decolonization*, New York and London: M. E. Sharpe, 2003.
2 For a more detailed discussion on the term 'nation-of-intent', see Shamsul A. B., *Malaysia in 2020: One State Many Nations? Observing Malaysia from Australia*, the Seventh James Jackson Memorial Lecture, Malaysia Society, Australia, Bangi: Department of Anthropology and Sociology, Universiti Kebangsaan Malaysia,

1992; and Shamsul A. B., 'Nations-of-intent in Malaysia', in S. Tonnesson and H. Antlov (eds), *Asian Forms of the Nation*, London: Curzon and Nordic Institute of Asian Studies, 1996, pp. 323–47.

3 For useful and sociologically informed historical accounts on Malaysia, see B. Andaya and L. Andaya, *A History of Malaysia*, 2nd edn, Honolulu: University of Hawai'i Press, 2001; T. N. Harper, *The End of Empire and the Making of Malaya*, Cambridge: Cambridge University Press, 1999; Shamsul A. B., 'The making of a plural society in Malaysia: a brief survey', in D. Wu, H. McQueen, and Y. Yamamoto (eds), *Emerging Pluralism in Asia and the Pacific*, Hong Kong: Institute of Pacific Studies, 1997, pp. 67–83; and Shamsul A. B., 'Development and democracy in Malaysia: a comment on its socio-historical roots', in H. Antlov and T. W. Ngo (eds), *The Cultural Construction of Politics in Asia*, NIAS Democracy in Asia Series No. 2, Surrey: Curzon Press, 2000, pp. 86–106.

4 See Federation of Malaysia, *Federal Constitution*, Kuala Lumpur: International Law Books Services, 1995. For an informed analysis on the contradictions within the Malaysian constitution, see M. Suffian, H. P. Lee, and F. A. Trindade, *The Constitution of Malaysia: Its Development 1957-1977*, Kuala Lumpur: Oxford University Press, 1978.

5 Not only in theorizing about the 'modern state' and 'nation-state', Europe and European thought have been influential in shaping ideas and explanations in many more spheres of non-European thought system. A Chicago-based Indian scholar asks: 'Can European thought be dislodged from the center of the practice of history in a non-European place?' This was the question that was asked and answered in a most interesting book by D. Chakrabarty, *Provincializing Europe: Postcolonial Thought and Historical Difference*, Princeton, NJ: Princeton University Press, 2000. For a comment on the Malaysian experience, see Shamsul A. B., 'Ethnicity, class, culture or identity? Competing paradigms in Malaysian studies', *Akademika*, 1998, no. 53, 33–60.

6 See, E. Gellner, *Nations and Nationalism*, Oxford: Oxford University Press, 1983, p. 1.

7 For further elaboration on these themes and subthemes in the subsequent pages, see Shamsul A. B., 'Debating about identity in Malaysia: a discourse analysis', *Tonan Ajia Kenkyu*, 1996, vol. 34, no. 3, 566–600; Shamsul A. B., 'The making of a plural society'; Shamsul A. B., 'The construction and transformation of a social identity: Malayness and Bumiputeraness re-examined', *Journal of Asian and African Studies*, 1996, no. 52, 15–33; Shamsul A. B., 'The economic dimension of Malay nationalism', *Developing Economies*, 1997, vol. 35, no. 3, 240–61. Also see the contribution of C. Hirschman, 'The making of race in colonial Malaya: political economy and racial category', *Sociological Forum*, Spring 1986, 330–61; and C. Hirschman, 'The meaning and measurement of ethnicity in Malaysia: an analysis of census classification', *Journal of Asian Studies*, 1987, vol. 46, no. 3, 555–82.

8 For a comparison of Malay and Chinese experience of identity formation in Malaysia, see Shamsul A. B., 'Identity contestation in Malaysia: a comparative commentary on "Malayness" and "Chineseness",' *Akademika*, 1999, no. 55, 17–37.

9 For detailed analyses on Dr M. Mohamed's rule as a Prime Minister of Malaysia, see B. T. Khoo, *Paradoxes of Mahathirism: An Intellectual Biography of Mahathir Mohamed*, Kuala Lumpur: Oxford University Press, 1995; B. T. Khoo, *Beyond Mahathir: Malaysian Politics and Its Discontents*, London: Zed Press, 2003; I. W. Hwang, *Personalized Politics: The Malaysian State under Mahathir*, Singapore: Institute of Southeast Asian Studies, 2003; B. Welsh (ed.), *Reflections: The Mahathir Years*, Washington, DC: Southeast Asian Studies Program, John Hopkins University, 2004.

10 See B. Anderson, *Imagined Communities*, London: Verso, 1983.
11 See Shamsul A. B., *Malaysia in 2020*.
12 For further elaboration and application of the concepts of 'embedded' and 'embeddedness', see Shamsul A. B. and A. Aziz, 'Political Islam and governance in Southeast Asia: a Malaysian viewpoint', Asian Cultures and Modernity Research Report No. 8, Stockholm: Department of Oriental Languages and Department of Political Science, University of Stockholm, 2004, pp. 4–6.

8 Some states of Asia compared from afar

Laurence Whitehead

Western political thought, at least since Machiavelli, has generated a varied and complex array of definitions and theoretical debates revolving around an abstract and idealized conception of 'the state'. More recent discussions have focused on various qualifiers – the nation-state, the modern state, the liberal state, the market state, the developmental state, and so on. The empirical referents for this cascade of concepts and categories are not timeless and universal, but rather firmly located in certain specific historical and geographical contexts (with different contexts implicitly invoked by each overlapping category). Much of the literature on 'the state' in abstract actually takes as its reference point the post-Westphalian (1648) distribution of power in Western Europe. The nation-state mostly refers to those societies most affected by the legacy of the French Revolution of 1789, and/or the disintegration of multinational empires as a result of the Great War of 1914–18. The modern state assumes mass literacy, the effective administration of uniform rights for all citizens throughout the jurisdiction, and other features associated with civilized society. The liberal and market states are especially geared to post-Cold War conditions (real or imagined). The 'developmental state' is the only subclassification with an implicit Asian content. (There may be developmental states outside Asia, but no general discussion would be complete if it ignored the so-called 'East Asian developmental states' that flourished between, say, 1960 and 1990.)

Some of the most influential authorities on the theory of the state have been quite explicit about the geographical and temporal context that has inspired their theorizing. Max Weber is worth noting here:

> The state in the sense of the rational state has existed only in the western world. Under the old regime in China a thin stratum of so-called officials, the mandarins existed above the unbroken power of the clans and commercial and industrial guilds. . . . Such an official performs no administrative work himself. . . . The mandarin is continually transferred from one place to another to prevent his obtaining a foothold in his administrative district, and he could never be assigned to his home province. As he does not understand the dialect of his province he cannot

communicate with the public. A state with such officials is something different from the occidental state.[1]

These theorists have viewed 'the state' as a European (or possibly a 'Western') sociohistorical construct, and have questioned the extent to which it can be expected to 'travel' beyond its place of origin. Weber himself elaborated a detailed account of a non-Western 'Other' that may not carry complete conviction with the contemporary reader. But at least he thought seriously about the limited geographical scope of his theories.[2] More often nowadays concepts abstracted from one small portion of the history of humanity are stretched, transferred, and naturalized by contemporary social scientists until it is taken for granted that they also apply (or ought to apply) in other settings. This can even apply to settings where the preconditions for their existence have never been investigated, and where the local population may be accustomed to using quite different concepts to organize their self-understanding. What, for example, do the people of Bhutan or Brunei understand by the concept of 'the state' as it applies to their contemporary circumstances? In particular, how are they to adapt a rich, complex, and profoundly embedded historical consciousness (imbued with a mythical, religious, and philosophical significance anterior to any encounter with Western universalizing categories and assumptions)[3] so as to relocate themselves within a system of thought populated by centralized territorially bounded administrations competing in a secularized global system? Insofar as a Weberian model of the state has been extended beyond Europe to the whole world, this has generally been brought about either through colonialism – formal or otherwise – or through 'modernizing' revolutions – nationalist, communist, or otherwise. In parts of Latin America indigenous populations may express their disconformity with what the prevalent language of 'the state' implies about their history, identity, and rights by adopting a counterdiscourse, and by denouncing 'the colonial' state. More generally, national state forms have proved far more transient and indeed malleable (even in Europe) than was imagined by the classical European theorists who propagated this model in the first half of the twentieth century. Indeed, antistatism has made most of the running since the decolonization wave of the 1960s, and since the collapse of state socialism in the Soviet bloc, exponents of a Weberian model of state organization are under even more pressure both from economic and political liberals ('globalizers') and from communitarian critics.

Notwithstanding these phenomena of genealogy and social bias, the contemporary world is in fact divided into a comprehensive grid of territorial units, each with its own boundaries, administrative capacities, and externally recognized authorities that we can designate as 'states'. Even those societies in Asia that were never subjected to direct European colonization have been remolded to conform to this standard template. Democratization has tended to reinforce this pattern since fair electoral contests require predefined territorial units with effective administration throughout a given jurisdiction.

And where conditions emerge that might appear to nullify this conceptual map (populations or territories without some minimum of administration, boundary enforcement, or identifiable locus of collective authority) the assumption of stateness is preserved through the invocation of residual categories ('failed' states, 'humanitarian emergencies', etc.). This is as true of Europe (for example in Bosnia and Kosovo) as of the rest of the world. It highlights the way the 'states' of Asia can be distributed along a continuum that applies equally well to non-Asian jurisdictions. It means that without insisting on a strong unitary and stipulative definition of what 'the state' must contain we can engage in broad exercises in inter- and intraregional comparison using a 'minimum kit' specification of the units under examination.

Classical European writers on the state have offered a variety of 'minimum kit' formulations, some emphasizing the enforcement side of state authority, others emphasizing its discursive character. Thus, Alexander Passerin d'Entrèves refers to the 'basic and essential features of the State' as 'being an organization endowed with the capacity of exerting and controlling the use of force over certain people and within a given territory'.[4] But Ernest Gellner comments that this idea 'is not entirely satisfactory. There are "states" – or at any rate institutions which we would normally be inclined to call by that name – which do not monopolize legitimate violence within the territory which they more or less effectively control'. He nevertheless concludes that 'The "state" is that institution or set of institutions specifically concerned with the enforcement of order (whatever else they may also be concerned with). The state exists where specialized order-enforcing agencies, such as police forces and courts, have separated out from the rest of social life. They *are* the state.'[5] Such institutions require resources, administration, and territorial limits, even if they are not very legitimate or do not exercise a full monopoly over the means of coercion. My view is therefore that more emphasis should be given to these organizational forms, and less to the state's coercive power. After all, as Iraq is demonstrating, an occupation force is not 'state' unless it can generate some degree of social acceptance as such.[6] Durkheim took this point much further, arguing that the state was 'a group of officials of a special kind, within which ideas and decisions are evolved which involve the whole society without being the creation of society'.[7] He thus privileged the state apparatus as an instrument of cognition and social ordering, rather than as an enforcement agency. My approach here leaves open the balance between force and persuasion, but stresses that in any case a durable state apparatus will be a specialized organization requiring resources, permanent administration, and a clearly demarcated territory.

I have therefore proposed that state organization can be studied and compared under three interrelated headings: territory; administration, and command over resources.[8] This inventory of the state's minimum kit is intended as a heuristic device, not a prescription and still less a platonic essence. In the post-Cold War setting that concerns us here it may be appropriate to add membership of international organizations as an additional criterion (but the examples of Hong Kong and Taiwan should caution us against too much formalism here). These are the units of state organization under inspection in this chapter (and also I believe in this volume). The purpose of this exercise is to 'revisit' the contemporary 'states' of Asia without importing too much conceptual baggage or Eurocentric assumptions. How much variation is there between these units, and how far do they diverge from a conventional social science template of what to expect of any modern 'state'? What added insights into their internal dynamics can be gained by trying to screen out stipulative and prescriptive assumptions from elsewhere?

In this volume on state making in Asia, all contributors specialize in at least some Asian countries or cultures. The only complete outsider was myself, and I was assigned the role of commenting on and comparing the various interpretations, presumably on the basis that I was equally distant from all of them. My field is comparative politics and I have written on the history of state organization in twentieth-century Latin America, as well as more general comparative topics that have included some Asian material. But this chapter is very much a nonspecialist view from afar. It relies on the expertise marshalled elsewhere in this volume, and the modest ambition is simply to order and interrogate those contributions as a sympathetic outsider might.

So let me present my initial observations in the form of a personal tour through the terrain laid out by these regional experts. My itinerary will take me from mainland China and Taiwan to Malaysia, before ending up in Japan. These are obviously only a sample of the states of Asia, and it is especially important to highlight at this point the omission of South Asia, and the very incomplete coverage of the Asian community of states. Nevertheless the comparison is strong enough to support some substantive generalizations, which will be offered after the completion of my tour. Still, the comparativist should always make explicit the *locus* of the enquiry. So the first step in my journey must be to pose the most basic of questions about the terrain to be revisited. Where is Asia and what (today) is an 'Asian state'? For my purposes, Asia extends as far west as India (but perhaps not Pakistan, and certainly not post-Soviet 'central Asia', let alone what the Romans first labeled 'Asia minor'). To the south it extends as far as Indonesia, and to the east it embraces Japan (but not the eastern half of the island of New Guinea, let alone Micronesia, or Polynesia). Both Koreas (or a future reunited Korea) must therefore be included. But on this view the heartland of Asia must be China. With over 190 member states of the United Nations to choose from, and virtually the whole of the globe now parceled out between territorial regimes that practice mutual recognition of each other's boundaries and legal sovereignty, it might at least seem straightforward to determine what is currently understood by the term 'Asian state'. But there is the question of Hong Kong, Taiwan, the Koreas, and even the Tibetan diaspora. So UN membership hardly seems the defining characteristic of contemporary statehood. In any case this 'Asian state' label is extended to cover Singapore as well as the

People's Republic of China. What are the implications of bracketing such dissimilar political entities within a unitary conceptual framework?

Since China seems to be the heartland of this Asian journey this may be the best place to begin probing the conception of stateness that is at issue, and how it has developed.[9] In this volume R. Bin Wong classifies China as 'the only state ruling a nation that roughly corresponds to the territory of a former agrarian empire. Other empires were broken up into smaller national states. The Chinese state has managed its survival, despite the collapse of its cultural hegemony, and its recognition of a multiethnic and multicultural nation.' He explains this singularity in terms of the often underestimated effectiveness of the strategies of rule and principles of social organization promoted during China's late imperial period. And he explores the extent to which this continuity of formal stateness since agrarian imperial times serves to shape China's political possibilities over the more recent past and into the present. But what are we to understand by this reference to 'the state' as the source of Chinese continuity? How does it relate to Western conceptions of the state or other Asian manifestations of this political structure, and how can it be distinguished from that vaguer but still compelling source of continuity in Chinese history which we refer to as its 'civilization'? One indication of the singularity of 'the state' as used in this long-run analysis is the fact that in late imperial times, however active and effective the then prevailing strategies of rule may have been, the self-image of China's political system was far removed from a Westphalian conception of stateness. Historically, China was not regarded by most Chinese as one among a collection of parallel entities, each of which was constrained by competition with its neighbors to create a standardized set of state institutions. (More generally, neither Korea, Japan, nor even Siam could have viewed themselves as 'states' in the European sense as early as the eighteenth century. The process by which this self-definition was transformed through intensified interaction with the West over the ensuing two centuries involves the creation, or even importation, of an initially unfamiliar conception and set of practices from elsewhere as stressed in Mark Ravina's account of the rise of the modern Japanese state.)

Moreover, as Wong stresses, imperial China not only lacked European-style boundaries and competition from neighboring states.[10] In addition, internally it was an ancient agrarian empire, meaning that its ruling beliefs, sources of cohesion, and modes of interaction with its subjects were also distinctive, and different from those presumed by the Eurocentric categories of statehood. For example, as I understand it, the Chinese language typically portrays the rulers as an extension of the family hierarchy.[11] The Chinese word for 'the state' (*guojia*) is the family or household of the country.[12] If Chinese politics have been characterized by the degree of continuity suggested by Wong, that inertia must surely reside in such cultural legacies as the language and practices of socialization (which may have proven resilient) rather than in the continuity of the state apparatus – at least if it is viewed in narrowly Weberian terms. In Europe, too, dynastic rulers often presented themselves to their subjects in patrimonial terms, and in Europe, too, wars, republics, and invasions interrupted the administrative continuity of many a state apparatus. But in Europe, in contrast to China, there was an extranational source of culture and socialization which bound the rival states into a common civilization ('Christendom'),[13] and in Europe impersonal institutions (courts and parliaments) progressively encroached upon the privileges of the hereditary ruling strata, an ideological transformation consecrated by the French Revolution. The modern European state may be regarded as a distinctive product of these peculiar regional dynamics. If so, no traditional dynastic agrarian empire in Europe could survive the rise of the resulting impersonal citizen-based conceptions of nationality and political cohesion. But in China, where the language, the dynasty, and the civilization were conjoined instead of counterposed; where hierarchical values were never so frontally contested as in Enlightenment Europe;[14] and where the mandarinate had long operated in an equilibrium with hereditary power and privilege, such indigenous sources of modern state making were weak or absent. In addition, we are told, China had no tradition of municipal autonomy, or of corporate elites, so it lacked the basis for an autonomous 'public sphere'. As a result of all this distinctiveness, the agrarian empire was not broken into a succession of separate states despite the heavy and repeated blows it received from without. This is the particularity of the Chinese state, as presented to us by Wong.

This is a challenging assertion of Chinese distinctiveness, and seems to me generally quite persuasive. There may however be some risk of overstating the continuities of Chinese traditional civilization, and of downplaying the impact of 'modern' influences derived from the European Enlightenment, at least as concerns state building after the Empire (post-1911). The rupture with traditional norms (stasis, order, ethics as the fulcrum of society) was far-reaching at the level of government and administration, even if new elites were more rapidly socialized into 'modernity' than much of Chinese society at large. How would such an analysis apply to the 'state' of Taiwan? Although no longer a member of the United Nations, and increasingly isolated in terms of formal diplomatic recognition, democratic Taiwan is not so completely beholden to the mainland as SAR Hong Kong. It belongs to APEC (under the designation 'Chinese Taipei') and the ADB, and in 2002 it obtained *de facto* membership of the WTO (formally as a 'customs territory' rather than a sovereign state). As Jenn-hwan Wang points out in his chapter, between 1949 and 1970 the government of Taiwan was unique among the internationally recognized states within the UN system for claiming a sovereignty that was vastly discrepant with the limited scope of its actually ruled territory. The eventual consequence of that gross impertinence was that the tables were turned. Now its 'really existing' territorial authority substantially exceeds its jurisdiction as generally recognized by the international community. Yet again standard notions of statehood have to be distorted beyond recognition to accommodate the anomalous power relations of post-revolutionary China. Wang also invokes what he calls the 'Listian' state model and the 'Schumpeterian' state model, as guides to the roles of military security and economic competitiveness respectively, in the evolution of Taiwanese politics before and after the democratization of the 1980s and 1990s. However, the degree of discontinuity between these two models may have been exaggerated, and pessimism about Taiwan's capacity to overcome what is described as the current 'crisis' may be overdrawn. In comparative and theoretical terms the key point in Wang's chapter is that the standard model of the 'developmental state' fails to capture key features of Taiwan's political economy – even in the pre-1980 period – because it downplays the autonomy of political processes (including 'state building' through patronage) and it underestimates the security ('state survival') imperative. In short, it is too ahistorical and reductionist.[15]

From my distant standpoint all these comparative oddities are instructive and direct attention to important aspects of Taiwanese political history. Nevertheless, from the outside it remains striking that Taiwan's state apparatus was either adapted from the inheritance of the Japanese colonial state (in the case of local governance) or imported wholesale from the mainland (in the case of peak institutions including the security apparatus). After 1949 the KMT set to work transforming an outlying province into an economic and military powerhouse, which not only survived for half a century but adapted to an extraordinary sequence of constraints and opportunities, and even evolved into a recognizably liberal democratic system of government. Despite its increased internal legitimacy there is certainly a risk that it may be extinguished by future developments, either through vulnerabilities in the economic realm or through geopolitical adversity. But perceived danger is the greatest stimulus to state building, and – unlike Hong Kong – Taiwan faces no externally fixed time limit, nor any last resort control from without. As a democratic state, it possesses the capacity to join a larger political community through an act of domestic choice, and if the PRC made itself a sufficiently attractive partner this path to reunification could become viable. But if its citizens cannot be persuaded voluntarily to exchange their hard-won autonomy for something else, then the state structures they have inherited give them considerable margin or continued survival as a separate polity. However unusual the past history of their state, the island's current predicament arises not from the exceptionalism of the Taiwanese state, but rather from its convergence towards 'normal' statehood, and the cognitive dissonance that processes evoke in this nonstandard region.

South Korea provides further evidence on the inadequacies of the 'developmental state' model as an account of state organization and development in this part of Asia, and on the extent to which standard Western analyses of 'the state' need to be stretched to accommodate regional realities. Both geography and history worked together to generate a unified Confucian Kingdom on the Korean peninsula by 1392 – that is, well before most European states had acquired their present frontiers. Even under Japanese colonial rule after

1910, this political and administrative continuity was not disputed, and in December 1943 the Allies pledged a 'free and independent' Korea would emerge from their victory. The demilitarized zone which marks the frontier of today's South Korea originated from what may well have been no more than the administrative convenience by which the Japanese forces were instructed to surrender to the Americans (south of the 38th parallel) or to the Russians (north of that line). Thus, although there are two bitterly counterposed states (still technically at war with each other) there is only one Korean nation. Once again standard assumptions about the permanence and legitimacy of statehood are falsified by this artificial Asian improvisation. Despite its remarkable success and indeed its longevity, the South Korean state is no more than a provisional construct awaiting an eventual national reunification (like some parts of Italy before 1860, or indeed China after the First World War).

Both conventional statists and their revisionist (and neopluralist) critics treat state and market as analytically distinct entities, and theorize about their interactions in unduly static and apolitical terms. But it would also be possible to adopt an integrated view of a 'state–market condominium' which evolves over time and through symbiosis. On this view both the forms and the developmental functions of the state should therefore be viewed as permanently evolving, modified by the consequences of economic development and the societal power balance. This interpretation could be buttressed by examination of the evolution of industrial policy and sectoral outcomes in the four dynamic 'tiger' economies. Such comparative work would be likely to highlight the diversity of state–business relations in different economies and the variations over time within each country. So rather than uncovering symbiosis and functional adaptation, a comparative survey of the four tigers would tend to indicate imperfect coordination between state and market, and to confirm the potential for even the most symbiotic of relationships to degenerate into friction either when growth slows, or when democracy advances. If so, rather than rescuing the 'developmental state' thesis from its failings this perspective could be expected to reinforce the conclusion that it provides no more than a highly schematic and fleetingly relevant approximation to East Asian realities.

The chapter devoted specifically to Malaysia confirms that it is necessary to look far beyond this state's activities as promoter of economic development in order to grasp its social role and its changing priorities and capabilities. It provides one of the most in-depth historical case studies of Asian state formation. It is also theoretically informed, and helps to situate the Malaysian case comparatively. From my itinerant standpoint, however, it neglects the crucial dimension of shifting territorial coverage, which – as we have already seen – is characteristic of so many Asian states. This 'Malaysia', whose developmental projects and nations-of-intent are so vividly evoked, was in fact a shifting combination of directly ruled ports (Penang and Singapore) and indirectly ruled sultanates. It began as a combination of the Straits Settlements and the Federation of Malay States. During the 1940s it was successively a component of the Japanese imperial system, a short-lived unitary administration within the British Empire, then a colonial 'federal state'. In the decade following independence (in 1957), its territorial coverage was first extended to include Sarawak and Sabah, then contracted to exclude Singapore. Admittedly since 1965 this territorial dimension of state formation has been stabilized, but taking the longer view Malaysia can be bracketed with the other Asian states discussed above, as another political apparatus with shifting boundaries despite its temporal continuity.

In their chapter Shamsul A. B. and Sity Daud make the revealing observation that despite their nationality, in order for them to travel within Malaysia (from the peninsula to the Borneo states) they need to carry a passport. Here is an empirical indicator of state activity worthy of further examination across the whole Asian region. What documents or permissions are needed by which categories of citizens in order to travel both within and between the various states covered by the Leiden conference? Which boundary prohibitions are effectively enforced, and which are porous?[16]

Malaysia's present territorial configuration may be more permanent than that of the various Chinese and Korean states already considered, but both Malaysia's internal dynamics and its interactions with neighboring states (such as a fissiparous Indonesia) still provide some grounds for unease about the present state's long-term integrity. This anxiety underlies the Vision 2020 project, and indicates why rival elites within Malaysia compete with alternative '*bangsa idaman*' (translated rather approximately by Shamsul and Daud as 'nations-of-intent' – national projects, nationalist ideologies). According to the authors, developmentalism is not enough to secure national integration. Their chapter offers a rich array of conceptual tools for characterizing the Malaysian state, and for explaining its temporal progression.

Shamsul and Daud also shift the focus from the material to the discursive dimensions of state formation, and from the 'authority-defined' (or top-down) perspective to one that gives equal weight to the 'everyday-defined' idea of a nation. But in practice the notion of 'nations-of-intent' leads them to highlight totalizing projects that can only be promoted through the pursuit of state power, and this leads them to the disconcerting conclusion that 'it is impossible for the state . . . to impose totally its presence on the more diffused and fragmented everyday social reality of the masses except in a draconian and authoritarian way'. They may have underestimated the extent to which the state in Malaysia has achieved greater national integration than, say, most ex-British colonies in Africa. More comparative work on British colonialism would be rewarding here. From my perspective, in any case, the only way that Gellner's 'national principle' could be fulfilled in Malaysia (that is, 'making the cultural and political unit congruent') would be by dialogue and syncretism rather than one-sided imposition. Both liberals and Gramscians may have something to add about this politico-cultural dimension of state formation, a dimension that may be assisted by strong economic performance, but one which requires quite as much state activism and creativity, albeit in the non-economic realm.

The last Asian state on this itinerary is arguably the only one that has really achieved the Gellnerian (or idealized European) fulfillment of the national principle through an indubitable territory and an unquestionable congruence between the political and the cultural components of its nationality. Richard Boyd's chapter on the sectionalism and transcendence of the Japanese bureaucracy provides the ideal finishing point in my tour. Japanese experts have portrayed an Asian state which was the closest replica we are likely to find of what Western analysts take to be a classical modern state. And yet, at the same time, they also pointed to crucial respects in which even the postwar constitutional Japanese state does not entirely conform to this abstract model.

Japan's insular status evidently helps to ensure congruence between politics and culture within the society. But of course even island states can have boundary problems (as exemplified by Britain and the boundary in northern Ireland). Japanese nationalists remain very sensitive about the issues of Okinawa and the Kuriles, even though these are extremely minor and peripheral blemishes on their territorial integrity (at least by comparison with the problems of the other Asian states considered here). During the twentieth century, the Japanese state obviously did not confine its presence to this core territory, but sought to conquer and control vast adjacent lands in Korea, China, and eventually throughout Asia. This explosive expansion of the geographical reach of the state was of course followed by an extremely violent and rapid contraction back to its core territory in 1945. But from a comparative perspective there was nothing unique (or uniquely Asian) about this expansion and contraction. Several major European states (including Britain, France, and Holland) followed similar trajectories, albeit in a more gradual fashion.

Mark Ravina draws attention to all the respects in which after the Meiji Restoration the Japanese state absorbed and replicated characteristic features of late nineteenth-century state organization in the West. In that respect it could be described as the last and best 'Victorian-era' state structure. From this very broad and long-run standpoint, then, Japan may be regarded as a fairly representative exemplar of European patterns of state formation rather than some deviant or regionally specific Asian variant. But these resemblances of form may disguise substantial contrasts in interpretation, understanding, and meaning. For example, a nation with a long proud and insular tradition of self-government may borrow the trappings of Western statehood in order to occupy its place in the world, without necessarily internalizing all their European connotations. Indeed the same may apply when it imitates European imperialism, or it assimilates a Constitution imposed under US occupation.

Boyd extends this analysis to generate an overall interpretation of the Japanese political system. The familiar landmarks of parties, elections, parliaments, and ministries may all be on display, but how they really operate is not so evident. The key, from Boyd's standpoint, is that the postwar Japanese state lacks what, borrowing from Finer, he calls a 'paramount organ'. Analysts therefore focus on the 'bureaucracy', studied in an unduly aseptic and decontextualized manner, and so they fail to grasp what makes the whole system behave so distinctively. Much of the chapter highlights 'sectionalism', the tendency for each bureaucratic agency to act as a law unto itself, not coordinated either through the office of the Prime Minister, or the cabinet (no collective cabinet responsibility) or through parliament, or the ruling party. This part of the analysis parallels John O. Haley's point about the weakness of legal enforcement powers, and the consequent reliance of each agency on forms of private ordering that favor collusion between bureaucrats and the dominant private interests in each sector.[17] The extreme manifestation of this pattern is when competing agencies go so far as to kidnap potential recruits. Faced by the impossibility of establishing an authoritative source of hierarchical coordination, the agencies respond to policy paralysis by proposing the creation of yet more agencies, each specialized in covering a deficiency created by the lack of collective authority. Boyd emphasizes that this pattern of sectionalism dates back to at least the beginning of the twentieth century, if not earlier. In principle, the Emperor could bypass these obstacles by issuing imperial decrees, but in practice such decrees would remain a dead letter unless taken up by the relevant ministry. Western nations' standard view of 'insulation', 'embeddedness', and 'privatization' all misunderstand or fail to capture the spirit of this system, which effectively subverts what outside observers presume to be the workings of a conventional modern state.

Boyd brackets sectionalism with a second, equally crucial and distinctive, feature of the Japanese state, which he refers to as 'transcendence'. In its narrowest sense this just refers to lack of bureaucratic accountability to the public, and can be illustrated in a conventional manner by reference to the absence of freedom of information provisions, citizen participation in decision making, or oversight of public works procedures, and so on. But Boyd proposes a broader interpretation. Transcendence in this sense refers to the bureaucracy's basic conception of its own role, a conception in which instrumentality and subordination shine by their absence. So this cannot be a Weberian rational modern state, since it is not geared to means-end rationality (program or service delivery). Again Boyd stresses the continuity between pre- and postwar Japan. Indeed, he traces the Japanese bureaucratic ethos back to the Tokugawa period (1600–1868).[18] Since the Emperor was the embodiment of a moral principle, he could not embody agency. If the Japanese nation was to be affirmed, and the Japanese state was to be built, it could only be by the rule of officials acting under the moral sanction of the Emperor, and the moral ideal he embodied. This required a hierarchical tradition of authority and close identification between bureaucrats and scholars. Bureaucrats were called on not to obey, but rather to enact. On this view Japan lacked an effective sovereign (a true counterweight to the bureaucracy) even during the Tokugawa and Meiji periods.[19] The bureaucracy cannot be the instrument of such a sovereign, although it derives its right to rule from its proximity to sovereign moral authority. Indeed, bureaucratic sectionalism arises from the fact that each agency could compete with its rivals for direct authorization from the ultimate state entity. Westerners may have supposed that after 1945, when the Emperor declared himself human and accepted the occupation and the constitution, this tradition of nationalist transcendence must have come to an end. Boyd's key claim about the distinctiveness of the Japanese state is that, on the contrary, the Emperor only reconfirmed his moral authority, and his consequent detachment from political agency. The rule of bureaucrats, unchecked by any paramount organ or requirement of instrumental rationality (let alone by any system of popular sovereignty) was thereby reaffirmed and perpetuated.

This emphasis on sectionalism and transcendence enables us to view the Japanese state comparatively, without underplaying the contrast between conventional 'Western' state forms and their locally rooted meanings. It promotes a long-run and holistic analysis of the Japanese state, and avoids the imposition of one-sided constructs (such as 'Weberian rationality'). But perhaps it overstates the inevitability of traditional Japanese practices after 1945. Bureaucrats and Emperors may both display continuities with their counterparts in the Tokugawa period as does the British House of Lords, and yet the transformative effects of 'modernity' have surely been operating on these state institutions with relentless effect for more than a century. I could not resist comparing his interpretation with what Masao Maruyama wrote in 1947 about the new dawn of a Japanese science of politics:

> Now for the first time it is possible to criticize rationally the very hub of state power, which hitherto had been shrouded in secrecy. The groups that were politically powerful under the *ancien regime* have been liquidated. The complicated process of forming the national will, which formerly carried out in obscurity has been opened to the public. The Diet has been made the 'highest organ of state power' and the parliamentary cabinet system has been fully adopted. The Emperor has withdrawn from his position as source of substantive values and become a 'symbol'. The neutral and formal character of State power has been proclaimed. At long last a political struggle, in the proper sense of the term, has emerged, carried on in an open arena and overtly aiming at control of State power.[20]

With hindsight we know that these hopes of a modern, neutral, and democratic state in Japan were not fully realized. (Maruyama was, after all, steeped in German theories of statehood and state formation, which obviously did not completely transfer to Japan.) But perhaps it would be a mistake to underestimate the long-term potential of this thwarted experiment. My impression is that the Cold War contributed as much to its relative failure as the inertia of Japanese traditionalism. Perhaps, despite everything that Boyd rightly underscores about the gap between formal appearances and the tacit conventions of Japanese policy making, the gap is not entirely unbridgeable. Perhaps Japan, more than any of the other Asian states covered by my itinerary, does already possess most of the attributes of a conventional Western state, and could incorporate the rest without extreme disruption.

Finally then, standing back from the particularities of the individual Asian states covered in my rapid *tour de horizon*, it seems appropriate to highlight the following general conclusions:

1   Modern states in contemporary Asia may diverge in significant respects from some of the standard assumptions about 'stateness' that are built into prevailing social science discourse (especially that expressed in the English language). But even if this is so, we can only compare and differentiate between states on the basis of some minimum conceptual agreement. Divergences of usage often arise not so much between Asian and Western scholars as between competing disciplinary perspectives. So for the sake of clarity, and without wishing to impose my stipulations on those from other backgrounds in this discussion I follow a fairly standard comparative politics approach, according to which at least the following minimum conditions are implied by 'the modern state': (a) sufficient command over resources and organizational capacity to assert significant economic and if necessary military control over a bounded territory; (b) a large enough population base for the maintenance over time of a specialized structure of administration (a 'state apparatus' – which probably requires a minimum of say 50,000 subjects);[21] (c) some at least tacit recognition by other states (in a modern world of states) of the existence of the state apparatus in question, and of its claimed territorial jurisdiction; (d) therefore some state persona, not so much an identifiable head of state (necessary though that may be) as a discursive claim to a collective identity, a historical presence, backed by a cognitive capacity to represent and administer the subject population within the claimed territorial boundaries. If these minimum conditions are not met, then we are not dealing with what I understand as a 'state'. There may perhaps exist a band, a chieftainship, or even some limited version of a kingdom, but without passing the threshold into modern state formation.

2   Some would say these minimum conditions have been set too low, but my aim is not to dichotomize, only to identify an outer boundary beyond which the term should not be applied. Within these limits there is abundant space for variation and development. When classifying and comparing our analysis should benefit from exposure to the full richness of historical and regional diversities.[22] Despite such diversities all modern states display the following shared morphological characteristics: complexity, temporal continuity, and multifacetedness. At least three key analytical dimensions of this multifacetedness can be identified: the

state as an idea; the state as an organization; and the state as a social formation. At the organization level we have already identified interconnected dimensions of the state as a structure: its territorial control; its command over resources; and its capacity for administration of its subjects. Holistic comparisons of states across time and space (and between regions) must take into account the interrelatedness of various dimensions of stateness. Clearly, then, this terminology generates an elaborate and specific concept, while at the same time allowing for much variation and development.

3   Following J. P. Nettl,[23] this perspective involves treating the state as what he called 'a conceptual variable'. But if it can vary (along multiple dimensions) in its intensity, this also raises the possibility that it can also weaken or degenerate. Schematically, therefore, we must allow for the emergence of 'failing' or even 'failed' states. This approach also allows for states that only manage to preserve their continuity and 'persona' thanks to external protection. This possible weakness refers primarily to the potential failure of a state as an organization, even though it may persist as a powerful idea, and may even retain inexpugnable social allegiances. Afghanistan, East Timor, etc., provide recent illustrations of this from the fringes of contemporary Asia. None of the states included in my Asian itinerary fell into this category, but some were still dominated by the fear that they could fail to survive (Hong Kong, Taiwan) or that they might disintegrate (Indonesia, Malaysia, perhaps even the PRC). Thus the possibility of failure may influence state behavior far beyond the limited incidence of actual breakdown.

4   The alternative possibility thrown up by our multifaceted characterization of the state is that a strong organization may exist which, however, does not correspond to the associated idea or persona of that state, or with a congruent social formation. Thus, for several decades the KMT state ruthlessly administered the territory of Taiwan, promoting only limited political engagement with most of the population of the island while insisting that its true persona was that of China as a whole. Likewise, the two states of Korea, both highly organized and administratively effective within their respective boundaries, each compete in championing rival ideas of a united Korea, which neither have ever been in a position to control. More generally, the modern states of Asia seem often to have acquired very impressive administrative capacities which are applied within territorial limits that are not yet entirely fixed, while embodying ideas of statehood that are substantially disconnected from their current activities.

5   Various typologies can be derived from this morphology of the state as a concept, and modern Asia provides some good exemplars of the range of variation that is possible. If so, all ahistorical and reductionist perspectives on the Asian state will exclude from analysis much that is essential, and will therefore fail to work even in their own narrow terms. Let us

consider one very simple, yet fundamental, dimension of the range of variation – population size. The People's Republic of China has a current population of approximately 1,300 million or approaching one-fifth of the total of humanity. Single provinces within China (such as Guangdong and Sichuan) each govern around 80–90 million subjects. By contrast we can properly regard Hong Kong as a major state-like entity even though its population is less than one-tenth as great. Singapore has only about four million subjects (which would hardly count as a significant unit of local government within the PRC). Singapore in turn has 40 times the population of Tonga, which, however, can also be viewed as a state and included within the range of units under comparative examination. Given these vast disproportions it is essential to recall how little the politics we label as 'states' may have in common. In particular, it is stretching the concept of 'the state' to apply it to an entity so vast, so internally differentiated, and so difficult to control from the center as mainland China. Undoubtedly there is a powerful and assertive state organization operating out of Beijing, and it would be foolhardy for those in outlying provinces to disregard its powers. And yet it would be still more misleading to impose a set of state-centric assumptions on our reading of how China is governed, when not only history, culture, and geography, but also administrative practicalities and subjective under-standings all conspire to limit (and even frustrate) a Weberian or indeed a Durkheimian model of functional and hierarchical centralization.

6   One strong message from this comparative project was that we should not limit our attention to the narrow focus adopted in the 'developmental state' debate. The state is not just a structure for accelerating the pace of economic development, and indeed even when it claims legitimacy on those grounds skepticism is in order. The state always has other purposes as well (security, ideology, the balancing or promotion of sectional inter-ests, perhaps even the development of citizenship). Moreover, even when a state is presented as developmental, and achieves economic success, the direction of causality cannot be assumed. Indeed, the sources of eco-nomic dynamism could be quite unrelated to state-led initiatives. More generally, the state-economy linkage is better understood as an inter-action than a one-way flow of causality. Similarly with state-society, and state-ideology and state-political linkages. Without underestimating the potential of a state organization to remold society, to rationalize the economy, or to project totalizing images of the community, a historical perspective indicates that there are always some external constraints that do not yield to state action, there is always feedback, and outcomes are heavily conditioned by contingency as much as by centralized direction. This gives rise to a complex typology of possibilities, most of which can be exemplified from contemporary Asia. For example, on the state–economy axis we can find developmental states, rentier states, market states, and predatory states. On the state–society axis there are insulated

states (colonial Hong Kong), there are ethnicized states (the *bumiputera* state in Malaysia), and there are society-immersed states (the Philippines). On the state–ideology axis there are Confucian-inspired states, Islamic states, and secular-nationalist states. On the state–political axis there are single-party states, constitutional democracies, absolute monarchies (Brunei), and military-dominated states (Burma). These are only schematic examples, to demonstrate the range of variation, and all are, of course, subject to contestation and historical change. It is even possible that this could all converge, under common external influences, towards a gradually more uniform and broad-based market democracy variant of state organization.[24]

7   All these types of state can be illustrated with examples from Asia. But nearly all types can also be found outside Asia. So, is there a distinctively Asian type of state, or some key respect in which Asian states as a cluster can be differentiated from their Western counterparts? Most theorists on the Asian states in our debate are of non-Asian origin, and although they may have purported to be manipulating universal categories they mostly distilled their social theory from the distinctive historical experiences of post-Westphalian Europe. Perhaps European imperialism in Asia was sufficient to universalize these ideas and to blot out any alternative analytical traditions, even in those societies not subject to direct rule from the West.[25] But Clifford Geertz, for one, has used Asian historical experience to interrogate and even attempt to reconfigure Western political theory. His study of the 'theater state' in nineteenth-century Bali concludes as follows:

Each of the leading notions of what the state 'is' that has developed in the West since the sixteenth century – monopolist of violence within a territory, executive committee of the ruling class, delegated agent of popular well, pragmatic device for conciliating interests – had had its own sort of difficulty assimilating [the symbolic dimensions of state power]. None has produced a workable account of its nature. Those dimensions of authority not easily reducible to a command-and-obedience conception of political life have been left to drift. . . . And the connection between what Bagehot called the dignified parts of government and the efficient ones has been systematically misconceived.[26]

So what this asserts is not that a tour of the states of Asia may uncover some eccentric exceptions to an almost universal European model, but rather that the study of such Asian particularities can help us elaborate richer and more varied conceptualizations of stateness in universal history. Both practice and theorization of the state extends far beyond Westphalian Europe.

After all, almost 2,000 years before Machiavelli and Hobbes, and in the midst of the 'warring states' era, the Confucian legalist scholar Han Feizi was already elaborating his concept of sovereign authority; his vision emphasized the vigorous administration of the law conceived as a single uniform system applicable equally to nobles and to serfs; his emphasis was on statecraft; and his advice to princes was to control the 'two handles of government' (commendation and chastisement). If other features of the European theory of the state were absent from his teaching, this was probably just because his point was to unify the civilized world under a single imperial system, and he knew of no external state that could test and challenge what would subsequently become China from without. Surely, therefore, one feature of the state in Asia that must differentiate it from the Western state is that it possesses its own long and separate tradition of self-reflection, embedded in the history and language of the major Asian civilizations. Perhaps tradition has been overshadowed by the universalizing pretensions of the Western imaginary. Perhaps it has even been temporarily lost in translation. But it is hard to pretend that it never existed, or to suppose that it can never resurface.

The historical reality of state formation is a patrimony of humanity, not the exclusive property of any one limited geographical region. So also our theorizing about the nature of the modern state should be drawn equally on Asian as much as on Western experience, and should be informed by a knowledge of both traditions of self-understanding.

Thus, my brief tour of some Asian states has been sufficient to convince me that much more comparative work and more crosscultural theory building remains for us (collectively) to do.

We have been able to identify a set of minimum necessary conditions for 'the modern state', delineating a defensible outer boundary of this concept that perhaps allows crossregional and longitudinal comparisons. It is not the only possible definition, but it seems useable both in Asia and the West. However, we have also seen that more precise definitions tend to accentuate one or other feature (for example, enforcement, centralized administration, persona, rationality) to the detriment of equally valid alternatives. And our tour of Asian examples has demonstrated that these different competing features can coexist (and conflict with each other) in a wide variety of diverse historical and geographical settings. Boundaries can be extremely clear and fundamental (as in insular Japan), but they can also be fluid and porous. Within a single state it is possible for territorial demarcations to become almost as salient as at the international frontiers (as in Malaysia). Hierarchical administration does not necessarily involve ultimate centralization (competing hierarchies can clash and subvert each other at the center). Huge and populous states like China may be more absorbed by internal differentiation and competitive peripheral pressures than by their outer territorial limits. The 'imagined community' invoked by a state may be radically different from the actual population under its jurisdiction at any particular time (Taiwan under the KMT, the two Koreas). In summary, the really existing states of contemporary Asia present us with a colorful menagerie that is far removed from the standardized attributes of stateness commonly found in Western-originated social theory.

Notes

This essay has benefited from the suggestions and ideas of many Asia experts. It is therefore invidious to mention names, but I need to recognize the input of Richard Boyd, Graham Hutchings, Rana Mitter, and Tak-Wing Ngo.

1 M. Weber, *General Economic History*, New York: Collier Books, 1961, p. 249. This text was reconstructed from the notes taken by his students shortly before his death in 1920.

2 Weber traced the rise of the 'rational' state to the early modern period when European cities came 'under the power of competing national states in a condition of perpetual struggle for power in peace or war. This competitive struggle created the largest opportunities for modern western capitalism. The separate states had to compete for mobile capital, which dictated to them the conditions under which it would assist them to power. Out of this alliance of the state with capital, dictated by necessity, arose the national citizen class, the bourgeoisie in the modern sense of the word. Hence it is the closed national state [of Europe] which afforded capitalism its chance for development.' See ibid., p. 249.

3 For an illuminating interpretation of one precolonial state tradition in Asia (much more about ceremony and ritual than about government or the concentration of hard power), see C. Geertz, *Negara: The Theatre State in Nineteenth-Century Bali*, Princeton: Princeton University Press, 1980. On p. 4, Geertz explains '*negara*' as a Sanskrit loanword, originally meaning 'town', also used in Indonesia more or less simultaneously and interchangeably to mean 'palace', 'capital', 'state', and 'realm'.

4 A. Passerin d'Entrèves, *The Notion of the State: An Introduction to Political Theory*, Oxford: Oxford University Press, 1961, p. 32.

5 E. Gellner, *Nations and Nationalism*, Oxford: Blackwell, 1983, pp. 3–4.

6 Every state apparatus – however weak or incipient – asserts its claim to 'legitimacy' within its claimed jurisdiction, and tries to back this claim with force if challenged. Some behaviorists may prefer the objective test of 'compliance' to the more subjective test of 'social acceptance'. But this is unsatisfactory for a comparativist, since it excludes the politically significant possibility of behavioral compliance without subjective acceptance (as in nineteenth-century partitioned Poland, or perhaps in Aceh, Kashmir, Tibet, etc.).

7 E. Durkheim, *Leçons de Sociologie* (Lessons in Sociology), Paris: Presses Universitaires de France, 1950, p. 61, as translated by S. Lukes, *Emile Durkheim: His Life and Work*, Harmondsworth: Penguin, 1973, p. 269.

8 L. Whitehead, 'State organisation in Latin America since 1930', in L. Bethell (ed.), *The Cambridge History of Latin America*, vol. 6, part 2, Cambridge: Cambridge University Press, 1994.

9 As a comparativist I started out on my tour equipped with a very ancient guidebook, provided by the 'modernization' school. J. Watanuki contributed the chapter on Asia entitled 'Nation-building at the edge of an old empire: Japan and Korea', in S. N. Eisenstadt and S. Rokkan (eds), *Building States and Nations*, vol. 2, New York: Sage, 1973. On p. 253, he compared just three very long-standing 'politico-cultural systems' – China, Korea, and Japan: 'Looking at the different routes followed by these three East Asian countries in the modern world, one is impressed with the fact that a long, historical existence of cultural and political unity per se was not a sufficient condition for building or developing a nation or state capable of surviving or developing in the modern world.' Thirty years later one may instead be impressed by the strength of such historical traditions, and the evanescence of judgements about 'routes to modernity' which extrapolate from just a few decades of historical turbulence.

10 However, Rana Mitter warns against overstating the point about territoriality. He

points out that, at least in principle, leaving Chinese territory was punishable by death in the high imperial Qing era, so there was a defined boundary between what was and wasn't within the *guojiao* (state) (personal communication, June 2004).

11 According to the Xinhua News Agency when Premier Wen Jiabao visited the UK in May 2004 he told Chinese nationals resident in Britain that if a person does not love his/her motherland that person would not love anything. A person who forgets the motherland will surely forget his/her parents, relatives, and old friends (communicated by Graham Hutchings).

12 At least according to S. Ogden, *Inklings of Democracy in China*, Cambridge, Mass.: Harvard University Asia Center, 2002, p. 46. Graham Hutchings comments that 'relatively speaking *guojia* is a neologism. Most Chinese up to the late nineteenth century would probably have answered the question "What nationality are you?" by saying "I am of this/the ruling dynasty" (*Woshi benchao de ren*).

13 However, Rana Mitter points out that the tribute system which China applied to Japan, Korea, and South-East Asia used Confucian norms they all shared.

14 R. B. Wong goes so far as to refer to monthly moral lectures for the common people in eighteenth-century China 'through which Confucian discourse permeated society'.

15 Perhaps this is somewhat too dismissive of the standard model. Certainly the debate on the developmental state prompted by Taiwanese and South Korean experience has enriched the literature on comparative politics. See, in particular, A. Amsden, 'The state and Taiwan's economic development', in P. B. Evans, D. Rueschemeyer, and T. Skocpol (eds), *Bringing the State Back In*, pp. 78–106, Cambridge: Cambridge University Press, 1985.

16 The mainland authorities who police the border with Hong Kong sometimes turn back prominent persons, included elected representatives, on the grounds that they held 'unpatriotic' views. They are therefore refused permission to enter what is legally their own country.

17 See J. O. Haley, 'The paradox of weak power and strong authority in the Japanese state', in R. Boyd and T. W. Ngo (eds), *Asian States: Beyond the Developmental Perspective*, pp. 67–82, London: RoutledgeCurzon, 2005.

18 Perhaps even this understates the historical distinctiveness of Japan. The Japanese state might be traced back to imitations of the Chinese imperial court and administration that were over a thousand years old. But whereas Chinese monarchs might lose the 'Mandate of Heaven', the Japanese Imperial dynasty remained unbroken. So the holder of the throne was sacrosanct. But this could only be achieved by passivity, which placed the Emperor above all criticism, a moral symbol, but not a decision-maker.

19 In an appendix to his study of the absolutist state in Europe, Perry Anderson highlighted the reasons why within his typology neither the Tokugawa state nor the Meiji state was an absolutism. On the one hand, Tokugawa tightly policed movements along the main highways by the use of internal passports and roadblocks. It also required the nobles to maintain a residence in the capital, and to leave family hostages there. However, within their own domains the 'feudal' lords issued laws, administered justice, raised taxes, and maintained troops without central control. Power was 'parcelized'. P. Anderson, *Lineages of the Absolutist State*, London: New Left Books, 1974, pp. 435–61.

20 M. Maruyama, *Thought and Behaviour in Modern Japanese Politics*, Oxford: Oxford University Press, 1963, p. 233, a translation of an essay first published in 1947.

21 Thus, for example, the Kingdom of Tonga, with a population of 101,000, may possess just about the rudimentary basis of a modern state, in my lexicon.

22 For broad comparative purposes the 'modern' state embraces almost all the states to be found in the contemporary world. But some theories of the modern state

assert a more specific claim – it is seen as an agency of rationality, meritocracy, progressive teleology, etc. As can be seen from my Asian itinerary, not all contemporary states are unambiguously 'modern' in this sense. Indeed, this ideal type is an empirical rarity, both in Asia and elsewhere.

23 J. P. Nettl, 'The state as a conceptual variable', *World Politics*, 1968, vol. 20, no. 4, 559–92.

24 For an illuminating discussion of both the potential for 'democratic' development states, and the structural impediments to such a desirable configuration, see M. Robinson and G. White (eds), *The Democratic Developmental State*, Oxford: Oxford University Press, 1998.

25 Schrecker thinks otherwise. He has retrieved the traditional Chinese distinction between *fengjian* and *junxian*, and has used it not only to structure an analytical history of China linking the pre-1800 experience to the subsequent two centuries of interaction with the West, but also to re-evaluate Western political influences using Chinese interpretative categories, '*junxian* society is run from the center with the country divided up into local units administered through bureaucrats appointed by the King'. J. E. Schrecker, *The Chinese Revolution in Historical Perspective*, New York: Greenwood Press, 1991, p. 4.

26 Geertz, *Negara*, pp. 121–2.

References

Alcock, R., *The Capital of the Tycoon: A Narrative of a Three Years' Residence in Japan*, 2 vols, New York: The Bradley Company, 1863.

Amsden, A., 'The state and Taiwan's economic development', in P. Evans, D. Rueschemeyer, and T. Skocpol (eds), *Bringing the State Back In*, pp. 78–106, Cambridge: Cambridge University Press, 1985.

Andaya, B. and Andaya L., *A History of Malaysia*, 2nd edn, Honolulu: University of Hawai'i Press, 2001.

Anderson, B., *Imagined Communities*, London: Verso, 1983.

Anderson, L., 'Understanding our global present: international issues and area knowledge', paper for the American Council of Learned Societies Annual Meeting, May 2003, Philadelphia.

Anderson, L., *Pursuing Truth, Exercising Power: Social Science and Public Policy in the Twenty-First Century*, Columbia: Columbia University Press, 2003.

Anderson, P., *Lineages of the Absolutist State*, London: New Left Books, 1974.

Antlöv, H. and Ngo, T. W., 'Politics, culture, and democracy in Asia', in H. Antlöv and T. W. Ngo (eds), *The Cultural Construction of Politics in Asia*, pp. 1–18, Surrey: Curzon Press, 2000.

Ardant, G., 'Financial policy and economic infrastructure of modern states and nations', in C. Tilly (ed.), *The Formation of National States in Western Europe*, Princeton: Princeton University Press, 1975.

Arnason, J. P., *Social Theory and Japanese Experience*, London: Kegan Paul International, 1997.

Arzt, D. E., *Refugees into Citizens: Palestinians and the End of the Arab-Israeli Conflict*, Washington: Brookings Institution Press, 1997.

Avedon, J. F., *In Exile from the Land of Snows*, London: Michael Joseph, 1984.

Ballentine, J., *Formosa: A Problem for U.S. Foreign Policy*, Washington: Brookings Institution Press, 1952.

Barker, E., *The Development of Public Services in Western Europe 1660-1930*, London: Oxford University Press, 1944.

Barnett, M. N., *Confronting the Costs of War: Military Power, State and Society in Egypt and Israel*, Princeton: Princeton University Press, 1992.

Bates, R., Greif, A., Levi, M., Rosenthal, J. L., and Weingast, B., *Analytic Narratives*, Princeton: Princeton University Press, 1998.

Bayart, F., 'Finishing with the idea of the Third World: the concept of the political trajectory', in J. Manor (ed.), *Rethinking Third World Politics*, pp. 51–71, New York: Longman, 1991.

Beker, M. and van Oordt, R., *The Palestinians in Lebanon: Contradictions of State-Formation in Exile*, Amsterdam: Middle East Research Associates, 1991.

Bellah, R. N., *Tokugawa Religion: The Values of Pre-Industrial Japan*, Glencoe, CA: Free Press, 1957.

Bellah, R. N., *Imagining Japan: The Japanese Tradition and Its Modern Interpretation*, Berkeley and Los Angeles: University of California Press, 2003.

Belz, H., *A Living Constitution or Fundamental Law? Constitutionalism in Historical Perspective*, Lanham, Boulder, New York, and Oxford: Rowman and Littlefield, 1998.

Bendix, R. *et al.* (eds), *State and Society: A Reader*, Berkeley and Los Angeles: University of California Press, 1968.

Binder, L., 'The crises of political development', in L. Binder, J. S. Coleman, J. LaPalombara, L. W. Pye, S. Verba, and M. Weiner (eds), *Crises and Sequences in Political Development*, pp. 3–72, Princeton: Princeton University Press, 1971.

Boli, J., 'Human rights or state expansion? Cross-national definitions of constitutional rights, 1870–1970', in G. M. Thomas, J. W. Meyer, F. O. Ramirez, and J. Boli (eds), *Institutional Structure: Constituting State, Society, and the Individual*, pp. 41–70, London: Sage Publications, 1987.

Bourdieu, P., *Practical Reason*, Stanford: Stanford University Press, 1998.

Boyd, R., 'Rents and economic outcomes in Japan and Taiwan', in L. Tomba (ed.), *On the Roots of Growth and Crisis: Capitalism, State and Society in East Asia*, Annale Feltrinelli No. 36, pp. 151–91, Milan: Giangiacomo Feltrinelli Editore, 2002.

Boyd, R., 'The rule of law or law as an instrument of rule? Law and the economic development of Japan with particular regard to industrial policy', in C. Antons (ed.), *Law and Development in East and South East Asia*, pp. 154–96, London: RoutledgeCurzon, 2002.

Boyd, R., Galjart, B., and Ngo, T. W. (eds), *Political Conflict and Development in East Asia and Latin America*, London: Routledge, forthcoming 2006.

Boyd, R. and Nagamori, S., 'Industrial policy making in practice: electoral, diplomatic and other adjustments to crisis in the Japanese shipbuilding industry', in S. Wilks and M. Wright (eds), *The Promotion and Regulation of Industry in Japan and Her Competitors*, pp. 167–206, London: Macmillan 1992.

Boyd, R. and Ngo, T. W., 'Emancipating the political economy of Asia from the growth paradigm', in R. Boyd and T. W. Ngo (eds), *Asian States: Beyond the Developmental Perspective*, pp. 1–18, London: RoutledgeCurzon, 2005.

Brand, L. A., *Palestinians in the Arab World: Institution Building and the Search for a State*, New York: Columbia University Press, 1988.

Bruce, J., 'Paradox in the politics of Taiwan', *Politics*, 1978, vol. 13, no. 2, 239–47.

Campbell, J. C., *How Policies Change: The Japanese Government and the Aging Society*, Princeton: Princeton University Press, 1992.

Carlile, L. E., 'Administrative reform in Japan: twilight of the developmental state?', paper presented at the Annual Meeting of the Association for Asian Studies, San Diego, California, 9–12 March 2000.

Carneiro, R. L., 'A theory of the origin of the state', *Science*, 1970, vol. 169, 733–8.

Centeno, M. A., *Blood and Debt: War and the Nation-State in Latin America*, Philadelphia: Pennsylvania State University Press, 2002.

Centeno, M. A. and Lopez-Alves, F. (eds), *The Other Mirror, Grand Theory through the Lens of Latin America*, Princeton: Princeton University Press, 2001.

CEPD (Council for Economic Planning and Development), *Taiwan Statistical Data Book*, Taipei: CEPD, 2002.

Chakrabarty, D., *Provincializing Europe: Postcolonial Thought and Historical Difference*, Princeton: Princeton University Press, 2000.

Chang, M. K., *Shehui yundong yu zhengzhi zhuanhua* (Social movements and political transition), Taipei: Taiwan National Policy Center Press, 1990.

Chen, M. T., *Paixi zhengzhi yu Taiwan de zhengzhi bianqian* (Factional politics and Taiwan's political change), Taipei: Yue-dan Press, 1995.

Chen, M. T. and Chu, Y. H., 'Quyu xinglian he duzhan jingji, difang paixi, yu shengyiyuan xuanju: yixiang shengyiyuan houxuanren beijing ziliao fenxi, 1950–1986' (Regional oligopoly, local factions, and provincial assembly elections: an analysis of the socio-economic background of candidates, 1950–1986), *National Science Council Proceedings - Social Sciences and Humanities*, 1992, vol. 3, 77–97.

Cheng, T. J., 'Democratization of a quasi-Leninist regime in Taiwan', *World Politics*, 1989, no. 41, 477–99.

Cheng, T. J. and Haggard, S. (eds), *Political Change in Taiwan*, Boulder: Lynne Rienner, 1992.

Chow, T. T., *The May Fourth Movement: Intellectual Revolution in Modern China*, Stanford: Stanford University Press, 1967.

Chu, Y. H., 'Guazhan jingji yu weiquan zhengzhi tizhi' (The oligopolistic economy and authoritarian political system), in M. H. H. Hsiao (ed.), *Longduan yu boxiao: weiquan zhuyi de zhengzhi jingji fenxi* (Monopoly and exploitation: the political economy of authoritarianism), pp. 136–60, Taipei: Taiwan Research Foundation, 1989.

Chu, Y. H., *Crafting Democracy in Taiwan*, Taipei: Institute for National Policy Research, 1992.

Claessen, H. and Skalník, P., 'The early state: theories and hypotheses', in H. Claessen and P. Skalník (eds), *The Early State*, pp. 533–96, The Hague: Mouton, 1978.

Clough, R. N., *Island China*, Cambridge: Harvard University Press, 1978.

Cohen, R., 'State origins: a reappraisal', in H. Claessen and P. Skalník (eds), *The Early State*, pp. 31–75, The Hague: Mouton, 1978.

Cohen, R., 'Evolution, fission, and the early state', in H. Claessen and P. Skalník (eds), *The Study of the State*, pp. 87–115, The Hague: Mouton, 1981.

Cohn, B., *Colonialism and Its Forms of Knowledge: The British in India*, Princeton: Princeton University Press, 1996.

Coleman, J. S., 'Conclusion: the political systems of the developing areas', in G. A. Almond and J. S. Coleman (eds), *The Politics of the Developing Areas*, pp. 532–76, Princeton: Princeton University Press, 1960.

Corrigan, P. and Sayer, D., *The Great Arch: English State Formation and Cultural Revolution*, Oxford: Blackwells, 1985.

Cox, R. H., *The State in International Relations*, San Francisco: Chandler, 1965.

Curtis, G., 'Japanese political parties: ideas and reality', Discussion Paper Series 04-E-005, Research Institute of Economy, Trade and Industry (RIETI).

Dalai Lama XIV, *Constitution of Tibet*, New Delhi: Bureau of His Holiness the Dalai Lama, 1963.

Dalai Lama XIV, *Freedom in Exile: The Autobiography of the Dalai Lama*, New York: HarperCollins, 1990.

Das, S. C., *A Tibetan- English Dictionary*, Delhi: Sri Satguru Publications, 1902.

Davis, W., *The Moral and Political Naturalism of Baron Katō Hiroyuki*, Berkeley: Institute of East Asian Studies, University of California, 1996.

Devoe, D. M., 'Keeping refugee status: a Tibetan perspective', in S. Morgan and E. Colson (eds), *People in Upheaval*, pp. 54–65, New York: Center for Migration Studies, 1987.

Deyo, F. (ed.), *The Political Economy of the New Asian Industrialism*, Ithaca and London: Cornell University Press, 1987.

Deyo, F., *Beneath the Miracle: Labor Subordination in the New Asian Industrialism*, Berkeley and Los Angeles: University of California Press, 1989.

Doornbos, M. and Kaviraj, S. (eds), *The Dynamics of State Formation: India and Europe Compared*, New Delhi: Sage Publications, 1997.

Dower, J., *Empire and Aftermath, Yoshida Shigeru and the Japanese Experience, 1878-1954*, Cambridge, MA, and London: Harvard University Press, 1988.

Drucker, P. F., 'In defense of Japanese bureaucracy', *Foreign Affairs*, September/October 1998, vol. 77, no. 5, 68–80.

Duara, P., *Rescuing History from the Nation: Questioning Narratives of Modern China*, Chicago: University of Chicago Press, 1995.

Duara, P., 'Civilizations and nations in a globalizing world', in D. Sachsenmaier and S. N. Eisenstadt (eds), *Reflections on Multiple Modernities: European, Chinese, and Other Interpretations*, pp. 79–99, Leiden: Brill, 2002.

Dunn, J., *The Cunning of Unreason: Making Sense of Politics*, London: Harper-Collins, 2000.

Durkheim, E., *Leçons de Sociologie* (Lessons in Sociology), Paris: Presses Universitaires de France, 1950.

Duus, P., 'Bounded democracy: tradition and politics in modern Japan', unpublished article.

Dyson, K., *The State Tradition in Western Europe*, New York: Oxford University Press, 1980.

Eastwood, A. D., 'International terms: Japan's engagement in colonial control', PhD dissertation, University of Chicago, 1998.

Eisenstadt, S. N., *The Origins and Diversity of Axial Age Civilizations*, New York: State University of New York Press, 1986.

Eisenstadt, S. N., *Japanese Civilization, A Comparative View*, Chicago and London: University of Chicago Press, 1996.

Eisenstadt, S. N. and Roniger, L., 'Patron-client relations as a model of structuring social exchange', *Comparative Studies in Society and History*, 1980, no. 22, 42–75.

Elias, N., *The Civilizing Process: Sociogenetic and Psychogenetic Investigations*, Oxford: Blackwells, 1994.

Elliott, M., *The Manchu Way: The Eight Banners and Ethnic Identity in Late Imperial China*, Stanford: Stanford University Press, 2001.

Emura, E., *Nihon kindai shisō taikei 9: Kenpō kōsō, Nihon Kindai Shiso Taikei 9*, Tokyo: Iwanami shoten, 1989.

Evans, P., *Embedded Autonomy: States and Industrial Transformation*, Princeton: Princeton University Press, 1995.

Federation of Malaysia, *Federal Constitution*, Kuala Lumpur: International Law Books Services, 1995.

Ferguson, J., *The Anti-Politics Machine: Development, Depoliticization, and Bureaucratic Power in Lesotho*, Cambridge: Cambridge University Press, 1990.

Finer, S. E., *The History of Government from the Earliest Times 1: Ancient Monarchies and Empires*, Oxford: Oxford University Press, 1997.

Finer, S. E., *The History of Government from the Earliest Times III: Empires, Monarchies and the Modern State*, Oxford: Oxford University Press, 1997.

Forbes, A., *Settlements of Hope*, Cambridge: Cultural Survival, 1989.

Foucault, M., *Power: Essential Works of Foucault 1954- 1984*, vol. 3, New York: The New Press, 2000.

Frechette, A., *Tibetans in Nepal: The Dynamics of International Assistance among a Community in Exile*, New York: Berghahn Books, 2002.

French, R., 'The new snow lion: the Tibetan government-in-exile in India', in Y. Shain (ed.), *Governments-in-Exile in Contemporary World Politics*, New York: Routledge, 1991.

Frey, M., Pruessen, R. W., and Tan, T. Y. (eds), *The Transformation of Southeast Asia: International Perspectives on Decolonization*, New York and London: M. E. Sharpe, 2003.

Friedman, E., 'Reconstructing China's national identity: a southern alternative to Mao-era anti-imperialist nationalism', *Journal of Asian Studies*, 1994, vol. 53, no. 1, 67–91.

Frisch, H., *Countdown to Statehood: Palestinian State Formation in the West Bank and Gaza*, Albany: State University of New York Press, 1998.

Frost, P., *The Bakumatsu Currency Crisis*, Harvard East Asian Monographs No. 36, Cambridge: East Asian Research Center, Harvard University, 1970.

Fujitani, T., *Splendid Monarchy: Power and Pageantry in Modern Japan*, Berkeley and Los Angeles: University of California Press, 1996.

Garon, S., *Molding Japanese Minds: The State in Everyday Life*, Princeton: Princeton University Press, 1997.

Geertz, C., *Negara: The Theatre State in Nineteenth-Century Bali*, Princeton: Princeton University Press, 1980.

Gellner, E., *Nations and Nationalism*, Oxford: Blackwell, 1983.

Gerth, H. H. and Wright Mills, C. (eds), *From Max Weber, Essays in Sociology*, London: Routledge and Kegan Paul, and Oxford: Oxford University Press, 1970.

Giddens, A., *The Nation-State and Violence: Volume Two of a Contemporary Critique of Historical Materialism*, Berkeley and Los Angeles: University of California Press, 1985.

Gold, T., *State and Society in the Taiwan Miracle*, New York: M. E. Sharpe, 1986.

Gold, T., 'Taiwan's quest for identity in the shadow of China', in S. Tsang (ed.), *In the Shadow of China: Political Development in Taiwan since 1949*, pp. 169–92, London: C. Hurst & Co., 1993.

Goldstein, M., 'Serfdom and mobility: an examination of the institution of "human lease" in traditional Tibetan society', *Journal of Asian Studies*, 1971, vol. 30, 521–34.

Goldstein, M., *Tibetan- English Dictionary of Modern Tibetan*, Kathmandu: Ratna Pustak Bhandar, 1983.

Goldstein, M., 'Freedom, servitude, and the servant-serf Nyima: a re-rejoinder to Miller', *The Tibet Journal*, 1989, vol. 14, 56–61.

Goldstein, M., *The Snow Lion and the Dragon: China, Tibet, and the Dalai Lama*, Berkeley and Los Angeles: University of California Press, 1997.

Goodman, B., 'Democratic calisthenics: the culture of urban associations in the New Republic', in M. Goldman and E. J. Perry (eds), *Changing Meanings of Citizenship in Modern China*, pp. 70–109, Cambridge: Harvard University Press, 2002.

Gordon, L., 'The welfare-state: towards a socialist-feminist perspective', *Socialist Register*, London: Merlin Press, 1990.

Gow, J., 'Shared sovereignty, enhanced security: lessons from the Yugoslav war', in S. Hashmi (ed.), *State Sovereignty: Change and Persistence in International Relations*, University Park: The Pennsylvania State University Press, 1997.

Gramsci, A., *Selections from the Prison Notebooks*, London: Lawrence and Wishart, 1971.

Grew, R., 'Comparing modern Japan: are there more comparisons to be made?', *New Global History*, July 2002, 1–41, <http://web.mit.edu/newglobalhistory/articles.html> (accessed 30 May 2004).

Guru-Gharana, K., 'Strategies for poverty alleviation in Nepal and the role of foreign aid', paper presented at a seminar on the political economy of small states, Kathmandu, Nepal, 1995.

Hagen, T., *Building Bridges to the Third World: Memories of Nepal, 1950-1992*, Delhi: Book Faith India, 1994.

Haggard, S., *Pathways from the Periphery*, Ithaca and London: Cornell University Press, 1990.

Haley, J. O., *Authority without Power: Law and the Japanese Paradox*, Oxford: Oxford University Press, 1991.

Haley, J. O. 'The paradox of weak power and strong authority', in R. Boyd and T.-W. Ngo (eds), *Asian States: Beyond the Developmental Perspective*, pp. 67–82, London: RoutledgeCurzon, 2005.

Harper, T. N., *The End of Empire and the Making of Malaya*, Cambridge: Cambridge University Press, 1999.

Harrison, H., *The Making of the Republican Citizen: Political Ceremonies and Symbols in China 1911-1929*, New York and Oxford: Oxford University Press, 2000.

Hashimoto, M., '*Chihō*: Yanagita Kunio's "Japan"', in S. Vlastos (ed.), *Mirror of Modernity: Invented Traditions in Modern Japan*, pp. 133–43, Berkeley and Los Angeles: University of California Press, 1998.

Hashmi, S., 'Introduction', in S. Hashmi (ed.), *State Sovereignty: Change and Persistence in International Relations*, University Park: The Pennsylvania State University Press, 1997.

Hawthorn, G., 'Waiting for a text?', in J. Manor (ed.), *Rethinking Third World Politics*, pp. 24–50, New York: Longman, 1991.

Hayao, K., *The Japanese Prime Minister and Public Policy*, Pittsburgh and London: University of Pittsburgh Press, 1993.

Heller, M., *Toward a Palestinian State*, Tel Aviv: Jaffee Center for Strategic Studies, 1997.

Herbst, J., *States and Power in Africa: Comparative Lessons in Authority and Control*, Princeton: Princeton University Press, 2000.

Heydemann, S., *Authoritarianism in Syria: Institutions and Social Change, 1946-70*, Ithaca and London: Cornell University Press, 1999.

Hirschman, C., 'The making of race in colonial Malaya: political economy and racial category', *Sociological Forum*, Spring 1986, 330–61.

Hirschman, C., 'The meaning and measurement of ethnicity in Malaysia: an analysis of census classification', *Journal of Asian Studies*, 1987, vol. 46, no. 3, 555–82.

Ho, S., *Economic Development in Taiwan, 1860-1970*, New Haven: Yale University Press, 1978.

Hobsbawn, E., *Nations and Nationalism since 1780*, 2nd revised edn, Cambridge: Cambridge University Press, 1990.

Hoffman, P. T. and Norbert, K., *Fiscal Crises, Liberty, and Representative Government, 1450-1789*, Stanford: Stanford University Press, 1994.

Hsiao, M. H. H. (ed.), *Bianqian zhong de Taiwan shehui de zhongchan jieji* (Taiwan's middle class and social change), Taipei: Ju-liu Press, 1989.

Hsiao, M. H. H., 'Formation and transformation of Taiwan's state-business relations: a critical analysis', *Journal of Ethnology*, 1993, no. 74, 1–32.

Hsu, C. K. and Shong, W. L. (eds), *Taiwan xinxing shehui yundong* (New social movements in Taiwan), Taipei: Ju-liu Press, 1989.

Huntington, S., *The Third Wave: Democratization in the Late Twentieth Century*, Norman: University of Oklahoma Press, 1991.

Huntington, S., *The Clash of Civilizations and the Remaking of World Order*, New York: Simon and Schuster, 1996.

Hwang, I. W., *Personalized Politics: The Malaysian State under Mahathir*, Singapore: Institute of Southeast Asian Studies, 2003.

Ikuta, T., *Kanryō, Japan's Hidden Government*, translated by H. Yanai, New York, Tokyo, Osaka, and London: ICG Muse, Inc., 1995.

Inoguchi, T., 'The pragmatic evolution of Japanese democratic politics', in M. Schmiegelow (ed.), *Democracy in Asia*, pp. 217–32, New York: St Martins Press, 1997.

Inoki, T., 'Japanese bureaucrats at retirement: the mobility of human resources from central government to public corporations', in H. K. Kim, M. Muramatsu, T. J. Pempel, and K. Yamamura (eds), *The Japanese Civil Service and Economic Development: Catalysts of Change*, pp. 213–34, Oxford: Clarendon Press, 1995.

Inoue, K., *Tennōsei* (Emperor system), Tokyo: Tokyo Daigaku Shuppankai, 1958.

Inoue, S., 'The invention of the martial arts: Kanō Jigorō and Kōdōkan Judo', in S. Vlastos (ed.), *Mirror of Modernity: Invented Traditions in Modern Japan*, pp. 163–73, Berkeley and Los Angeles: University of California Press, 1998.

Isomura, E. and Kuronuma, M., *Gendai Nihon no gyōsei* (Contemporary Japanese administration), Tokyo: Teikoku Chihō Gyōsei Gakkai, 1974.

Jackson, R. H., *Quasi-States: Sovereignty, International Relations, and the Third World*, Cambridge: Cambridge University Press, 1990.

Jacoby, N., *U.S. Aid to Taiwan: A Study of Foreign Aid, Self-Help, and Development*, New York: F. A. Praeger, 1966.

Jansen, M. B., *Sakamoto Ryōma and the Meiji Restoration*, Princeton: Princeton University Press, 1961.

Jaspers, K., *The Origins and Goal of History*, New Haven: Yale University Press, 1953.

Jepperson, R. L., 'Institutional logics: on the constitutive dimensions of the modern nation-state polities', Working Paper 2000/36, Florence: Robert Schuman Centre for Advanced Studies, European University Institute, 2000.

Jessop, B., 'Bringing the state back in (yet again): reviews, revisions, rejections, and redirections', paper presented to the International Political Science Association conference, Quebec, 2000, pp. 1–23. Available online at http: <www.comp.lancs. ac.uk/sociology/papers/jessop-bringing-the-state-back-in.pdf> (accessed 10 May 2001).

Jin, G. and Liu, Q., *Kaifang zhong de Bianqian* (Changes during openness), Hong Kong: Chinese University Press, 1992.

Johnson, C., 'Japan: who governs? An essay on official bureaucracy', *Journal of Japanese Studies*, 1975–76, vol. 2, 1–28.

Johnson, C., *MITI and the Japanese Miracle*, Stanford: Stanford University Press, 1982.

Johnson, C., *Japan: Who Governs? The Rise of the Developmental State*, New York and London: W. W. Norton & Co., 1995.

Joshi, H. D., *A History of the Tibetan Refugees in Nepal*, Kathmandu: Swiss Association for Technical Assistance, 1983.

Kallgren, J. K., 'Nationalist China: the continuing dilemma of the mainland philosophy', *Asian Survey*, 1963, no. 3, 11–16.

Kaviraj, S., 'On state, society and discourse in India', in J. Manor (ed.), *Rethinking Third World Politics*, pp. 72–99, New York: Longman, 1991.

Kaviraj, S., 'The modern state in India', in M. Doornbos and S. Kaviraj (eds), *The Dynamics of State Formation: India and Europe Compared*, pp. 225–50, New Delhi: Sage Publications, 1997.

Kaviraj, S., 'In search of civil society', in S. Kaviraj and S. Khilnani (eds), *Civil Society, History and Possibilities*, pp. 287–323, Cambridge: Cambridge University Press, 2001.

Kerr, G., *Formosa Betrayed*, Boston: The Riverside Press, 1965.

Khilnani, S., *The Idea of India*, New York: Farrah Strauss Giroux, 1997.

Khoo, B. T., *Paradoxes of Mahathirism: An Intellectual Biography of Mahathir Mohamed*, Kuala Lumpur: Oxford University Press, 1995.

Khoo, B. T., *Beyond Mahathir: Malaysian Politics and Its Discontents*, London: Zed Press, 2003.

Kitschelt, H., 'Political opportunity structures and political protest', *British Journal of Political Science*, 1986, vol. 16, 57–86.

Knaus, J. K., *Orphans of the Cold War: America and the Tibetan Struggle for Survival*, New York: Public Affairs, 1999.

Koh, B. C., *Japan's Administrative Elite*, Berkeley and Los Angeles: University of California Press, 1989.

Krader, L., *Formation of the State*, Englewood Cliffs: Prentice-Hall, 1968.

Krasner, S., *Sovereignty: Organized Hypocrisy*, Princeton: Princeton University Press, 1999.

Krasner, S., 'Problematic sovereignty', in S. Krasner (ed.), *Problematic Sovereignty: Contested Rules and Political Possibilities*, pp. 1–23, New York: Columbia University Press, 2001.

Kyōgoku, J. I., *The Political Dynamics of Japan*, translated by N. Ike, Tokyo: University of Tokyo Press, 1987.

Lawrence, S. and Dean, J., 'A whole new conflict', *Far Eastern Economic Review*, 18 December 2003, 16–21.

Lee, Y. J., *Taiwan gonghui zhengce de zhengzhi jingji fenxi* (The political economy of Taiwan's union policy), Taipei: Ju-liu Books, 1992.

Lerman, A. J., 'National elites and local politicians in Taiwan', *American Political Science Review*, 1977, vol. 71, no. 4, 1406–22.

Lin, C. L., 'Weiquan shicong zhengti xia de Taiwan fandui yundong' (Opposition movement under an authoritarian clientelist regime), *Taiwan: A Radical Quarterly in Social Studies*, 1989, vol. 2, no. 1, 117–43.

Loewenstein, K., 'Report on the Research Panel on Comparative Government', *American Political Science Review*, 1944, vol. 38, no. 2, 540–8.

Lopez-Alves, F., *State Formation and Democracy in Latin America 1810-1900*, Durham: Duke University Press, 2000.

Lopez-Alves, F. (ed.), *War, Institutions and Social Change in the Middle East*, Berkeley and Los Angeles: University of California Press, 2001.

Lukes, S., *Emile Durkheim: His Life and Work*, Harmondsworth: Penguin, 1973.

Madsen, R., 'The struggle for sovereignty between China and Taiwan', in S. Krasner (ed.), *Problematic Sovereignty: Contested Rules and Political Possibilities*, pp. 141–93, New York: Columbia University Press, 2001.

Malkki, L., 'Citizens of humanity: internationalism and the imagined community of nations', *Diaspora: A Journal of Transnational Studies*, 1994, vol. 3, 41–68.

Malkki, L., *Purity and Exile: Violence, Memory, and National Cosmology among Hutu Refugees in Tanzania*, Chicago: University of Chicago Press, 1995.

Manor, J. (ed.), *Rethinking Third World Politics*, New York: Longman, 1991.

March, J. and Olsen, J., *Ambiguity and Choice in Organizations*, Bergen: Universitets-forlaget, 1976.

Maruyama, M., *Thought and Behavior in Modern Japanese Politics*, Oxford: Oxford University Press, 1963.

Maruyama, M., 'The structure of Matsurigoto: the *basso ostinato* of Japanese political life', in S. Henny and J. P. Lehmann (eds), *Themes and Theories in Modern Japanese History*, pp. 27–43, London: Athlone, 1988.

Marvin, C., Ingle, D. W., Alexander, J. C., and Seidman, S. (eds), *Blood Sacrifice and the Nation: Totem Rituals and the American Flag*, Cambridge: Cambridge University Press, 1999.

Masayoshi, M., *Report on the Adoption of the Gold Standard in Japan*, New York: Arno Press Inc., [1899] 1979.

McLaren, W. W. (ed.), *Japanese Government Documents*, 2 vols, Washington: University Publications of America, [1914] 1979.

McVeigh, B., *The Nature of the Japanese State: Rationality and Rituality*, Japanese Studies Series, London and New York: Nissan Institute/Routledge, 1998.

Meyer, J. W., 'The world polity and the authority of the nation-state', in G. M. Thomas, J. W. Meyer, F. O. Ramirez, and J. Boli, *Institutional Structure: Constituting State, Society, and the Individual*, pp. 41–70, Newbury Park: Sage Publications, 1987.

Meyer, J. W., 'The changing cultural content of the nation state: a world society perspective', in G. Steinmetz (ed.), *State/Culture: State Formation after the Cultural Turn*, pp. 123–44, Ithaca and London: Cornell University Press, 1999.

Meyer, J. W., Boli, J., and Thomas, G. M., 'Ontology and rationalization in the Western cultural account', in G. M. Thomas, J. W. Meyer, F. O. Ramirez, and J. Boli, *Institutional Structure: Constituting State, Society, and the Individual*, pp. 11–37, Newbury Park: Sage Publications, 1987.

Meyer, J. W., Boli, J., Thomas, G. M., and Ramirez, F. O., 'World society and the nation-state', *American Journal of Sociology*, 1997, vol. 103, no. 1, 144–81.

Migdal, J. S., 'The state in society: an approach to struggles for domination', in J. S. Migdal, A. Kohli, and V. Shue (eds), *State Power and Social Forces: Domination and Transformation in the Third World*, pp. 4–36, Cambridge: Cambridge University Press, 1994.

Mitchell, T., 'Society, economy, and the state effect', in G. Steinmetz (ed.), *State/Culture: State Formation after the Cultural Turn*, pp. 76–97, Ithaca and London: Cornell University Press, 1999.

Miyachi, A., *Bringing Accountability to Japan's Bureaucracy*, National Institute for Research Advancement, Spring 1999, <http://www.nira.jp/pub/review/99spring/miyachi.html> (accessed 30 June 2004).

Mizuno, K., 'Gyokaku Kaigi: Kanryō to no Kobo' (The Administrative Reform Council: fights with bureaucrats), *Bungei shunjuu*, October 1997, pp. 105–7.

Muramatsu, M., *Sengo Nihon no Kanryōsei* (The bureaucratic system in postwar Japan), Tokyo: Tōyō Keizai, 1981.

Mydans, S., 'Pressed by I.M.F., Indonesia accepts economic reforms', *New York Times*, 15 January 1998.

Mydans, S., 'Indonesia agrees to I.M.F.'s tough medicine', *New York Times*, 16 January 1998.

Nadel, S. F., 'The Kede: a riverain state in northern Nigeria', in M. Fortes and E. E. Evans-Pritchard (eds), *African Political Systems*, pp. 164–95, London: Oxford University Press, 1940.

Najita, T., *Japan, The Intellectual Foundations of Modern Japanese Politics*, Chicago: University of Chicago Press, 1974.

Nakamura, M., Ishii, K., and Kasuga, Y. (eds), *Nihon Kindai Shisō Taikei 8*, Tokyo: Iwanami shoten, 1988.

Nakasone, Y., *The Making of the New Japan: Reclaiming the Political Mainstream*, translated and annotated by L. Connors, Richmond: Curzon, 1999.

Nettl, J. P., 'The state as a conceptual variable', *World Politics*, 1968, vol. 20, no. 4, 559–92.

Ngo, T. W., 'The political bases of episodic agency in the Taiwan state', in R. Boyd and T. W. Ngo (eds), *Asian States: Beyond the Developmental Perspective*, pp. 83–109, London: RoutledgeCurzon, 2005.

Nihon keiryō kyōkai (ed.), *Keiryō Hyakunen Shi*, Tokyo: Nihon keiryō kyōkai, 1978.

Nowak, M., *Tibetan Refugees: Youth and the New Generation of Meaning*, New Brunswick: Rutgers University Press, 1984.

Odagiri, N., 'Kokka Kimigayo Kōwa', in K. Shigeshita and T. Sato (eds), *Kimigayo Shiryō Shūsei*, 5 vols, Tokyo: Kyoeki shōsha shoten, 1991.

Ogden, S., *Inklings of Democracy in China*, Cambridge: Harvard University Asia Center, 2002.

Ohmae, K., *The End of the Nation State: The Rise of Regional Economies*, New York: The Free Press, 1995.

Okada, T., 'The unchanging bureaucracy', *Japan Quarterly*, 1965, vol. 12, 168–76.

Oksenberg, M., 'The issue of sovereignty in the Asian historical context', in S. Krasner (ed.), *Problematic Sovereignty: Contested Rules and Political Possibilities*, pp. 83–104, New York: Columbia University Press, 2001.

Ooms, H., *Tokugawa Ideology: Early Constructs, 1570-1680*, Princeton: Princeton University Press, 1985.

Palmer, R. R., *A History of the Modern World*, New York: Knopf, 1952.

Passerin d'Entrèves, A., *The Notion of the State: An Introduction to Political Theory*, Oxford: Oxford University Press, 1961.

Philpott, D., 'Ideas and the evolution of sovereignty', in S. Hashmi (ed.), *State Sovereignty: Change and Persistence in International Relations*, pp. 15–49, University Park: The Pennsylvania State University Press, 1997.

Philpott, D., *Revolutions in Sovereignty: How Ideas Shaped Modern International Relations*, Princeton: Princeton University Press, 2001.

Planning Council of the Central Tibetan Administration of His Holiness the Dalai Lama, *Tibetan Resettlement Community Integrated Development Plan, 1995-2000*, Dharamsala, India: Central Tibetan Administration, 1994.

Poggi, G., *The Development of the Modern State*, Stanford: Stanford University Press, 1978.

Przeworski, A., 'Some problems in the study of transition to democracy', in

G. O'Donnell, P. C. Schmitter, and L. Whitehead (eds), *Transitions from Authoritarian Rule*, pp. 47–63, Baltimore: The Johns Hopkins University Press, 1986.

Przeworski, A., *Democracy and the Market: Political and Economic Reforms in Eastern Europe and Latin America*, Cambridge: Cambridge University Press, 1991.

Ravina, M., *Land and Lordship in Early Modern Japan*, Stanford: Stanford University Press, 1999.

Republic of China, Mainland Affairs Council (MAC), *Cross-Strait Economic Statistics*, Taipei: MAC, 2002.

Republic of China, Ministry of Economic Affairs (MOEA), *Investment Commission Statistics*, Taipei: MOEA, 2002.

Robinson, G., *Building a Palestinian State: The Incomplete Revolution*, Bloomington: Indiana University Press, 1997.

Robinson, M. and White, G. (eds), *The Democratic Developmental State*, Oxford: Oxford University Press, 1998.

Roniger, L. and Ayes, G., *Democracy, Clientelism, and Civil Society*, Boulder: Lynne Rienner, 1994.

Rose, R. 'What is lesson-drawing?', *Journal of Public Policy*, 1991, vol. 11, no. 1, 3–30.

Rosenau, J. N., 'The state in an era of cascading politics: wavering concept, widening competence, withering colossus, or weathering change?', in J. A. Caporaso (ed.), *The Elusive State: International and Comparative Perspectives*, pp. 17–48, Newbury Park: Sage Publications, 1989.

Rudolph, S. H., 'Presidential address: state formation in Asia – prolegomenon to a comparative study', *The Journal of Asian Studies*, 1987, vol. 46, no. 4, 731–46.

Rudolph, S. H. and Rudolph, L. I., 'Authority and power in bureaucratic and patrimonial administration: a revisionist interpretation of Weber on bureaucracy', *World Politics*, 1979, vol. 31, 195–227.

Sahashi, S.,'Kanryō shokun ni chokugen suru' (Straight talk to the gentlemen of the bureaucracy), *Bungei shunjuu*, July 1971.

Saigō Takamori zenshū henshū iinkai (ed.), *Saigō Takamori Zenshū*, 6 vols, Tokyo: Yamato shobō, 1976–80.

Sangay, T., 'Tibet: exiles' journey', *Journal of Democracy*, 2003, vol. 14, 119–30.

Sanger, D. E., 'U.S. is set to lend $3 billion to help bolster Indonesia', *New York Times*, 31 October 1997.

Sanger, D. E., 'U.S. warning to Indonesia: comply on aid', *New York Times*, 8 January 1998.

Schaffer, B. B., 'Deadlock in development administration', in C. Leys (ed.), *Politics and Change in Developing Countries*, pp. 177–212, Cambridge: Cambridge University Press, 1969.

Schiff, B., *Refugees into the Third Generation: UN Aid to Palestinians*, Syracuse: Syracuse University Press, 1995.

Schmitter, P., 'Still the century of corporatism?', *Review of Politics*, 1974, no. 36, 85–131.

Schmitter, P., 'Civil society: East and West', in L. M. Diamond, M. F. Plattner, H. M. Tien, and Y. H. Chu (eds), *Consolidating the Third Wave Democracies*, vol. I., pp. 239–62, Baltimore: Johns Hopkins University Press, 1997.

Schram, S. (ed.), *Foundations and Limits of State Power in China*, Hong Kong: Chinese University Press, 1987.

Schrecker, J. E., *The Chinese Revolution in Historical Perspective*, New York: Greenwood Press, 1991.

Scott, J. C., *Seeing Like a State: How Certain Schemes to Improve the Human Condition Have Failed*, New Haven: Yale University Press, 1998.

Shain, Y., *The Frontier of Loyalty: Political Exiles in the Age of the Nation-State*, Middletown: Wesleyan University Press, 1989.

Shakya, T., 'Politicisation and the Tibetan language', in R. Barnett and S. Akiner (eds), *Resistance and Reform in Tibet*, Bloomington: Indiana University Press, 1994.

Shamsul A. B., *Malaysia in 2020: One State, Many Nations? Observing Malaysia from Australia*, The Seventh James Jackson Memorial Lecture, Malaysia Society, Australia, Bangi: Department of Anthropology and Sociology, Universiti Kebangsaan Malaysia, 1992.

Shamsul A. B., 'Debating about identity in Malaysia: a discourse analysis', *Tonan Ajia Kenkyu*, 1996a, vol. 34, no. 3, 566–600.

Shamsul A. B., 'Nations-of-intent in Malaysia', in S. Tønnesson and H. Antlöv (eds), *Asian Forms of the Nation*, pp. 323–47, London: Curzon and Nordic Institute of Asian Studies, 1996b.

Shamsul A. B., 'The construction and transformation of a social identity: Malayness and bumiputeraness re-examined', *Journal of Asian and African Studies*, 1996c, no. 52, 15–33.

Shamsul A. B., 'The economic dimension of Malay nationalism', *Developing Economies*, 1997a, vol. 35, no. 3, 240–61.

Shamsul A. B., 'The making of a plural society in Malaysia: a brief survey', in D. Wu, H. McQueen, and Y. Yamamoto (eds), *Emerging Pluralism in Asia and the Pacific*, pp. 67–83, Hong Kong: Institute of Pacific Studies, 1997b.

Shamsul A. B., 'Ethnicity, class, culture or identity? Competing paradigms in Malaysian studies', *Akademika*, 1998, no. 53, 33–60.

Shamsul A. B., 'Identity contestation in Malaysia: a comparative commentary on "Malayness" and "Chineseness" ', *Akademika*, 1999, no. 55, 17–37.

Shamsul A. B., 'Development and democracy in Malaysia: a comment on its socio-historical roots', in H. Antlöv and T. W. Ngo (eds), *The Cultural Construction of Politics in Asia*, pp. 86–106, NIAS Democracy in Asia Series No. 2, Surrey: Curzon Press, 2000.

Shamsul A. B. and Aziz A., 'Political Islam and governance in Southeast Asia: a Malaysian viewpoint', Asian Cultures and Modernity Research Report No. 8, pp. 4–6, Department of Oriental Languages and Department of Political Science, University of Stockholm, 2004.

Shi, T., *Political Participation in Beijing*, Cambridge: Harvard University Press, 1997.

Shibusawa, E. and Nihon shiseki kyōka (eds), *Tokugawa Yoshinobu kō den shiryō hen*, 3 vols, Tokyo: Tōkyō daigaku shuppankai, 1975.

Shillony, B. A., *Politics and Culture in Wartime Japan*, Oxford: Clarendon Press, 1981.

Silberman, B. S., 'Bureaucratic development and the structure of decision-making in the Meiji period: the case of the *genrō*', *Journal of Asian Studies*, 1968, vol. 27, 81–94.

Silberman, B. S., 'The bureaucratic role in Japan, 1900–1945: the bureaucrat as politician', in B. S. Silberman and H. D. Harootunian (eds), *Japan in Crisis: Essays in Taisho Democracy*, pp. 183–216, Princeton: Princeton University Press, 1974.

Silberman, B. S., 'Bureaucratization of the Meiji state: the problem of succession in the Meiji Restoration, 1868–1900', *Journal of Asian Studies*, 1976, vol. 35, 421–30.

Silberman, B. S., 'The bureaucratic state in Japan: the problem of authority and legitimacy', in T. Najita and J. V. Koschman (eds), *Dimensions of Conflict in Modern Japan*, pp. 226–57, Princeton: Princeton University Press, 1982.

Silberman, B. S., *Cages of Reason: The Rise of the Rational State in France, Japan, the United States, and Great Britain*, Chicago: University of Chicago Press, 1993.

Silberman, B. S., 'The structure of bureaucratic rationality and economic development in Japan', in H. K. Kim, M. Muramatsu, T. J. Pempel, and K. Yamamura (eds), *The Japanese Civil Service and Economic Development, Catalysts of Change*, pp. 135–73, Oxford: Clarendon Press, 1995.

Slaughter, A.-M., 'The real New World Order', *Foreign Affairs*, 1997, vol. 76, 183–97.

Smith, A., *The Ethnic Origin of Nations*, Oxford: Blackwell, 1986.

Spruyt, H., *The Sovereign State and its Competitors: An Analysis of Systems Change*, Princeton: Princeton University Press, 1994.

Stein, B., 'Review of Sangam polity', *Indian Economic and Social History Review*, 1968, vol. 5, 109–15.

Stein, B., 'The segmentary state in South Indian history', in R. G. Fox (ed.), *Realm and Region in Traditional India*, pp. 3–51, Durham: Duke University Press, 1977.

Stein, B., *Peasant State and Society in Medieval South India*, New Delhi: Oxford University Press, 1980.

Steinmetz, G. (ed.), *State/Culture: State Formation after the Cultural Turn*, Ithaca and London: Cornell University Press, 1999.

Subrahmanyam, S., *The Makings of Early Modern Asia: A Polycentric Approach*, Boulder: Westview Press, 1998.

Subrahmanyam, S., *Prenumbral Visions: The Making of Polities in Early Modern South India*, Ann Arbor: University of Michigan Press, 2001.

Suffian, M., Lee, H. P., and Trindade, F. A., *The Constitution of Malaysia: Its Development 1957- 1977*, Kuala Lumpur: Oxford University Press, 1978.

Thompson, L. A., 'The invention of the *Yokozuna* and the championship system, or, Futahaguro's revenge', in S. Vlastos (ed.), *Mirror of Modernity: Invented Traditions in Modern Japan*, pp. 174–87, Berkeley and Los Angeles: University of California Press, 1998.

Tilly, C., 'Reflections on the history of European state-making', in C. Tilly (ed.), *The Formation of National States in Western Europe*, pp. 3–83, Princeton: Princeton University Press, 1975.

Tilly, C., *Coercion, Capital, and European States, AD 990- 1990*, Cambridge: Blackwell, 1990.

Tsang, S. (ed.), *In the Shadow of China: Political Development in Taiwan since 1949*, London: C. Hurst & Co, 1993.

Tsou, T., *The Cultural Revolution and Post-Mao Reforms: A Historical Perspective*, Chicago: University of Chicago Press, 1986.

Tsuji, K., *Gendai Nihon no Seiji Katei* (Political processes in contemporary Japan), Tokyo: Iwanami Shoten, 1958.

Tsukahara, Y., 'Meiji No Kyūchū Gyōji Saihen to Gagakuka (Reijin) No Seiyō Ongaku Kenshū', in H. Matsushita (ed.), *Ibunka kōryū to kindaika* (Cultural encounters in the development of modern East Asia), pp. 214–21, Tachikawa-shi: 'Ibunka kōryū to kindaika' Kyōto kokusai seminā, 1996; soshiki iinkai, 1998.

Tu, W., 'Beyond the enlightenment mentality: a Confucian perspective on ethics, migration, and global stewardship', *International Migration Review*, 1996, vol. 30, 58–75.

Van Wolferen, K., *The Enigma of Japanese Power*, London and Basingstoke: Macmillan, 1989.

Vlastos, S., 'Agrarianism without tradition: the radical critique of prewar Japanese modernity', in S. Vlastos (ed.), *Mirror of Modernity: Invented Traditions in Modern Japan*, pp. 79–94, Berkeley and Los Angeles: University of California Press, 1998a.

Vlastos, S., 'Tradition: past/present culture and modern Japanese history', in S. Vlastos (ed.), *Mirror of Modernity: Invented Traditions of Modern Japan*, pp. 1–18, Berkeley and Los Angeles: University of California Press, 1998b.

Vlastos, S. (ed.), *Mirror of Modernity: Invented Traditions of Modern Japan*, Berkeley and Los Angeles: University of California Press, 1998c.

Wade, R., *Governing the Market: Economic Theory and the Role of Government in East Asia*, Princeton: Princeton University Press, 1990.

Wagner, R., 'Political institutions, discourse and imagination in China at Tiananmen', in J. Manor (ed.), *Rethinking Third World Politics*, pp. 121–44, New York: Longman, 1991.

Wakabayashi, B. T., 'Kato Hiroyuki and Confucian natural rights, 1861–1870', *Harvard Journal of Asiatic Studies*, 1984, vol. 44, no. 2, 469–92.

Waldner, D., 'From intra-type variations to the origins of types: recovering the macro-analytics of state building', paper presented for the conference on Asian Political Economy in an Era of Globalization, Dartmouth College, 10–11 May 2002.

Wallerstein, I., *The Modern World System: Capitalist Agriculture and the Origins of the World Economy in the Sixteenth Century*, New York: Academic Press, 1975.

Wang, J. H., 'Taiwan de zhengzhi zhuanxing yu fandui yundong' (Political transformation and the opposition movement in Taiwan), *Taiwan: A Radical Quarterly in Social Studies*, 1989, vol. 2, no. 1, 71–116.

Wang, J. H., 'Guojia jiqi, ziben han Taiwan de zhengzhi zhuanxing' (The state, capital and Taiwan's political transition), *Taiwan: A Radical Quarterly in Social Studies*, 1993, no. 14, 123–64.

Wang, J. H., *Shui tongzhi Taiwan: zhuanxing zhong de guojia jiqi yu quanli jiegou* (Who rules Taiwan: the transformation of the state and power structure), Taipei: Ju-Liu Books, 1996.

Wang, J. H., 'Labor regimes in transition: changing faces of labor control in Taiwan: 1950s–1990s', in A. Y. Hing, C. T. Chang, and R. Lansbury (eds), *Work, Organization, and Industry: The Asian Experience*, pp. 250–74, Singapore: Armour, 1998.

Wang, J. H., 'Civil society, democratization, and governance in Taiwan', in National Science Council, Taipei, Bonn Office (ed.), *Conference Prague 1999: Transitional Societies in Comparison: Central East Europe vs. Taiwan*, pp. 17–34, Frankfurt am Main: Peter Lang, 2000.

Watanuki, J., 'Nation-building at the edge of an old empire: Japan and Korea', in S. N. Eisenstadt and S. Rokkan (eds), *Building States and Nations*, vol. 2, pp. 250–65, New York: Sage, 1973.

Weber, M., *General Economic History*, New York: Collier Books, 1961.

Weber, M., *Economy and Society: An Outline of Interpretive Sociology*, vol. 1, edited by G. Roth and C. Wittich, Berkeley and Los Angeles: University of California Press, 1978.

Weiss, L., *The Myth of the Powerless State*, Ithaca and London: Cornell University Press, 1998.

Weiss, L. and Hobson, J., *States and Economic Development*, Cambridge: Polity, 1995.

Welsh, B. (ed.), *Reflections: The Mahathir Years*, Washington, DC: Southeast Asian Studies Program, Johns Hopkins University, 2004.

Westney, D. E., *Imitation and Innovation: The Transfer of Western Organizational Patterns to Meiji Japan*, Cambridge, Mass.: Harvard University Press, 1987.

Whitehead, L., 'State organisation in Latin America since 1930', in L. Bethell (ed.), *The Cambridge History of Latin America*, vol. 5, Part 2, pp. 3–95, Cambridge: Cambridge University Press, 1994.

Winckler, E., 'National, regional and local politics', in E. Ahern and H. Gates (eds), *The Anthropology of Taiwanese Society*, pp. 13–37, Palo Alto: Stanford University Press, 1981.

Winckler, E., 'Institutionalization and participation on Taiwan: from hard to soft authoritarianism', *The China Quarterly*, 1984, no. 99, 481–99.

Winichakul, T., *Siam Mapped: A History of the Geo-Body of a Nation*, Honolulu: University of Hawai'i Press, 1994.

Wittfogel, K., 'The theory of oriental society', in M. Fried (ed.), *Readings in Anthropology, Volume II: Cultural Anthropology*, pp. 179–200, New York: Crowell, 1968.

Wong, R. B., 'Great expectations: the "public sphere" and the search for modern times in Chinese history', *Chūgoku shi gaku*, 1993, vol. 3, 7–50.

Wong, R. B., *China Transformed: Historical Change and the Limits of European Experience*, Ithaca and London: Cornell University Press, 1997.

Wong, R. B., 'Citizenship in Chinese history', in M. P. Hanagan and C. Tilly (eds), *Extending Citizenship, Reconfiguring States*, pp. 97–122, Lanham: Rowman and Littlefield, 1999.

Wong, R. B., 'Two kinds of nation, what kind of state?', in T. Brook and A. Schmid (eds), *Nation Work*, pp. 109–23, Ann Arbor: University of Michigan Press, 2000.

Wong, R. B., 'Formal and informal mechanisms of rule and economic development: the Qing empire in comparative perspective', *Journal of Early Modern History*, 2001, vol. 5, no. 4, 387–408.

Wong, R. B., 'The social and political construction of identities in the Qing empire', in L. Blussé and F. Fernández-Armesto (eds), *Shifting Communities and Identity Formation in Early Modern Asia*, pp. 61–72, Leiden: CNWS Publications, Leiden University, 2003.

Woo-Cumings, M., 'National security and the rise of the developmental state in South Korea and Taiwan', in H. Rowen (ed.), *Behind East Asian Growth: The Political and Social Foundation of Prosperity*, pp. 319–37, London: Routledge, 1998.

Woo-Cumings, M., 'Introduction: Chalmers Johnson and the politics of nationalism and development', in M. Woo-Cumings (ed.), *The Developmental State*, pp. 1–31, Ithaca and London: Cornell University Press, 1999.

Woo-Cumings, M. (ed.), *The Developmental State*, Ithaca and London: Cornell University Press, 1999.

Woodward, S. L., 'Compromised sovereignty to create sovereignty: is Dayton Bosnia a futile exercise or emerging model?', in S. Krasner (ed.), *Problematic Sovereignty: Contested Rules and Political Possibilities*, pp. 252–300, New York: Columbia University Press, 2001.

Wright, M., *Japan's Fiscal Crisis: The Ministry of Finance and the Politics of Public Spending, 1975- 2000*, Oxford: Oxford University Press, 2002.

Wu, J. M., 'Zhengzhi zhuanxing qi de shehui kangyi: Taiwan 1980 niandai' (Social protests in political transition: Taiwan in the 1980s), MA thesis, National Taiwan University, 1990.

Wu, Y. P., *A Political Explanation of Economic Growth: State Survival, Bureaucratic*

Politics, and Private Enterprises in the Making of Taiwan's Economy 1950- 85, Harvard East Asian Monographs, Cambridge: Harvard University Press, 2005.

Young, C., *The African Colonial State in Comparative Perspective*, New Haven: Yale University Press, 1994.

Young, L., 'Colonizing Manchuria: the making of an imperial myth', in S. Vlastos (ed.), *Mirror of Modernity: Invented Traditions in Modern Japan*, pp. 95–109, Berkeley and Los Angeles: University of California Press, 1998.

Yu, X., 'Citizenship, ideology and the PRC constitution', in M. Goldman and E. J. Perry (eds), *Changing Meanings of Citizenship in Modern China*, pp. 288–307, Cambridge: Harvard University Press, 2002.

Yui, M. and Obinata, S. (eds), *Nihon kindai shisō taikei 3: Kanryōsei keisatsu*, Tokyo: Iwanami shoten, 1990.

Index

eBooks

eBooks – at www.eBookstore.tandf.co.uk

A library at your fingertips!

eBooks are electronic versions of printed books. You can store them on your PC/laptop or browse them online.

They have advantages for anyone needing rapid access to a wide variety of published, copyright information.

eBooks can help your research by enabling you to bookmark chapters, annotate text and use instant searches to find specific words or phrases. Several eBook files would fit on even a small laptop or PDA.

NEW: Save money by eSubscribing: cheap, online access to any eBook for as long as you need it.

Annual subscription packages

We now offer special low-cost bulk subscriptions to packages of eBooks in certain subject areas. These are available to libraries or to individuals.

For more information please contact webmaster.ebooks@tandf.co.uk

We're continually developing the eBook concept, so keep up to date by visiting the website.

www.eBookstore.tandf.co.uk